the *Virgin* gardener

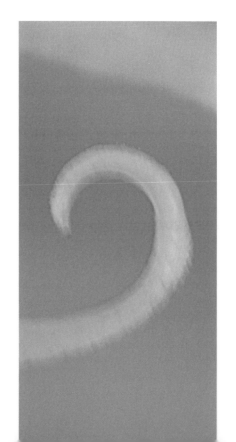

the Virgin gardener

Everything the Beginner Needs to Know to Create, Maintain, and Enjoy a Garden

JONATHAN EDWARDS

VIKING STUDIO

To Liz and Sonja for all their help and support

Created and produced by:

Carroll & Brown Limited
20 Lonsdale Road, Queen's Park, London NW6 6RD

Editor Caroline Uzielli

Art Editor Gilda Pacitti

Designer Vimit Punater

Photography David Murray

VIKING STUDIO
Published by the Penguin Group
Penguin Putnam Inc., 375 Hudson Street, New York, New York 10014, U.S.A.
Penguin Books Ltd, 27 Wrights Lane, London W8 5TZ, England
Penguin Books Australia Ltd, Ringwood, Victoria, Australia
Penguin Books Canada Ltd, 10 Alcorn Avenue, Toronto, Ontario, Canada M4V 3B2
Penguin Books (N.Z.) Ltd, 182–190 Wairau Road, Auckland 10, New Zealand

Penguin Books Ltd, Registered Offices: Harmondsworth, Middlesex, England

First published in 2000 by Viking Studio, a member of Penguin Putnam Inc.

1 3 5 7 9 10 8 6 4 2

Library of Congress Cataloging-in-Publication Data
Edwards, Jonathan, 1959-
        The virgin gardener : everything the beginner needs to know to create, maintain,
        and enjoy a garden / Jonathan Edwards
p. cm.
        ISBN 0-670-89243-2
            1. Gardening. I. Title

        SB453.E38 2000
        635.9—dc21   00-020747

Reproduced by Colourscan, Singapore. Printed and bound by New Intelitho Italia SPA

Foreword

Gardening is infectious—once you have been bitten by the bug you will be an enthusiast for life. From the day you buy your first plant or sow your first seed it is a continuous learning experience.

The beauty of gardening lies in the fact that you don't need extensive knowledge to get started and yet you can spend a lifetime absorbed in the passion, learning more and more about the subject each day.

Like life itself, gardening has its ups and downs. Of course, you will get the occasional disappointment, but you can be certain that you will always get another chance to get it right. One of the great joys of gardening is that it never fails to surprise. At the very heart of its appeal is the excitement and uncertainty of what may be appearing just around the corner. No matter how experienced you become or how often you carry out a particular task, there is always something new and fascinating to learn.

Gardening is an evolving pastime that grows along with your knowledge—not only in the literal sense, as your garden matures, but the range of challenges you set yourself will extend as your skills increase. Indeed, the completion of your first garden should be viewed as the starting point of your learning experience; something that will evolve and develop seamlessly with your changing needs and interests. Above all else, gardening should be enjoyable.

Jonathan Edwards

contents

introduction

As a novice gardener, you may be overwhelmed by all the available information on this enormous subject. Not only might you have to cope with a barren plot or overgrown jungle, but also with finding a helpful guide that will explain everything thing you need to know to get started and to make gardening less of a chore.

The Virgin Gardener has been specifically written with you in mind. While it concentrates on the creative aspects of designing with plants as well as the practical science of growing them, it also contains many special features (see the list opposite) to make this information readily graspable and easy to put into practice.

The structure of the book

Chapter 1 describes how to plan your garden from scratch or renovate and improve an existing garden with confidence. There are lots of ideas for making dramatic improvements from day one. It also includes tips on choosing and buying plants for your garden as well as advice on the essential tools and useful equipment that will save you a lot of time and effort.

The essential features of a garden are outlined in chapter 2—what your options are when covering the ground, the various types of boundary available, and which plants to choose to get color and interest all year. It also explains how to make the most of patios and water features within your design. Each section in this chapter is accompanied by case studies which describe how representative Virgin Gardeners have put expert advice into practice. Some are new gardeners who have tackled completely empty gardens from scratch—creating an established-looking design that meets their particular needs. On pages 50–51, for example, Joe and Marsha produce an easy-care garden with a lawn and paving to suit all the family, while on pages 68–69 Judy and Chris create a perennial paradise in a heavily shaded town garden.

There are also examples of Virgin Gardeners who have made drastic improvements to existing designs,

Facing the challenge

This barren plot is very long and narrow and has an unsightly wall at one end (right), which dominates the garden design and spoils the view from the house. What's needed here is a design that focuses the eye within the center of the garden and makes the most of available space.

This ingenious design (far right) transformed the look and feel of the garden. It has solved the problems by disguising the boundaries with plants and incorporating a large ornamental pond as the main central feature. Changes in color and texture from the sunny terrace to the shady border at the bottom of the garden are linked by an eye-catching blue-stained arbor.

Choice boundaries for a modern garden page 108

Flower borders page 58

Planting containers page 114

Planning a garden re-design page 162

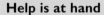

either by adapting or changing features to suit their own taste and lifestyle or by completely renovating an overgrown jungle. On pages 106–107, for example, Meg and Paul tackle a plot crammed with overgrown shrubs and create space for a wider variety of plants as well as a sun-deck. In the water gardening section, an old garden is transformed by Kevin and Joanna into a contemporary design with the addition of a dramatic water feature, novelty seats and a sunken patio area (see pages 142–143).

Each real-life example illustrates how a barren plot or overgrown chaos can be transformed quickly, easily and within any budget. Here is proof that you don't have to be an expert to make genuine improvements to your garden.

Chapter 3 explains how to keep your garden looking good all year, listing all the essential tasks for each season as well as handy hints on solving common problems that might occur.

All the basic techniques you need to know to get started are detailed in the final chapter. It includes an easy-to-follow guide to planning your garden, improving your soil and recycling waste materials. There are also tips on caring for your plants, with advice on feeding and watering, plus the best ways to tackle weeds, pests and diseases, including an at-a-glance guide to identifying many common plant problems.

Help is at hand
Throughout this book, special boxes highlight essential information that will make gardening quick, easy and efficient for the Virgin Gardener.

FAQs—Frequently Asked Questions
Anticipating those questions a new gardener is most likely to ask, here are straightforward answers in easy-to-understand language on those subjects you need to know when you start gardening for the first time.

Steps to success
Essential information about the project at hand is summarized in these quick-reference guides.

Virgin Gardener's best bets
Recommended trouble-free plants giving the best displays are listed; these are grouped according to their cultural needs, to help you choose the right plant for your garden.

Expert tips
Simple techniques, tried and tested by the experts, have been highlighted throughout the book—these tips will save you time, money and a great deal of effort.

Green tips
Where appropriate, handy hints are provided to help you garden in an environmentally friendly manner.

Planting and supporting climbers page 76

Constructing arches and arbors page 92

Making a mowing strip page 49

Reshaping lawns page 46

Adding plants and fish page 138

Building a new pond 136

Using colorful paints and stains page 30

Easy-care garden surfaces page 50

Creating a private terrace page 122

the virgin gardener's jargon buster

USEFUL TERMS

Acclimatization see *Hardening off.*

Algae A primitive plant that forms a green slime over paving and containers that remain damp for long periods. One form of algae causes pond water to turn green and a floating type, known as blanketweed, covers the surface.

Algaecide A chemical to control *algae.*

Alpines Plants adapted to growing in the mountains, usually low-growing and compact. They are traditionally grown together in a special rock garden, but also can be used to fill gaps between paving slabs.

Annual A plant that takes a year to complete its life cycle: the seed grows into a plant, then flowers, produces seed and dies in one year.

Aquatic plant A plant that lives in water.

Bedding Plants that are often used in large quantities as temporary additions to a garden to provide a seasonal display.

Biennial A plant that takes two years to complete its life cycle: forming a plant in the first year, then flowering and setting seed and dying in the second.

Biological control A method of controlling pests by introducing a natural enemy of the pest which is harmless to other insects and the crop.

Bog garden An area either constructed or natural that has marshy soil which can grow moisture-loving plants such as rushes. Often associated with a pond or water feature.

Bud A growing point that can produce either leaves, stems or flowers during the growing season.

Bulb A generic term used to describe any rounded plant storage organ, including true bulbs such as daffodils, *corms* such as crocus, *rhizomes* such as bearded iris, and *tubers* such as cyclamen.

Burlap Sacking material that is used to line aquatic planting baskets.

Capillary matting An absorbent material that holds water. Plants in containers that are placed on the matting can draw water from it by capillary action.

Chemical control A method of controlling pests and diseases using specially formulated chemicals.

Climber Any plant that can grow up a vertical surface. They can be self-clinging, such as ivy, or twining such as clematis, but also include plants such as climbing roses that need to be tied onto their support. Also known as vines.

Cloche A protective dome-shaped cover made from glass or plastic, which can be moved around the garden to protect vulnerable plants from weather.

Compost bin A special container designed to make garden compost from organic waste materials.

Conifer A tree or shrub, usually evergreen, that produces its seed in cones.

Corm A solid, underground stem that stores food during the dormant season. See also *Bulb.*

Crown The area where stems and roots meet at ground level.

Cutting A short piece of stem used to propagate a new plant.

Damping off A disease which causes seedlings to flop over and die.

Deadheading A method of removing old blooms from a flowering plant to prevent seeding, tidy the display and encourage a further flush of flowers.

Deciduous Plants that lose their foliage in the fall.

Division A method of propagating large, established clumps by splitting the roots.

Dormant period The time when plant growth slows as temperatures fall during winter.

Evergreen Plants, of any color, that don't lose their foliage in winter. The leaves are still shed, but not all at once, so it usually goes unnoticed.

Fern A non-flowering plant which reproduces by spores.

Fertilizer A material that is added to the soil to improve plant growth.

Foliar feed A fast-acting dilute fertilizer that is applied as a liquid to the leaves of a plant.

Frost A layer of frozen condensation that may form on plants and other surfaces when temperatures fall below 32°F (0°C).

Fungicide A chemical formulated to kill fungal diseases.

Garden compost An organic material produced by the decomposition of plant waste materials from the garden. Usually in a compost bin.

Germination The sprouting of a seed.

Groundcover plants Low-growing ornamental plants that produce dense growth used to cover the soil and suppress weeds.

Hardening off A method of gradually acclimatizing plants raised in warm or protected areas to the harsher conditions outside. Also known as *acclimatization.*

Hardy A term used to describe a plant that can survive cold; plants, however, vary greatly in their cold tolerance (see page 160).

Herbaceous plants Perennials that produce soft, non-woody growth and die down to the ground each winter. New shoots are then produced each spring from the underground root system.

Hormone rooting powder A compound that is used to stimulate cuttings to produce roots.

Insecticide A chemical used to kill garden insect pests.

Layering A method of propagating by rooting stems while they are still attached to the parent plant.

Leafmold Animal waste which, after aging, is useful for using as a *mulch* or for improving the soil structure.

Manure An organic material made from decomposed animal and plant waste that is used to improve soil structure and to add nutrients that are essential for plant growth.

Mowing strip A permanent edge or narrow paved border around the perimeter of a lawn and level with its surface, so that a lawnmower can mow straight over the edge.

Mulch A material laid on the surface of the soil to suppress weeds and prevent moisture loss through evaporation. There are three types: loose organic mulches, such as *leafmold*, wood chips and grass clippings; loose inorganic mulches, such as gravel and pebbles; and fabric sheet mulches made from permeable materials.

Organic A system of gardening that uses natural materials. Or any chemical compound that contains carbon. Organic fertilizers, such as fish emulsion and bonemeal, are derived from natural sources; chemical fertilizers are man-made.

Perennial A plant that lives more than one year, usually applied to a plant that produces hardy, non-woody growth. Most are herbaceous and die down in winter, but some are *evergreen*. Tender perennials are killed by frost.

Pressure-treated wood Specially prepared softwood lumber that has been impregnated with a wood preservative. Treated wood does not require any further preservative.

Prune To control the growth of a plant by cutting its stems back.

Rhizome A horizontal underground stem. See also *Bulb*.

Rootball A term used to describe the root system of a plant grown in a container or that of a plant grown in the ground when dug up with the soil intact around its roots.

Rootstock The root system onto which a more ornamental variety is attached. Rose cultivars, for example, are often not grown on their own roots but joined onto the root system of an easy-to-grow but less desirable relative.

Scarifying Raking out of dead grass stems from the lawn.

Shards Pieces of broken terra cotta or stones that can be used to cover large drainage holes in a container to prevent soil from washing out.

Shrub A plant which produces woody stems but no central trunk.

Slow-release fertilizer A fertilizer that is coated in a special resin so that it releases nutrients over a period of time. The amount released increases as the temperature rises and with moisture levels, so plants get more food when growing rapidly. Also known as controlled-release fertilizer.

Sod A section of grass including its roots, cut for the purpose of making a new lawn.

Soil, potting A material in which plants are grown. Various types are produced, often based on peat or compost. There are special formulations for different stages of growth and for special needs, such as ericacious soil for acid-loving plants.

Spun row cover A porous fabric designed to be laid over young plants and seedlings to protect from cold and act as a barrier against flying pests. It also can be used to wrap established plants to protect them in winter.

Standard A plant with a rounded, bushy top, grown on a long straight stem.

Subsoil The layer of soil which lies underneath the *topsoil* and contains less nutrients and organic matter and is less well aerated.

Sucker A shoot produced from the roots or *rootstock* of a woody plant. Roses and lilacs often produce suckers.

Tap-root A succulent anchoring root, like that of a carrot.

Tender A plant that is killed by cold. As with hardy plants, the degree of cold tolerated varies from one species to another.

Thatch A term for the dead organic material that forms a dense mat at the base of grass blades in a lawn.

Thinning A method of increasing space between seedlings by removing seedlings that lie in between.

Three-four-five triangle A triangle made from rough timber with sides in the proportions of 3, 4 and 5, and with one corner of exactly 90 degrees. This is useful for checking right angles when constructing squares and rectangles in your garden.

Topsoil The surface layer of soil of which is most fertile.

Transplanting The term given to the moving of plants from one position to another to give them more room to grow.

Tuber A swollen mostly underground stem that bears buds and serves as a storage site for food. See also *Bulb*.

Variegated A term used to describe parts of a plant that have two or more colors.

Vermiculite A natural substance which forms very light, air-filled granules after heating. Useful when growing plants from seed (see page 178).

Vines see *Climber*.

Windbreak A barrier that protects an area from the prevailing wind. It can be made from a fence, hedge or a shelter belt of trees and shrubs, and even fabric.

making
plans

designing your garden

Garden design is one of the most challenging, yet most exciting, pursuits for the Virgin Gardener. It is rather like designing a room in your house, since the same principles of balance and harmony, sense of proportion and use of color and texture apply. Your garden, however, differs in one fundamental way—it changes with time. Unlike interior design, you have to take account of how the garden will look during the different seasons and how it will evolve over the years.

The definition of a well-designed garden is one that contains a combination of features that gel together in a way that reflects the individual personality and lifestyle of its owners and meets their particular needs. This means that every garden design is unique. All successful garden designs, however, conform to a few basic principles which are good starting points when designing your own garden.

Using shapes and contrast

All garden designs, no matter how big or small, how traditional or modern, are made up of simple interlocking shapes. These shapes should complement each other and combine to achieve the same central

3

1 2

theme or style. Your overall design should be clearly defined in appearance, whether you would like to create a formal garden with bold geometric shapes or an informal one with flowing curves.

A common problem with many gardens is that they are confusing to look at, especially when filled with an uncoordinated mass of color, form and texture. To appreciate any particular feature, you need to bring some sort of order to the chaos so that the overall effect has cohesion and individual elements stand out from the crowd. This means choosing features that both complement and contrast with each other —combine plants and features that offer different outlines, textures, colors and overall sizes, so that each can be appreciated in its own right.

Focal points and vistas

To create a well-designed garden, you also must include points of focus which help to provide definition. Statues and ornaments make good focal points, as do plants with bold outlines. Don't be restricted to focal points within the garden. If you have a stunning view, for example, incorporate this into your garden design.

Small features also can be made into focal points by emphasizing them. For instance, you can help lead the eye to a simple sundial using an attractive path, or make the most of a small statuette by framing it from a distance through an arch set partway down the garden.

Focal points can be used in other ways, too. They are useful for highlighting certain features, such as a pool or a rockery, or drawing the eye away from less favorable areas, such as a shed or compost pile. They can add intrigue and mystery to a garden, inviting the casual viewer to explore further. This works particularly well when the feature is partially hidden from view. Don't overdo it, however, since if too many focal points can be viewed from the same position, they become self-defeating.

Exploit what you've got

A design will be all the more effective if it is developed with the garden's surroundings in mind. To some extent, your options should be dictated by the area in which your garden lies. In an urban situation, for example, there may be more need for privacy or to hide an ugly building—in the garden pictured opposite, a fabric canopy provides a modern solution in a contemporary design. In a country location you might want to preserve a view or keep out a sharp wind.

When choosing materials for any garden features, it is worth noting that they look far more striking if they are made of similar materials used elsewhere in your house.

It is also worthwhile making the most of any existing features such as slopes, walls or established trees and shrubs. Even seemingly problem areas can be turned to your advantage by choosing the right plants to grow in them (see page 72).

You should also consider how much time and money you can afford to spend both building your garden and maintaining it afterwards. Different styles and features as well as the plants you choose can have a big impact. Also, think about the sorts of tasks you will be able to carry out yourself and which you may prefer to leave to a professional gardener or builder.

When to start work

Building work is best scheduled for a period of settled weather. Leave planting until spring or fall. If you are redesigning an existing garden it is worth leaving it for a year before making any large changes so that you can note down the good and bad points during all the seasons. By doing this, you will find that you make few mistakes when drawing up your new garden design.

Striking designs
This secluded informal patio area **(1)** provides a focal point for the relaxing colorful planting scheme; fabric canopies and awnings provide privacy for this roof garden **(2)**, while mood lighting, decking and minimal plants create a calming, yet modern, environment, ideal for entertaining; strong geometric shapes and architectural plants form a highly contemporary garden style, which requires minimum upkeep **(3)**.

designing with plants

Choosing the right plants is the key to any successful garden design. The plants need to be able to cope with the conditions in your garden, however (see pages 20–23).

Plants can be used in many ways to create a variety of effects. Some are there to provide a permanent backdrop and to form the backbone of beds and borders. These include hedges, evergreen vines and specimen trees and shrubs. Others are more decorative, producing brilliant flowers, colorful foliage or berries. They are often short-lived, taking the limelight for just a month or two. Most annuals, herbaceous perennials, bulbs and some flowering shrubs and vines fall in this category. A garden is not complete without a few reliable filler plants that hold the design together— evergreen plants and many shrubs are good examples.

Creating structure

When choosing plants for your garden, consider what function you want each to perform and how you perceive the end result.

If you are looking for a dramatic effect, architectural plants with spiky and fountain-shapes such as yucca, phormium and pampas grass are perfect. For even more drama, look for tall, narrow, upright-shaped plants such as columnar ornamental trees and conifers.

Low-spreading plants, such as ground-hugging prostrate conifers and heathers, and mat-forming herbaceous plants can create a more calming atmosphere. So too can vines and wall-hugging shrubs, which help break up the stark appearance of walls and fences.

To add bulk and form to your design, include rounded, dome-shaped plants, such as hebes,

evergreen barberry and viburnum. If it's humor you want, there are several unusually shaped or colored plants you could choose, such as corkscrew rush, contorted hazel and zebra grass. You should use these with discretion, however.

Mood planting

A garden should be a sensual experience and so you need to consider how your chosen plants

will appeal to the various senses. Color is perhaps the most important, but texture and scent should not be neglected.

To choose color combinations, think logically and in stages. The predominant color in most gardens is green, so use this as your background color. Then add colors that appeal, but how you organize them will have a significant effect on the mood you create. To make combining colors easier, separate the color spectrum into two groups: blues, deep reds and purples; and yellows, pinks, bright reds and oranges. If you want to create a harmonious scheme, combine colors from different groups. If, however, you prefer clashing, vibrant schemes, choose colors from the same group. White flowers can be combined with any shade.

Textures are easier to combine because the worst effect you can produce is no effect at all. To make an impact, put together plants with strikingly different textures, such as frothy grasses or soft ferns next to plants with strong outlines—a bold hosta or castor-oil plant, for example. It's not just foliage that can provide texture since bark, stems, flowers, seedpods and berries also can be used.

Place scented plants where they can be appreciated—next to a seating area, near an entrance or alongside a well-trodden path, for example. Avoid exposed sites because the fragrance will be carried away in the wind. The plants you choose should be a matter of personal preference. As a general rule, however, those that produce a strong scent, such as *Lilium regale*, mock orange and wisteria, are best appreciated from afar where their alluring perfume can be carried toward you by a breeze. For a sheltered corner or by the patio, plants with less overpowering scents are better, such as primroses, dianthus and clematis.

Imaginative planting ideas
A large, rounded statue and curved pots combine with spiky bronze carex and *Agave americana* 'Variegata' **(1)** to form a bold design in this seaside garden; bamboo conceals an Oriental statue and creates a mysterious Eastern mood **(2)**; a mass of colorful plants produces a traditional-looking country garden **(3)**, but a modern "twist" is provided by the sculptural metal gate in the background; architectural forms dominate this contemporary roof garden **(4)**, which has a simple planting scheme focusing on a strikingly colorful bougainvillea.

growing your own food

For the Virgin Gardener, having your own garden opens up many opportunities and one of the most exciting is the chance to grow some food. Contrary to popular belief, you don't need a vegetable plot or fruit garden to do this—a whole range of fruits, vegetables and herbs can be grown in ordinary borders mixed in with the flowers, and many others are worth growing in containers (see page 126).

There are drawbacks to mixing crops in with your flower borders, however. Perhaps the most important is that the crop will be in competition with other plants for soil moisture and nutrients. This will slow the crop's development and reduce potential yields. Access is also poor, making it more difficult for you to plant, tend and harvest your crops. When a leafy vegetable such as lettuce is harvested, it can also leave an ugly gap in your flowering display. Fortunately, all these difficulties can be overcome by choosing the right crops for the right locations and adapting the way you grow them.

Productive borders

At the back of a flower border you could try planting an apple tree. Choose a relatively easy to grow variety, such as 'Liberty' or 'Golden Delicious', and the tree will not only be productive, but will also offer decorative displays of blossom in early spring and colorful fruit in late summer. To get the best crop of tasty apples you need to prevent competition from the surrounding plants until the tree has become well established. Don't plant any nearer than 3 feet from the tree and cover the ground around the tree with a piece of landscaping fabric (available from garden centers) to prevent weeds and keep the soil moist. Fan- and espalier-trained fruit trees are a better choice at the back of a shallow border where there is a suitable fence or wall. Runner beans and other vining vegetable crops such as squashes are also worth planting in this position, where they can be trained over canes or other supports. With all back-of-the-border crops, lay stepping stones to make training and harvesting easier.

Edging crops

Some vegetables, such as ruby chard, carrots and frilly leaf lettuce, are so attractive that they can be used as a summer bedding

Attractive harvests

Strawberries and drought-tolerant herbs are combined in this collection of terra cotta pots on a balcony **(1)**; a vine of small pumpkins has been trained along a low paling fence **(2)** with flowering passion flower; add flowering plants to a dedicated vegetable plot **(3)** and you can turn it into an attractive feature.

substitute at the front of a border. A few crops, such as ruby chard and leaf lettuce, can be used in formal schemes because only the outside leaves are harvested, leaving the plant to grow on. If you want to grow crops, such as head lettuce, where the whole plant is harvested, create a less organized feel to the border by mixing up crops, so any harvested plant will go unnoticed. Ever-bearing strawberries are also worth growing at the front of your borders where they will be easy to harvest.

Attractive vegetable plots

You can make an attractive feature out of a vegetable plot by adding flowers and herbs. Some, such as marigolds, rosemary, lavender and garlic, are not only attractive but may also reduce the incidence of common pests. They either confuse the pests by masking the smell of the crops they feed on, or provide food for beneficial insects that naturally prey on the pests.

where and how to buy plants

The plants that you choose for your garden can make or break its overall appearance. To create reliable, long-lasting displays, you should choose plants that suit your garden's soil type and situation, as well as varieties that are hardy in your area. To get the greatest choice of plants you will need to visit a reputable garden center. If you want specific varieties or something a little out of the ordinary, however, you may need to visit a specialty nursery or buy from a catalog. Plant sales and garden shows are other good sources of plants. You will find the best selection during the spring.

Choosing a garden center

Before you buy your plants, first inspect the various garden retailers in your area. Supermarket-like garden centers are good places to start. They don't grow their own plants, but instead buy them from wholesalers. This means they can offer a wide range of plants usually categorized into types to make locating what you want a lot easier. The main area for outdoor plants is usually dedicated to an A–Z selection of shrubs (by their Latin name) with smaller zones for other categories such as annual flowers, herbaceous perennials, trees and water garden plants.

A good garden center should take into account a plant's requirements. For example, shade-loving plants, such as azaleas, camellias and ferns, should be displayed where they are protected from the sun. In frost-prone areas, tender plant varieties should be displayed inside away from cold drafts.

The outside display area of a good retailer should look neat and well-stocked. All container plants should be kept on a well-drained surface, ensuring that plants don't

Steps to success when buying plants
- Make a list in advance of the type of plants you want to buy.
- Choose a reputable garden center or plant nursery.
- Check that the plants are healthy and correctly labeled.

become waterlogged after periods of rain. There should be all-weather paths that are paved and uncluttered to make moving about with a cart more convenient. Beds should be clearly labeled, and groups of the same plant kept neatly together. All plants should be clearly labeled, too, and preferably accompanied by

Green tip

Protecting native plants
Wildlife gardens have become very popular and are often of particular interest to the Virgin Gardener. Many native plants are offered for sale by reputable nurseries, who have raised the plants from seed. Don't be tempted to dig up wildflowers in the country yourself, and do not accept or buy wildflower plants from other sources. Not only is this trade contributing to the destruction of the native wildflower populations, but the plants are less likely to thrive than plants propagated in a nursery from seed.

a color photograph and detailed planting and care requirements, which is an important source of information for the Virgin Gardener. For this reason, it is essential that you make sure that plants have been correctly labeled before you buy them.

Good garden centers care about their customers, and often provide information desks where you can get advice about different plants. This can be a good place to ask about plants that will suit your particular requirements, or to check whether the plant you have chosen has been correctly labeled. Don't be afraid to ask. You will invariably receive a helpful and, if you are lucky, a well-informed answer. Many garden centers also have reference books available, which you can check through before making your plant selection.

Plant nurseries

Most of the plants at local nurseries are grown on site. These nurseries are a tremendous resource of local knowledge for the Virgin Gardener, but they can be daunting places to visit because they are not always laid out in a logical fashion and, in general, are less user-friendly than garden centers.

Display beds are often poorly laid out and plants tend to be more variable in quality and less well labeled. It is still worth visiting your local nursery, however, because even though it tends to offer a much narrower range of plants, you can be certain that all the plants for sale are suitable for growing in your area. The staff are usually very well informed, so nurseries are good starting points if you have a problem with a specific plant.

Some local nurseries specialize in a particular group of plants, such as herbs, conifers or perennials. Again,

they usually grow all their own stock, but as specialists, they may sell a lot of their plants by mail-order. Despite this, you still can usually visit the nursery at set times or on particular days, but call before you go to check their opening hours. Also look for the large mail-order specialists who produce informative catalogs, as these can be a good source of information.

If you do want to buy plants by mail order, start by asking gardening friends where they get their plants and check out the advertisements in newspapers and gardening magazines. Then, call the nursery and ask for a catalog, price list and order form. Once you have made your plant selection, call to check the availability of the plants you want before submitting your order. Remember to check the sizes of plants with the nursery if it is not stated in the catalog and keep a copy of your order so that you can check the plants when they reach you. When they do arrive, open the package immediately to check that your order is complete and the plants are satisfactory. If there are any problems, contact the nursery as soon as you can, to tell them of your complaint. If not, plant as soon as weather conditions allow.

Garden shows

A good way of visiting a variety of specialist nurseries in one day is to attend a garden show. Retailers often bring a range of popular plants to sell at very reasonable prices, so bring plenty of boxes and make the most of the special offers.

Neighborhood and church sales and charity bazaars also can be good places to purchase common plants cheaply as well as introduce you to other gardening enthusiasts in your area. Gardening clubs and societies also are worth joining.

FAQs – BUYING PLANTS

Q How can I tell if the plant is suitable for my garden?

A First check the plant label. These days, most plants are supplied with color labels which clearly state the plants' soil and cultural requirements, as well as how big they will grow. If in doubt, ask an assistant for advice.

Q When is the best time to buy plants?

A Most garden centers have the widest range of new stock in spring when sales are highest. It is always worth checking when the retailer is due to get their next delivery, so that you have the best choice. This is particularly worthwhile if you want small plants, such as varieties of annuals and vegetable plants, that are sold for a short period only. As a general rule, try to visit your local garden center before the weekend rush.

Q Which is the best size to buy plants?

A It is worth buying large specimens of slow-growing plants, such as flowering trees and Japanese maple, especially if they are to be used in a prominent position, such as a focal point, in the garden. Most other plants are best bought as small, vigorous specimens that will be quick to establish and put on new growth.

Q Are plants worth buying in flower?

A Although beautiful displays of flowering plants can look tempting, it is generally best to buy plants before they are in full bloom. However, it is sometimes helpful to know what a new plant looks like in flower—when matching it to an existing a color scheme, for example. Also, some plants, such as potted bulbs, are worth buying as they come into bud to add an instant splash of color to your garden.

choosing healthy plants

Improvements in the production and care of plants in recent years has meant that the majority of specimens that reach garden centers are in peak condition. There are exceptions, however, so it is important to know what you are looking for when you buy plants.

Bulbs

These are ideal for the Virgin Gardener because they are guaranteed to flower in the first year provided they have not been badly treated and are stored correctly.

Your garden center will sell bulbs either loose or pre-packaged. Pre-packaged bulbs are particularly useful because they are clearly labeled with color photographs and a complete set of instructions. Loose bulbs, on the other hand, are often cheaper, but can be more variable in quality, so you will need to be more careful in selecting them. You also can buy bulbs by mail order from bulb specialists. This is particularly useful if you want specific or unusual varieties.

If you are buying bulbs loose, check them over carefully first. A good bulb should not feel light or hollow, but should be firm when squeezed between finger and thumb. There should be no sign of growth from the growing tip and the skin should be blemish-free and intact. The base of the bulb should be firm with no new root growth. Look for large "single nosed" bulbs rather than "multi-nosed" ones because the former will produce larger flowers and create a more reliable display.

Bedding plants

Hardy winter and spring bedding plants, such as pansies or ornamental cabbage, are available as potted plants from mid-fall onward. As when buying any potted plant, make sure these hardy bedding plants look vigorous and healthy so that they can be slipped into the garden for instant effect.

Tender summer bedding annuals (some of which are really tender perennials) and patio plants are sold from early spring at every stage of growth from seedlings to large flowering potted plants. The increasing popularity of these plants means that garden retailers are stocking an ever-expanding range of varieties packaged in increasingly tempting ways. They are usually given their own sales area, which should be protected from cold winds in frost-prone areas. Many popular varieties are also available as seedlings or tiny plants by mail order from seed specialists.

All bedding plants transplant best while young and not in flower. The clamor for instant color in recent times, however, has led to most varieties now being available in bud if not full bloom.

With very small plants, any buds that are forming are best pinched off before planting so the plant puts all its energies into getting established. With larger plants, look for lots of buds rather than flowers that have opened; it is the buds that will provide the display in your garden.

Don't buy plants with yellow leaves, which are signs of starvation, and avoid those with a bluish tinge, as this indicates stress caused by cold weather or a lack of water and nutrients. Try to avoid tall, lanky plants because this means that they have been grown too close together.

Hardy perennials

These plants are usually organized alphabetically by their Latin name in garden centers. Although they are available all year round, most are sold during the spring as small specimens when the fresh new growth emerges, or in the fall as large well-established plants. Plants delivered in early spring can still be on sale during late summer, so it is worth looking for signs of neglect, such as faded labels and weeds in the top of the soil.

Plants should be compact with fresh-looking foliage. Avoid any specimens with yellowing leaves, because this is a sign of starvation and check growing points and the undersides of leaves for pests. Also, make sure that the plants are well-established in their pots, but check that they don't have roots growing out of the drainage holes.

Trees, shrubs and vines

Garden centers have permanent displays of hardy trees, shrubs, vines and other climbers, such as climbing roses, throughout the year. Some shrubs, particularly conifers, are grown in the ground and lifted with soil around their roots (known as *rootballed*) and a few, notably hedging shrubs, are sold during the dormant season bare-root.

Check that all container-grown trees, shrubs and climbers are well-established in their pots, but don't buy any that have masses of roots circling the base of the pot. The foliage of all plants should look fresh and healthy. Make sure that variegated plants do not have any all-green shoots. Roots of bare-rooted plants should be moist while rootballed plants should have a large, firm rootball that is not breaking up.

Trees should have an upright leading shoot and a reasonably well-balanced canopy of branches. Many trees are propagated by joining them to the roots of another tree by a method called grafting. Most are grafted a few inches above the ground, but a few, such as weeping varieties, are grafted at the top of a straight stem to form a standard tree. Check that all grafts are well healed and the union is strong. Don't buy plants with shoots coming from below the graft.

Shrubs should be bushy with dense foliage and have a well-balanced shape. This is particularly important with evergreen shrubs.

essential tools and equipment

The number of gardening tools on the market is growing by the day. The best are based on designs that have stood the test of time. The only notable exceptions are the result of developing technology; a good example is the nylon-line trimmer, that's useful for neatening the edges of a lawn (see page 27).

The basic tools

As a Virgin Gardener, you need just ten essential tools to start gardening, less if you don't have a lawn. A variety of other tools are worth considering because they will save you time and labor; these include many powered versions that will tackle repetitive jobs quickly and easily (see pages 26–27). If your gardening gets more adventurous or you develop an interest in a specific area, then you may want to invest in a few specialist tools later on.

Pocket knife A good general-purpose garden pocket knife **(1)** is not usually thought of as an essential tool by many American gardeners, but it is nevertheless lightweight, easily portable, and capable of handling many small, everyday tasks. It can be used for light pruning tasks such as removing dead flower heads and for taking cuttings. The knife should have a straight blade of high-quality steel that folds away into the handle. Store it in a safe place and sharpen it regularly.

Shovel Also called a spade, a shovel is used for digging, scooping soil and planting large plants. Choose a shovel with a comfortable handle and a shaft that is long

Virgin Gardener's essential tools

10

Pocket knife
Shovel
Trowel
Hoe
Leaf rake
Pruners
Broom
Lawn mower
Edging shears
Hose

2

1

enough to prevent you from stooping—this can cause back problems. Long-handled versions are available for taller gardeners.

Trowel This is a small hand tool used for light cultivation between plants and for planting bulbs, bedding plants and vegetables. Check that the handle is smooth and comfortable to hold in your hand.

Hoe Used for chopping off or uprooting annual weeds by cutting through just below the surface of the soil using a pull and push action. Choose one that is comfortable to use, with a handle of the right length for your height.

Leaf rake This is used for clearing leaves **(2)**, raking gravel and scratching moss and dead grass clippings from the lawn. Check that its weight and balance is comfortable and choose one with closely spaced plastic or wire prongs.

Pruners These are ideal for cutting back woody stems up to ½-inch thick, removing dead flowers and

the general trimming of plants. Check that the handles are not too big for your hands when fully open and are comfortable to use.

Broom This is the best tool **(2)** for sweeping paved areas. Choose one with stiff bristles and make sure the head is securely fitted to the shaft.

Lawn mower For efficient mowing, choose a lawn mower that suits the size and style of your lawn. If you have a large lawn, select a mower with a wide blade; small lawns require narrower blades. There is a range of different models of lawn mower and each has its advantages and disadvantages, but the best all-rounder for the Virgin Gardener is probably the wheeled rotary mower, which is versatile enough to tackle short and long grass. Check that the handle height is right for you and make sure you get a demonstration before you buy.

Edging shears Used for trimming the edge of a lawn **(3)**, clipping small hedges and other general trimming tasks around the garden. Long-handled versions take the backache out of lawn trimming, but are unsuitable for other jobs.

Hose This is essential for delivering water to specific areas in your garden. Choose one that will reach all parts of your garden and doesn't kink when it is unraveled. Consider also buying a hose-reel for convenient storage and an adjustable nozzle to fit on the end so you can control the flow of water while you are using the hose. A hose wand is similar, but has a long spout that will effectively extend your reach, making easy work of watering hanging baskets and windowboxes.

FAQs – BUYING TOOLS

Q Where can I buy garden tools?

A To get the best selection, visit a large garden retailer during the spring when the store is well stocked. You also can buy tools by mail order or from commercial web sites on the Internet, but bear in mind that you will not be able to try them out before buying.

Q Do I need to buy new tools?

A No, second-hand tools that have been properly cared for are often as good and a lot cheaper than a new tool. The selection will be limited, so it is even more important to try them out to make sure they are comfortable. Check that tools are in good condition. Handles should be sturdy and blades straight for easy sharpening later. It is worth seeking expert advice before buying power tools second-hand.

Q What is the best way to care for garden tools?

A All tools need to be kept properly maintained if they are to work well. This means cleaning them immediately after they have been used. Scrape soil from cultivation tools, such as shovels, rakes and hoes, and clean off plant material and sap from the blades of trimming tools such as the lawnmower, shears or pruners.

Q How should I store tools?

A Any tools that are put away for long periods should be cleaned thoroughly, then all bare metal wiped with an oily rag to prevent rust. Sharpen dull blades before storage, so that the tool is ready to use when you need it, and have power equipment serviced. Store all tools in racks for convenience, in a dry, secure place, such as a locked garage or garden shed.

other useful equipment

As well as the ten basic tools (see pages 24–25), you may want to invest in or rent some other pieces of equipment. These are non-essential, but can make light work out of many tasks in your garden.

Digging, planting and weeding

To make these often labor-intensive tasks easier, you could invest in the following gardening tools.

Spading fork Ideal for most digging tasks, especially in stony soil where a shovel is less practical. A fork is very good for cultivating the soil between established plants because it will cause less root damage; it is also convenient for moving bulky materials such as garden compost.

Bow rake Used for spreading and leveling soil **(1)** before planting and sowing. Check that the prongs are evenly spaced and the rake head is securely fitted to the shaft.

Garden sieve Used for separating stones and other coarse debris from soil **(2)**. Those made from molded plastic with a mesh size of ¼-inch are perfectly adequate.

Rotary tiller Useful for cultivating large areas quickly, especially in neglected gardens. These are not worth buying unless you intend to dig large areas every year, such as a vegetable plot, but they can be rented by the day.

Watering and feeding

Ensuring that your plants are kept fed and watered can be an easy task if you have the right equipment.

Watering can If you have a very small garden or need to water just a few potted plants on a patio, a watering can may make more sense than a garden hose. They are also useful for feeding container plants with liquid fertilizer. A separate clearly marked watering can be used for applying diluted liquid weed killers.

Automatic watering If you have a lot of containers, consider installing a network of microbore tubing attached to the mains supply to make watering easier (see page 119). In warmer areas, a system of pop-up sprinklers could be laid to take the hard work out of watering elsewhere in the garden.

Hose-end sprinkler This small attachment screws on the end of a garden hose and sprays water evenly over a large area. Static, rotating, pulse and oscillating types are available. Hose-end sprinklers can be left unattended, so you can do other things in the meantime.

Gardening gloves

Although not essential, gloves make gardening safer and more pleasant. You should buy at least two pairs: a pair of general-purpose leather-palmed and fabric-backed gloves for weeding and working with soil and a thick thorn-proof pair for pruning and cleaning up around the garden. Water-proof rubber gloves are also worth investing in for mixing chemical concentrates and for messy jobs, such as cleaning out a pool.

1

2

3

Hose-end feeder This is an attachment that fits to the end of your garden hose, which contains concentrated fertilizer that is diluted as the water from the hose passes through it **(3)**. It is especially useful for applying a general fertilizer to large areas.

Cleaning up your garden

To keep your garden free of mess and clutter and looking its best all year, there is a huge range of tools and equipment available.

Compost bin This is used to recycle organic waste such as grass clippings, prunings and weeds into a useful soil improver. Choose one that contains about 1 cubic yard of compost and has a removable panel or slats so that you can access the compost easily. More compact, plastic rotating bins are worth considering in a small garden.

Ground cloths Use these for collecting and moving lightweight bulky materials, such as fallen leaves and hedge prunings. Make sure it is made from tough fabric and has carrying handles. Baskets and trugs are also worth considering for small amounts.

Garden cart This is worth buying if you want to move heavy, bulky materials. Choose a sturdy cart or wheelbarrow with pneumatic tire(s). It should be stable when full, and easy to maneuver when empty. You can buy an extension to increase the capacity, but these should only be used for carrying large quantities of light materials, such as leaves. If you wish to move a large quantity of heavy materials, such as paving, rent a special cart instead.

Loppers These are ideal for pruning woody stems between ½-1½ inches

thick. For stems over 1½-inches thick use a pruning saw. Long-reach versions on the end of a pole, which are designed for pruning high branches while still standing on the ground, may be useful if you have a fruit tree to prune.

Shredder This is used to chop woody prunings and tough garden waste into small pieces that can be composted or used as a mulch. Shredders can be heavy to maneuver and noisy to use, so ask for a demonstration before you buy.

Sprayer These pump-up pressure sprayers can be useful for misting plants or applying chemicals.

Leaf blowers and vacuums Both of these are useful for clearing up leaves in the fall and litter at all times. Leaf blowers are ideal for clearing large flat areas such as lawns, paving and drives, while vacuums **(4)** are more suitable for confined areas such as small courtyards and borders.

General lawncare

Green and lush lawns with neat edges can be easily achieved with the help of a couple of extra tools.

Nylon-line trimmer This is not an essential tool for the Virgin Gardener, but it makes edging lawns and trimming long grass and weeds elsewhere in the garden easier. Make sure the model you buy has an automatic line-feed so you don't have to keep stopping to adjust the length of the cutting line.

Dethatcher A powered rake that makes light work of scratching accumulated dead grass clippings and debris from the lawn. Usually unnecessary, but can be rented if you desire.

4

instant improvements

There are many ways of making instant and dramatic improvements to your garden. Trimming and edging the lawn neatly, cleaning the patio, even weeding and covering the soil with an attractive mulch will make a difference. Adding a touch of colored paint or stain to tired-looking fences and other garden structures is also quick and easy to do. If you want to go further, consider reshaping your lawn or adding one or two focal points such as a large terra cotta pot or a statue. Both these changes will alter the way visitors view your garden, guiding gazes from one feature to the next.

Before making any changes, however, take into account the surroundings and scale of your garden. Large features should be sited with care because they can be imposing and dramatically alter the overall appearance and focus of your garden.

Creating an atmosphere

First impressions are very important in gardening. If you create an attractive gateway into your front-yard and a welcoming path to the front door, your whole garden will be viewed in a new light by visitors. Use a combination of plants to provide year-round interest, so that regular visitors see something new with every visit. Position containers next to the front door and fill them with attractive displays to create a welcoming atmosphere. When planted with lush foliage, containers also can be used to soften areas of hard landscaping such as paving and walls. They can be used alone or in collections, or combined with another feature such as a set of steps or a garden seat (1).

Buy colorful annuals or bulbs, such as tulips or lilies, in flower to dramatically improve your garden overnight (2). Already planted hanging baskets and patio containers will also make an instant improvement.

Another way you can quickly transform the atmosphere in your garden is to buy plants that stimulate the senses. Add containers of scented plants along well-used paths and next to the patio or house where the aroma will be most

2

1

appreciated. Also try including furry plants next to seating areas where they can be touched, and aromatic plants in between paving stones where they will be crushed underfoot and release their pungent scent (see page 56).

Adding focal points

By including one or two distinctive elements, such as an attractive container, ornament or dramatic-looking plant, you can instantly add points of focus in your garden.

Ornaments can be particularly useful for creating a sense of mystery, surprise or even humor in your garden. A pair of rock towers **(3)**, for example, adds height and a sense of drama as well as the humor of knowing that such an unnatural stack should instantly collapse.

Containers can be used as a focal element in their own right or planted with eye-catching displays of flowers and placed anywhere in the garden. A planter placed in a raised stand and filled with potted lilies and chrysanthemums, for example, can add a splash of color next to your house **(4).** The beauty of this arrangement is that when the flowers begin to fade they can

simply be removed and replaced with other potted plants or flowers which are just coming into bloom.

Make the most of small figurines by placing them on a column to raise them up or frame them in an arch to focus the eye. Larger human forms, such as bust or statue, tend to look most effective when partially hidden from view, among bamboos or grasses, for example. Animal figures usually look best positioned in a natural setting—a stork by water or a sleeping cat on a sunny wall are two good examples.

using colorful paints and stains

You can quickly turn drab features into something a bit special by using colorful paints and stains, which are widely available from do-it-yourself outlets. They can be used all around the garden on wood, metal, stone or terra cotta.

Choose a paint or stain that is suitable both for use out of doors and for the material you intend to cover. You must make sure that you prepare surfaces as directed, before applying the color.

Using colors effectively
One of the most striking ways to use paints and stains is to choose a color that already appears in your garden. This could be an existing paint or stain, the color of paving or walls or the shade of flowers or foliage. A trellis at the back of a border, for example, will look all the more co-ordinated with its planting scheme if it's painted in the same color as one of the main flowers within the border. Choose a flower that's in bloom for many weeks so that the effect is prolonged. Better still, add other plants with similar colored blooms that flower at other times of year. Not only will the blooms make the trellis look good but the trellis will reinforce the color of the flowers so that they stand out from the rest of the planting scheme. On the other hand, you could choose a contrasting but complementary color to make a feature out of a vine. If a wall painted bright yellow is

Dramatic backgrounds
An angular wall planter filled with theatrical foliage of yuccas contrasts with the deep orange-colored wall (above); blue-stained poles provide a striking backdrop to a casual meadow garden (right).

used to support a purple-flowering clematis, for example, the effect could be quite startling. Again, it will last only as long as the vine remains in flower.

As a rule, it is important not to have too many striking features in one garden. Otherwise they become counter-productive, effectively cancelling each other out. In areas where the summer sunshine is very strong and bleaches out subtle shades, however, you may need the dramatic contrast for the feature to be noticed at all.

Highlighting with color

Paints and stains can be used to emphasize the existence of certain features such as ornate screens, arches or gates. Alternatively, you can use colors to turn eyesores into stylish and colorful features in themselves. A dilapidated shed, for example, can be transformed by adding finials to the roof and fancy fretwork along the eaves, and a windowbox or two at the side, before being painted with bright colors for a festive look.

Paints or stains?

The range of colored wood stains available is increasing all the time. Make sure you use water-based stains around plants and their supports, to prevent harming them, and the more effective solvent-based stains elsewhere.

Oil-based paints also can be used as long as you dilute them with turpentine (use 1 part paint to 2 parts turpentine). Specially mixed paints are best if you wish to create an exact shade.

Mix and match
A blue-stained arbor and matching trellis stand out against this garden's predominantly green planting scheme.

changing shapes and perspectives

Illusions play a part in most gardens, adding a sense of the unexpected to intrigue visitors. There are various tricks you can use to alter the perceptions of visitors and increase the sense of space. Most are easy to achieve and can be used to great effect in any garden.

Simple shapes

All garden designs are made up of a few simple shapes which have a considerable impact on the way the garden is viewed. Straight borders running down either side of a short garden, for example, would make it seem even shorter. One deep border that curves across the garden and into the bottom corner, however, would emphasize the longest dimension of the garden, making it seem larger than it really is.

Paths are also very directional elements—your eye is naturally led to where they end. If a path cuts right through a narrow garden, the sense of space can seem claustrophobic. You can prevent this by introducing changes in direction or obscuring the end of the path from view. Alternatively, try adding a focal point or an arch partway down the garden to form a visual break (see page 54).

Altering perspectives

Every view has natural lines of perspective. In the garden, you can redraw these lines to create an unreal sense of space. A garden fence that gets progressively shorter the farther away it gets from the house, for example, will make the garden seem longer. Likewise, a straight path that narrows as it goes down the garden will have the same effect. Emphasize the illusion by introducing a curve or two to make the path longer.

Color and texture can be used to change the way we view a garden. Fine-textured plants, such as grasses and bamboos, or those with tiny leaves, such as boxwood and barberry, tend to seem further away, while those with large leaves and strong outlines, such as a yucca, will appear closer than they really are. Similarly, bright whites and hot colors such as red, orange and yellow stand out in a border, while cool colors such as blue, gray, lilac and mauve have the opposite effect. Use this natural deception to your advantage when choosing plants

1

and colors to create the illusion of space where you need it. Any effect is most pronounced in the soft light at either end of the day.

Breaking up boundaries

Bare fences and walls not only look stark but they clearly mark the boundary line so that the garden can seem boxed-in. Disguising the boundaries or hiding them with plants can have the opposite effect. In a small garden, you can use vines and wall shrubs as camouflage without taking up too much space. You don't need to clothe the whole boundary in foliage, but simply break up its strong outline. Further down the garden, a well-positioned specimen or two can do the trick. If your garden is larger, you can make the borders wider and include a range of trees and shrubs in your planting schemes.

When positioning plants, check they are having the desired effect from the places you are most likely to view the garden, such as from the patio or kitchen window. By varying the depth of borders and incorporating the tops of plants from neighboring gardens or views, you can make any garden seem larger. Choose plants that blend in with those that can be seen outside to create a seamless transition.

Make the most of small spaces
Covering the high walls of this narrow passage with foliage and flowers **(1)** prevents it from feeling boxed-in, while the cool secluded seating area invites you to pause; vine-clad trellis **(2)** screens out the world without reducing the feeling of space in this roof garden; and tiers of hand-painted pots filled with clipped boxwood and grape hyacinths **(3)** help break up this imposing boundary.

creating mystery and drama

All the best gardens have a distinct sense of drama and mystery that invites the visitor to explore. You can do this in your own garden by adding mirrors, creating concealed areas within the design or using garden dividers.

Rooms for improvement

Dividing a garden into small areas or "rooms" using garden dividers is a good way of adding a sense of mystery. It also can make a small garden seem larger or a large garden more private.

Each "room" can be used to showcase different styles or features, thereby creating a surprise around every corner as well as extending your gardening scope. One "room," for example, could be a herb garden, another a vegetable garden and a third a wildlife area. Try to have a common theme linking all the areas—this could be the materials used to make the dividing screens, the paving materials, or the key plants within each "room."

In a small garden, a tranquil and secluded corner or "room" can be created by adding a garden seat and a few plants, or a piece of trellis and a vine or two. To be effective, the corner needs to be in sun or shade (depending on your preference), and away from dripping trees or the noise of traffic. It also needs privacy and shelter, so you may have to increase the height of your boundary fence. You don't need a large screen to be effective, it just has to block or partially block the view of a feature or area beyond. A simple post covered in climbers strategically positioned can suffice. To ensure that you want to spend time in your secluded corner, add close-up interest, such as intricately marked flowers and foliage, and if possible an attractive view. Such areas also associate well with water features (see page 130).

In a large garden, you can divide the garden into roughly equal "rooms" or have a main open area with hidden annexes slotted in around the edge. Where the garden is long and narrow, the area can be divided to form two or three roughly square compartments, with one leading onto the other. This is a good way of screening off unsightly utility areas used for storage—an ornamental garden with a lawn could lead onto a woodland garden which hides a shed or machinery at the end, for example.

Adding screens

Hedges, trellis and fences are the easiest way to divide a garden. Hedges can be neatly clipped for a formal garden or allowed to sprawl in an informal setting. Trellis and fences can be painted to stand out and as they take up little space, are ideal for small gardens. Trellis allows light to enter the garden, so it can be fairly tall without being imposing or claustrophobic.

Unexpected elements

Mirrors and perspective trellis (also called *trompe l'oeil*) can be used

either separately or together in different parts of your garden to create drama and mystery.

A mirror adds light and a sense of space to the garden and so is especially effective in confined spaces. Position the mirror so that the reflection makes it seem like the garden continues beyond the wall. Angle it slightly so that you cannot see your own reflection and hide the edges to make it convincing. It doesn't have to be big: if framed to look like a small window, it can be very effective.

Secret corners

With a surprise around every corner, the different sections in this design (right) mimic the rooms of a house with a table and chairs in the "dining room" and a bench in the "lounge." A gravel path or "corridor" links the grassy lawn, bordered by colorful flowers, to two "rooms"—a secluded seating area and a child's playground (below).

new approaches to garden design

Garden design has dramatically changed in recent years. The emphasis is no longer simply on the growing of plants, but on the expression of personality and the enjoyment of a convenient and pleasant outside space—a place to relax and reflect on our increasingly busy lives.

Rather than looking back to past glories for inspiration, most modern garden designers are pushing the boundaries of what we understand as gardening. They are using shapes, colors, textures, materials and proportion and, of course, plants in challenging ways.

Getting inspiration

At gardening shows, many settings have become works of art, where the statement or concept lying behind the work is more important than the practicality. As snapshots they are thought-provoking and thoroughly enjoyable. But, in the real world, you cannot expect to maintain a garden of this type—real gardens evolve all the time, changing with every season and from one year to the next. Indeed, you probably wouldn't even want a very design-based garden, because such garden designs tend to be very personal expressions of their

creators that are very unlikely to fit in with your particular needs or personality.

You always can learn from good design, however. Pick out individual elements that appeal, and build on those. Make a scrapbook of garden design ideas and features that you like. Cut out features from magazines and take photographs when visiting garden shows or friends' gardens. Visit famous gardens for inspiration, but most of all, experiment with your own ideas yourself. Don't be afraid to make mistakes—all the best gardeners and designers do.

1 2

Modern materials

Follow your own sense of style when choosing decorative elements for your garden. Natural focal points, such as an upright conifer or a pool, are always popular for garden highlights. Wood, stone, and metal sculptures have been joined by lightweight cast-resin or plastic decorations, which look like natural materials but are usually much less expensive and easier to maneuver. For pathways and sitting areas, conventional flagstone, pebbles, and bricks have been joined by inexpensive wood chips and by pre-cast pavers that make installation a cinch. Adventurous gardeners can have fun incorporating unusual elements like seashells or flea-market finds. Glass chips have become popular with some designers. They can be used to great dramatic effect in a still pool of water—either forming sweeping curves or, as here, heaped into neat conical mounds which represent the piles of drying salt that were a vivid image from the creator's childhood in Vietnam **(1)**.

Sculptures imitating nature are nothing new, but there is something quite challenging about replacing plants with timeless sculptures **(2)**. The use of heaped stone chips in various colors along with the vertical cypress trees gives this garden a futuristic, even lunar look.

The combination of contrasting materials is a popular innovation. The galvanized planter **(3)** contains plants with dark foliage as a counterbalance. The deep purple phormium and the black grass-like *Ophiopogon planiscapus* 'Nigrescens' provides dramatic foliage. Pebbles create a sense of balance while the wooden decking provides changes in texture and color.

New materials have enabled designers to challenge the thinking behind many traditional features, one of which is pools. For example, in the courtyard garden design **(4)**, a curved water tank is used at the front of a raised bed. Water, pumped through the tank to flow like an endless river, makes a gentle sound as it moves and creates a calming atmosphere. The bed behind the water tank is filled with sand and drought-tolerant plants, such as thrift, sedges and ornamental grasses, to provide a visual contrast to the running cool water alongside. The use of contrasting colors helps to emphasize the overall effect.

essential features

2

Ground cover

Grass, plants or paving—however you choose to cover the ground will largely determine what you can use your garden for and how much time it will take to maintain.

The style and type of ground cover you use also will have a profound influence on the very nature and appearance of your garden's design. A well-planned and maintained area of lawn, for example, can improve the ambience of your entire garden. It even can become a key feature in its own right, helping to integrate all the different elements.

As a Virgin Gardener, you have five basic ground cover options: a lawn or wildflower meadow; plants; loose gravel, stone, lava rock or rounded stones; wooden decking and various paving materials. Choosing one will produce a unified effect; combining them can create an exciting and modern design feature.

Before you make a final decision, it is important to decide what you want to use your garden for, how much time you are prepared to spend looking after it, and how much you can afford to spend on it. You also have to consider where your garden is sited. If it is in deep shade for much of the time, creating a lawn will be a struggle as the grass will become thin and patchy or be invaded by shade-tolerant weeds and mosses. Similarly, if your garden is on a steep slope, creating a lawn will be difficult and even dangerous to maintain—it would be better to create a ground covering of low-growing, well-behaved plants.

Bearing these things in mind, read on and use the design solutions outlined on the following pages to help you decide which material or materials will be most suitable for your garden floor.

plants or paving?

Though poets write of a garden as a green and pleasant place, and despite the obvious appeal and advantages of having a grassy outdoor patch, there are many other materials to choose from which are equally attractive and may be easier to maintain.

Lawns

Generally, lawns are easy to lay, require little gardening knowledge to maintain—as long as you have the right equipment (see page 24)—and offer a quick and attractive way of covering a large area of outdoor space for very little cost. Although it is possible to create a fine-quality, putting-green-style lawn, it takes a great deal of effort and some skill to achieve. For the Virgin Gardener, a far better bet is to opt for a hard-wearing, easily maintainable standard-quality lawn (often called a family or utility lawn).

To create a new lawn from scratch, you can either grow it from seed, small tufts (known as plant plugs or sprigs), or lay sod. Sowing seed is the cheapest and easiest option, but takes the longest to establish. If you want to create a lawn quickly, sod can be ready for use in a matter of weeks, but it takes more labor to lay and can be expensive. Sprigs and plant plugs fall roughly between the two.

Flowering lawns

If you have a large garden, covering the ground solely with grass may be impractical because this can take a lot of time to look after. If you really want a lawn, however, but do not have the time to maintain it, one option is to create a flowering lawn. To do this, either sow a special wildflower lawn mixture or plant native flowers and dwarf bulbs in groups in the existing lawn.

If you have very little spare time, try creating a wildflower lawn—one that you leave to grow naturally for most of the year. Filled with wildflowers, the grass needs cutting only twice: once during early spring and once after the flowers drop their seed (see page 44).

AT-A-GLANCE GROUND COVERING SELECTOR

TYPE	COST	WORK TO CREATE	WORK TO MAINTAIN	WEAR	GARDEN USES open areas	steep slopes	paths	patios & sitting areas
Family lawn	$$	•••	••••	•••	✓	✗	✓	✗
Fine-quality lawn	$$$	•••	•••••	•	✓	✗	✗	✗
Wildflower meadow	$	•••	•••	•	✓	✗	✗	✗
Concrete	$$	•••••	•	•••••	✓	✗	✓	✓
Flagstone	$$$$	•••••	•	•••••	✓	✗	✓	✓
Gravel	$$	••	•	••••	✓	✓	✓	✓
Bricks	$$$	••••	•	••••	✓	✗	✓	✓
Groundcover plants	$$$$	•••	••	•	✓	✓	✗	✗
Decking	$$$$	•••	••	••••	✓	✓	✓	✓
Bark or wood chips	$$$	••	••	•••	✓	✓	✓	✗

Successful partners
A combination of attractive paving materials with low-growing drought-tolerant plants help break up the appearance of this large area.

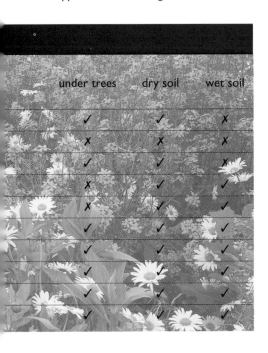

	under trees	dry soil	wet soil
	✓	✓	✗
	✗	✗	✗
	✓	✓	✗
	✗	✓	✓
	✗	✓	✓
	✓	✓	✓
	✓	✓	✓
	✓	✓	✓
	✓	✓	✓

Groundcover plants

Low-growing plants are ideal for covering areas where a lawn is impractical, such as over a steep bank or in deep shade. They also are ideal for the novice because, apart from the occasional clean up in spring and after flowering, ground-cover plants require little mainten-ance. There are many types to choose from. Like lawn grass, it is important to buy a species that suits the location and climate in which you live (see page 160).

Some groundcover plants, like herbs, can be used to produce a "virtual lawn." Bear in mind, however, that even tough ground-cover plants cannot be used in areas that are constantly walked on. If you have a patch that gets only occa-sional use, try planting aromatic herbs such as thymes, which release their pungent scent when they are trodden underfoot.

Paving

The wonderful selection of materials available today can enhance the appearance of a garden and provide a practical, easy-care all-weather surface. It is ideal for heavily worn areas or for providing a flat, durable surface for garden furniture or a grill. Paving, however, can be fairly expensive as well as difficult and hard work to lay, especially if the area is sloping. Once it is laid, however, it is virtually maintenance free.

Loose materials

Few modern garden designs are complete without at least a small area covered by gravel or loose stones. These materials are cheap, hard-wearing and easy to lay, so are ideal for areas where paving is impractical. Periodical weed control and raking maybe necessary to keep them tidy. Loose materials are easier

Steps to success when covering the ground

- If you want a lawn or ground-cover plants, it is important to select species that suit the light levels and climate in your garden.

- Choose the surface that best fits your available maintenance time and how you plan to use your garden.

- If your budget and time is limited, you should start with a low-cost, low-maintenance option; change when time and money permit.

on the eye than great expanses of paving. They can be used to blanket the ground between plants helping to prevent weeds. They lessen evaporation from the soil surface, thus reducing the need for regular watering.

Wood chips or shredded bark are good options if you want to create a natural-looking area around any trees or shrubs.

For a highly modern design effect, try crushed glass. This special glass is tumbled to remove any sharp edges and by using the many colors available you can create some exquisite designs.

Decking

If you want a natural look or to create a sitting area on a slope or a raised up platform, decking is the material of choice. It doesn't need to be constructed on a flat surface and the wood is cut to fit, so it can be tailor-made for any situation. Construction is fairly easy, and the deck can be stained any color you want. Decking tiles also can be laid directly on top of an existing flat surface such as an old patio or terrace.

planting a new lawn

There are several grades of lawn—each is made up of a different blend of several species of grasses. The one you choose should fit in with the climate in your area and how much time you are willing to spend maintaining it. If you want a general-purpose lawn that is easy to look after and is reasonably hard-wearing, choose a standard-quality grade. Special mixtures for shade and wildflower meadows also are available. The species of grasses used in the different blends will vary from area to area to suit the local growing conditions. Make sure you check the information on the seed bags and ask your local supplier for advice if you are unsure which blend to choose.

Preparing the site

Whether you sow seed or lay sod, thorough ground preparation is vital to prevent problems occurring later. The first task is to remove any perennial weeds, such as dandelion. Dig them out by hand, or if you prefer, apply an appropriate herbicide at least a month before sod is delivered or seed is sown. When the weeds are dead, the soil needs to be dug to the depth of a full spade's blade (about 8 inches) and all large clods broken up. The soil should then be roughly leveled using a soil rake and any large stones removed.

Leave the site to settle for a week, then firm the soil by treading the whole area using shuffling small steps with the weight on your heels.

After that, the soil should be raked to even out any lumps or hollows. About a week before sowing the seed or laying sod, scatter some general-purpose granular fertilizer, a handful per square yard, over the soil and rake it into the surface.

Laying sod

The best time to lay grass sod is when the grass is dormant—in early spring in cold-winter areas, as long as the soil isn't frozen or so wet that it sticks to boots and tools, or from fall through early spring in mild regions. You can also lay a lawn successfully in summer in temperate regions, but regular watering is necessary until the grass is established. If the area to be covered is

Sowing grass seed evenly

To get a good-looking lawn, it is important to scatter the seed evenly over the surface. Use the following method to get best results. Choose a warm day when the surface of the soil is dry, but moist underneath.

- Use string and bamboo canes to divide the area into one-yard-square blocks. Measure a quarter of the amount of seed required for each square yard in a plastic cup. Mark this level on the cup and use it as a quick measure.

- Begin walking east to west and carefully scatter the seed in your cup evenly over the first block. Refill, and repeat for each block.

- Then turn around and repeat this process walking from west to east. When you get to the end, each square will have received half of its seed.

- Now, repeat the whole process walking north to south and then south to north. Each square yard will now have received four quarter measures of seed sown as evenly as possible.

- Rake the seed into the surface and cover the area with fine-mesh netting to keep the birds off. Water the whole area with a garden sprinkler and keep well watered until the grass has become established.

- When the grass is about 2-inches high, walk over the lawn and remove any stones that have come to the surface. Then roll the lawn using a garden roller, which you can buy at a home supply store or rent for a day or two. Make the first cut when the grass is dry, the blades of the mower set high—at least 1½ inches.

not clearly defined, use sand to mark out the area. This will make it easier to estimate the number of sod pieces required. It is important to lay grass sod as soon as possible after delivery, preferably the same day. If weather conditions make laying the sod impossible, unroll each sod in a shady spot and give it a light watering to keep it moist, healthy and pliable.

Looking after a new lawn

Once laid, your lawn should be well watered using a garden sprinkler and kept moist until the sod pieces have knitted together. Keep the edges of the sod pieces especially moist because they are prone to drying out and can shrink to leave unsightly cracks. Don't walk on the lawn for at least a month, except to trim the grass with the blades of the lawnmower set high (check your mower's instructions for details). During periods of drought, the new lawn should be watered thoroughly every few weeks during its first growing season.

Flowering lawns and ground cover plants

Add color to the edge of your lawn by planting random groups of bulbs such as bluebells, crocuses, grape hyacinths, daffodils and snowdrops. Keep them in clumps to make them easier to mow around in spring. If you want the whole lawn to flower, either sow a wildflower and grass seed mixture, or add wildflower plants, such as violets or spring beauty (*Claytonia* spp.). If you want to create a spring meadow effect, you can encourage pretty lawn weeds such as diminutive blue speedwell, English daisies, buttercups and oxeye daisies. For a summer-flowering meadow garden, plant clumps of aggressive perennials and wildflowers among the grass. Beebalm, goldenrod, wild asters, perennial sunflowers, coneflowers, and many other plants are suitable; you can investigate the native species in your area.

Small areas of aromatic, low-growing herbs, such as chamomile and creeping thymes, make an inviting lawn, but are too delicate to withstand regular foot traffic. Some ornamental plants, including ajuga, heathers, hosta, groundcover roses, and vinca, all do a fine job of covering the ground with a solid sweep of foliage and occasional flowers.

Laying a new lawn with sod

Before you lay your grass sod, it is important to water the soil until it is thoroughly, but evenly, moist.

1 Roll out the first strip of sod along one side of your new lawn area using a straight edge, such as a board, as a guide. Lay out the second strip of sod, butting it up closely to the first. Press each strip down using the back of a spade. Continue to lay the strips, using two short boards to stand on the area of grass that you have already laid.

   To prevent the joints lining up together, stagger the sod in alternate rows, like bricks in a wall. Use whole sod strips at the edges and place any filler pieces within the main area where they are less likely to dry out.

2 Use a mixture of equal-parts soil and sand to fill any cracks between the sod. Trim the strips using a sharp shovel guided by a board along straight edges, and a stiff piece of hose around curves.

3 Flatten any lumps by jumping on the board, working your way across the lawn.

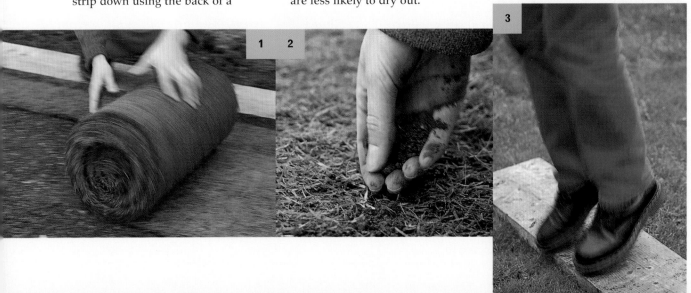

maintaining a perfect lawn

Whether you've planted a new lawn or need to maintain an existing one, it doesn't take much effort to keep it looking good.

Trimming and mowing

Regular trimming and mowing are the secrets to a healthy lawn. These can be fun and satisfying pastimes provided your equipment is well maintained and you don't let the grass get too long (see FAQs, opposite). Installing a mowing strip (see page 49) can make mowing easier and cut down on trimming.

Keep it simple

Lawns with sweeping curves are easier to mow and maintain as you don't have to maneuver the mower around corners.

If you have a particularly dense, lush lawn it is worth removing the build-up of dead grass shoots (known as *thatch*) before it smothers and weakens the grass. Do this by giving your lawn a vigorous raking (known as *scarifying*). You can use a wire rake to tackle small areas but would be better off renting a powered scarifier for larger ones. If your lawn contains moss, treat this first (see opposite). If your grass is growing well and has good color, ignore the thatch; it will naturally decompose and feed the lawn.

You also should clear your lawn of any fallen leaves because they can weaken the grass if left. If you have a small lawn, you can clear it using a wire rake or garden vacuum; larger areas are easier to clear using a leaf sweeper or a rotary mower with the blades set to the highest level (see operating instructions).

Weed control

Many gardeners prefer to tolerate or even learn to appreciate the diversity of weeds in their grass. However, if you want to improve the appearance of your lawn, remove isolated weeds by digging them out using an old kitchen knife, making sure you remove as much of the carrot-like, tap-rooted weeds as possible, or treat them using a dab-on weedkiller. If the weed problem is more widespread, treat the whole lawn with a special lawn weedkiller. Buy one that contains fertilizer, as

shape up your lawn

Lawns needn't be boring rectangles—you could jazz up your garden with a more interesting design. A lawn, however, should have a calming influence on a garden's structure and a simple shape will look best. Over-complicated designs are less easy on the eye, awkward to mow because you have to turn the lawnmower more often, and have more edges, so they take longer to trim.

Fortunately, changing the shape of a lawn is very easy. Mark out your shape using hose for curved lines and bamboo canes for straight ones. Stand back and view how it looks from all angles, making the necessary adjustments until you are completely satisfied. To get a perfect right-angle, make a 3-4-5 triangle out of rough timber (see page 11). To create a perfect circle, mark out the circumference using sand dribbling through a hole in the bottom of a container, guiding your hand with string tied to a stake at the circle's center.

this also will feed your lawn. You should apply weedkillers in early summer when the grass and weeds are growing strongly, but before the weeds flower and spread their seed.

Controlling moss

Moss can be a problem in a shady lawn or following a wet winter. Luckily, it is easy to eradicate using a chemical mosskiller; a combined feed and moss treatment can give your lawn a boost at the same time. If part or all of your lawn is regularly colonized by moss, you will need to deal with the main culprits—mowing too close, compacted or waterlogged soil and too much shade. So, adjust the cutting height of your mower, improve drainage (see below) and thin out canopies of overhanging shrubs.

The cutting edge

A neat edge is the *pièce de résistance* of a perfect lawn. If your soil is light or sandy and crumbles easily, it may be necessary to recut your lawn edge every spring to keep it sharp. To do this, make a vertical cut around the edge of your lawn about 3 inches deep using a sharp spade or a special half-moon edging tool. Use a board as a guide for straight lines or a hose for curved lines. Ease the handle of the cutting tool toward you to create an even gully with a vertical edge. Discard the trimmed pieces of grass to prevent them from rooting in the border, causing a weed problem.

Improving drainage

If your lawn is used regularly during the summer months, the soil underfoot can become compacted, preventing surface drainage and restricting the amounts of air and water that are available at root level. To overcome these problems, aerate your lawn during early fall using a garden fork for small areas or a powered aerator for large ones. Make sure the holes are at least 3 inches deep and spaced about 2 inches apart over the affected area. If you are using a garden fork, wiggle the handle around to enlarge the size of the hole. After aerating, apply a dressing of equal-parts sieved garden soil and sharp sand and brush into the holes.

FAQs – LAWNCARE

Q When should I start cutting my new lawn?

A In temperate regions, start mowing when the grass is about 2½ inches long. Set the cutting height of the mower to 1½ inches.

Q How often do I need to cut my lawn?

A During the growing season, cut the grass at least once a week if you have a family lawn, twice that for a fine quality lawn. Frequent mowing promotes thick and healthy grass that will be too dense to be colonized by weeds.

Q How short should I cut my lawn?

A Do not cut the grass too short because you will weaken it. After the first few cuts, aim to trim the grass by about one-third, cutting it no shorter than 1 inch for a family lawn and ½ inch for a fine-quality lawn. During a prolonged dry spell, raise the cutting height of your mower blades by ½ inch, to help the grass cope with drought. In the fall, raise the cutting height to this level anyway and continue to mow as necessary until the grass stops growing. Do not mow if the lawn is waterlogged or hit by frost.

Q Can I leave the clippings on the lawn?

A Provided you mow regularly, the clippings can be left on the lawn to feed the grass as they decompose. If the clippings are longer than ¾ inch, rake them up for the compost pile (see page 168).

Q How often should I trim the edges of a lawn?

A Trim the edges at least once every other cut to keep it looking its best. Use long-handled edging shears to save strain on your back. If you have a large lawn you may want to invest in a powered edger or a nylon-line trimmer to make the job easier. The latter is particularly versatile and can be used to cut rough grass and weeds all around the garden.

48

improving your lawn

A neglected lawn often contains bare patches, caused by overgrown trees and shrubs, straggly edges and bumps and hollows due to tree roots. It also may have obstacles that make mowing more difficult.

Treating bare patches
Trees and shrubs overhanging the edges of a lawn starve the grass of sufficient light and so it is weakened and it eventually dies. When this occurs, ugly bare patches develop and shade-tolerant weeds start to take over. In order to overcome this problem, you can either reduce the size of your lawn by recutting the edge away from the overhanging shrub, or thin out the canopy of the overhanging plant to allow more light through and re-seed the area with a shade-tolerant mixture of grass seed (see page 44).

If one area of your lawn is used more than any other, such as around the grill or under the swing set, you could provide reinforcement. Replace the grass with a more durable material—gravel or wood chips, for example—or protect the area with hard-wearing green plastic mesh. Buy this from your garden center, then simply peg it into position over the precut area of lawn and allow the grass to grow up through the mesh to hide it. Then, re-sow any bare patches.

Tackling troublesome roots
Hills and troughs can make a lawn look poorly maintained, especially during the summer when hills get scalped by the blades of the lawnmower and hollows show up as patches of lush, green grass. One of the main causes of a lawn's unevenness are tree roots growing just below the surface. Remove roots as described opposite ("Repairing lumps and hollows"), or raise the

Dealing with damaged edges

A carelessly placed foot while mowing or playing can damage the lawn edge. This can be repaired without recutting the outer shape.

1 Using a garden shovel, cut a rectangle of grass that includes the damaged area.

2 Use the shovel to cut under the grass evenly, so it is about 1-inch thick. Then, turn the grass patch around so the damaged area is within the lawn.

3 Now, fill the gap and any holes and cracks with good garden soil, and sow with a grass seed that matches the quality of your lawn (choose a shade-tolerant type for shady areas). Press the seed into the surface using the back of a soil rake.

Then water well using a watering can which produces a fine spray; take care not to wash away any seed. Finally, cover with spun polyester row cover material or fine-mesh netting held down by stones. This protects the seeded area from the birds and keeps it moist. Remove the protective covering once germination begins.

level of your lawn over a period of time. To do this, you should mix equal-parts of sieved soil and sand and sprinkle a thin layer evenly over the lawn every couple of months during the growing season. Do not add more than ½ inch at any one time, however, and never bury the grass completely.

Some trees also throw up shoots from roots (known as *suckers*) which can disfigure the appearance of a lawn. To remove these, you need to expose the root and point of origin of each sucker, and then pull off each sucker by giving it a sharp tug. Don't prune off the suckers at ground level, though, because this will simply encourage the roots to produce further, even more vigorous, suckers.

Making a mowing strip

Installing paving slabs or bricks around the edge of the grass can help to frame your lawn as well as provide all-weather access right around your garden. It will also mean you spend far less time trimming the edges and it makes mowing far easier.

To lay a mowing strip, dig a trench around the lawn, which is 3 inches deeper than your pavers or bricks. Fill the trench with a 3-inch layer of ready-mixed dry concrete. Place the pavers or bricks on top of the concrete, tapping them down to ensure that they are level with each other and the lawn. Now, brush dry mortar mix between the bricks or slabs, water well and allow to set. Mow over the the strip.

Repairing lumps and hollows

Individual lumps and hollows can be tackled in the following way. If, however, a large area of your lawn is uneven, you would be better off raising the level of the lawn instead (see "Tackling troublesome roots," left).

- For either a lump or hollow, make an H-shaped cut about 12 inches wide and 18 inches high. Use a sharp spade and center the cut over the offending area.

- Carefully cut under the grass on both sides to produce two even flaps about 1 inch thick. Then, peel back the flaps making sure they do not tear or crack.

- Using a garden fork, loosen the surface under the grass flaps and remove any buried debris, such as rocks, that could be causing the problem.

- Add or remove soil as necessary to level the area, before firming and relaying the two flaps of grass. Check the area is level with a straight piece of lumber.

- Finally, fill any cracks with an equal-parts mixture of sieved garden soil and sand, then water thoroughly.

Using a mowing strip
A line of bricks or slabs can make mowing easier. Make sure you run the mower right over the brick strip to keep the edges trim.

easy-care garden surfaces

J oe and Marsha Fraser have two sons aged eight and ten and wanted to turn their dreary suburban garden into an attractive place for the entire family to relax yet provide enough space for the children to play. They are a busy family, so couldn't afford to spend too much time on routine maintenance. Marsha is interested in foliage plants and the whole family was keen to have a lawn. They were looking for a design that would incorporate a range of low-maintenance features, which are easy to keep looking good and well able to withstand the wear and tear that comes with two energetic children. The garden is south facing and slopes slightly toward a copse of mature trees which casts quite a lot of shade, especially in winter.

Somewhere to sit

The Frasers wanted a patio where they could sit and enjoy the garden, but didn't want an ordinary patio. They liked the idea of gravel, but this wasn't a practical option so close to the house because there was no doubt that with two lively children the small stones would find their way inside.

If you are in a similar situation, a good alternative that offers the look and feel of gravel but the convenience of paving is called bonded gravel. Rather than being loose, the gravel is bound together by a resin, which keeps it in place and forms a firm surface; ask your local garden center or builders' merchant for details—you may want to get a professional contractor to lay it for you.

The Frasers needed quite a large area of paving, so to help break up the expanse they decided to create a patchwork effect using lines of frost-proof bricks to form borders between squares of paving. Marsha, who works as a movie editor, particularly liked the idea of continuing the same design for the path across the lawn because it gives the impression of a strip of negatives. This paving not only helps to link the patio and lawn areas, but also forms an all-weather path to the woodland play area at the bottom of the garden. A couple of the squares near the edge of the paved area have been planted with a range of drought-tolerant plants, such as ornamental grasses, to help soften the impact of the regimented lines.

Making the patchwork

Laying a path is a relatively easy task and well within the scope of the confident Virgin Gardener. Joe decided he would construct the paths himself, but hired a professional contractor to help him lay the paving patchwork.

To make the paths, Joe first needed to ensure that they were laid on strong foundations. To achieve this, he dug a 6-inch-deep trench, slightly wider than the length of a brick, along each line of the patchwork pattern. Next he placed a 3-inch-deep layer of dry concrete mix along each trench and then rammed it down firmly. Moisture from the soil was absorbed by the dry concrete mixture causing it to set firm. Once the concrete foundations had set, Joe laid the frost-proof bricks on a bed of mortar on top of the foundation layer, checking they were level and perfectly straight. He used spacers between the bricks to ensure that all the gaps were even. Lastly he filled the gaps with mortar, carefully smoothing the surface using a small piece of hose and clearing away any excess. The contractor firmed the base in each of the patchwork squares to leave the top inch to be filled with the bonded gravel.

Low-maintenance lawn

To make cutting the grass easier, bricks have been laid around the edges of the lawn to form a mowing strip (see page 49) so that the lawnmower could pass straight over the top when mowing—practically eliminating the need for edge trimming. Although quite dramatic in appearance, the design of the lawn is in fact very simple, making it remarkably quick and easy to maintain.

The existing lawn was so patchy that the Frasers wanted to start again. They decided to lay a new lawn using grass sod that contained a reasonably hard wearing blend of grasses. This type of lawn can cope with seasonal wear if you have children who enjoy playing in the garden, but still looks good. What's more, it doesn't need to be mown as often as a lawn containing finer grasses.

Long-lasting borders

The design contains two feature borders, one narrow and one deep, running down either side of the lawn. It is essential to cover all the bare soil with foliage so that weeds have less opportunity to become established. Before planting, the borders were thoroughly dug over and all the weeds, including the roots, were painstakingly removed. Marsha decided she wanted to grow a lot of foliage plants with some flowers providing seasonal variation and interest.

Instead of annual bedding plants that would need to be replaced every year, a combination of permanent edging plants are used in both borders. For foliage contrast, Marsha chose a variety of evergreen groundcover plants, including bergenia for its large rounded leaves, the variegated grass *Holcus mollis* 'Variegata' and the multicolored *Ajuga reptans* 'Burgundy Glow'. In the narrow border, long-living trouble-free perennials including euphorbias, sedums and hardy

geraniums have been added. In the deep border, they have included shrubs, such as variegated dogwood, photinia and euonymus, which do not require regular pruning, are not susceptible to pest and disease attack and are tough enough to cope with the occasional football. All the beds are covered with a 3-inch layer of bark chips to keep the ground moist and to suppress weeds.

At the bottom of the garden a 3-inch layer of bark chips was also used to cover the soil between the trees and shrubs at the end of the garden to enhance the woodland effect and prevent weeds.

Blurring the edges
The different ground covers of paving, lawn and plants in this garden have been integrated successfully by allowing one element to run into the other.

Woodland floor
Between the mature trees at the end of the garden (above), a layer of bark chips was put down to create a natural looking, weed-suppressing ground cover.

a sun deck for all seasons

Jenny and Matthew Lawrence have a young daughter, Helen, age three, and have bought a house on the outskirts of town with superb views of the nearby hills. The garden faces southeast, so the Lawrences would like to take full advantage of all the sun it gets. The favorable climate in their area means they can make use of an outside room for most of the year, but the area nearest the house gets hot in the height of summer, so the Lawrences are eager to introduce some form of shade. They also like to entertain, so they wanted a flat surface area at the back of the house large enough to accommodate a dinner party. Paving would be too hot in their situation, so they decided on decking. As well as being quick and fairly easy to install, decking is also very versatile and can be adapted to fit any garden.

The first decisions

If you are adept at making home improvements, installing decking in your garden will be well within your capabilities. Otherwise, it is a quick (and therefore relatively inexpensive) job for a contractor. Before you commit yourself to anything, however, you must first consider exactly where you want the decking, its overall dimensions, and how much you are prepared to spend. Decking can be constructed from the naturally durable Western red cedar or pressure-treated wood, both of which are available in kit form from decking suppliers. If your budget is tight, you can also build decking from rough-sawn softwood prepared for use outdoors, such as fence posts and boards that are available from lumber yards and fencing suppliers. These will create a more rustic effect.

The Lawrences decided upon a cedar deck to run the full width of their garden, with a stepped front edge so that they wouldn't need a hand rail that would interfere with the view. To provide shade in summer, they opted to include an arbor covering about half of the deck, and added outdoor lighting so the deck could be used well into the evening.

Designing the deck

Planning is the key to a well-designed and constructed deck, so it is a good idea to make an accurate plan of your garden on graph paper before you go any further. Permanent features such as drain access covers and trees should be indicated. To help them visualize their design, the Lawrences marked out the area on the ground with pegs and string and used a second line to indicate the level of the final surface.

Once you are happy with the overall design, you should consider making a detailed plan of the decking construction if you are intending to build the deck yourself; this will make it easier to estimate the amount of lumber you will need and, therefore, reduce waste later on. It is particularly important to get the overall width right, taking account of the width of each board and the spacing between the boards to allow for drainage.

Building the base and top

The Lawrences hired a couple of specialist decking contractors to build their deck, who made quick work of the job. They first put together a frame for the decking and fixed this to sturdy posts concreted into the ground. Next they covered the ground with a special weed-proof

All hands on deck

A large area of decking was constructed so that dinner parties could be enjoyed on warm, summer evenings. Most of the garden was planted in lawn with feature plants adding structure and colorful flowers offering seasonal interest.

snowdrops and snowflakes appear in the soil around the tree, complemented beautifully by spring-flowering crocuses and daffodils which have been planted in the surrounding lawn. To help the different elements of the design to blend together, lumber identical to the decking has been used to construct a garden seat and a series of frames down one side of the garden to support a variety of fruit crops. The shed at the end of the garden was converted into a playhouse for Helen and her friends. This has a small yard surrounded by a picket fence to keep them safe but still in view of her parents sitting on the deck at the other end of the garden.

landscape fabric to stop weeds growing underneath. The top of the deck was then encased with boards. The contractors fixed the two outermost boards in position first, and then laid the rest roughly in position, evenly spaced about ¼ inch apart. The boards were then hammered into place and trimmed to leave about a 1-inch overhang on all sides. So that a drain inspection cover could be easily accessed, the boards over its top were cut and then secured with rust-resistant screws (pictured far left).

Seasonal features

Color is provided in the form of potted plants. In the summer, the Lawrences used bedding plants such as coleus, marigolds, cineraria, and lobelia combined with spiky phormiums. In the spring and fall, they added bright and cheerful potted bulbs. A variety of vines have been encouraged to cover the arbor and other vertical surfaces. Up the posts in the middle of the deck, Jenny planted vines that would eventually be trained right over the top to provide extra shade, and jasmine for its delicious scent. Passion flowers were also planted in tubs and trained up the walls of the house.

The majority of the rest of the garden is planted in lawn with a multi-stemmed white birch as a focal point. The birch comes into its own in the spring when bulbs such as

A YEAR LATER. . . VINING PLANTS

Once vines have become established, they very quickly grow and cover their supports. Jenny used vertical wires attached to each post and along the overhead horizontal timbers of the arbor to make training the vines as easy as possible. The scented jasmine (pictured) planted against one of the posts in the middle of the deck is a particular favorite with visitors because it fills the evening air with its fragrance from early summer until fall.

Leading you
down the garden path

Paths are an important element of any garden design so should be given careful consideration. They not only provide access from one area to another, but their style will influence the rest of the garden.

Paths are very directional and suggest movement in the garden design. The straighter, narrower and flatter the path, the more it encourages us to move on. On the other hand, a gently curving path will invite the user to pause at every turn and appreciate his or her surroundings. A path, however, can be designed so that movement is not its primary focus. In the picture opposite, two contrasting paving materials have been combined to create a spiral mosaic half way down the path in the middle of the garden. The effect is quite startling; not only does it add visual humor to the scene but an ingenious central focus is given to the path.

Selecting a style

The style of path should reflect the overall design of the garden. It is a good idea to repeat the paving theme used elsewhere in the garden to help the different features to gel. In a formal garden, for example, a straight path laid in a regular pattern will reinforce the geometric shapes used elsewhere. However, if you want the paths to be less obvious, try combining two or more flat paving materials in various sizes and colors.

In an informal cottage garden, a path can simply meander between features. Use loose materials, such as gravel or wood chips, which are easy to lay in curves, or put down small block pavers or bricks in an informal pattern. Allow plants to spill over to hide the edges and, on occasionally used sections, plant the cracks with tough aromatic plants (see page 56).

Creating illusions

A straight formal path laid directly down the garden can make a short garden seem smaller. To counteract this effect in a formal garden design, incorporate a change in direction such as a zigzag, or create the illusion of depth by tapering the path so that it gets narrower the further away it is from the house. Another design trick is to use diagonal paths that run across the garden, making the plot seem larger. Or you can let the path disappear from view behind a garden feature and when it reappears, make it visually different by changing the material it is made from or its width.

Choosing materials

The frequency and type of use a path gets should influence the materials and type of construction. If, for example, the path is to withstand heavy weight, the foundations will need to be deeper and the paving material stronger. On the other hand, where a path gets only occasional foot traffic, simply laying pavers or other materials on firmed soil would suffice.

For a hard-wearing path that you can use in all weathers, choose bricks, blocks or concrete pavers; the latter are available in a range of sizes, shapes and finishes (see page 58). In an informal garden design, hard paving materials can be combined with loose gravel or pebbles, to soften their appearance. All-gravel paths are a practical option in many gardens because they are very easy to lay. Bear in mind, however, that pebbles on their own are uncomfortable to walk on, so suitable only for an occasional path. Another option for a rarely used path is grass. It is easy to lay but requires more maintenance than other path surfaces.

Wood has natural appeal, too, and can be laid to create formal or informal effects. It is reasonably easy to construct and very versatile so can be adapted to fit any situation. Wood can also be stained to complement or contrast with its surroundings. Rough-sawn lumber produces splinters and planed timber or wood blocks become slippery when wet or covered in frost, so it is a good idea to cover them with wire mesh to provide grip in shady areas. Alternatively, use specially prepared decking timber which is rot resistant and grooved to provide a non-slip surface.

Combining colors and textures
A spiral mosaic design using a variety
of materials focuses the eye on the middle of the garden (1); small-leaved ivies
have been cleverly trained along the risers
of a set of steps to soften the edges (2);
pieces of sawn lumber make a natural
edge to an informal path (3); and a
stained boardwalk adds color contrast to
a garden setting (4).

paved patios

A flat, hard and strong surface is a useful one on which to place a grill or an outdoor table and chairs. Ideally, a patio should be positioned close to the house where it is convenient to use in an area that gets sun for much of the day. This is easiest to achieve in south-facing gardens. If the best view is from the side of your house, however, there is no reason why you shouldn't build a patio in this position. If you have a north-facing back garden, the best place for a patio may be away from your house where it catches the sun for most of the day. Or you could have more than one paved area: a patio adjoining the house where you can dine outside on warm days and another hidden from view in a secluded part of the garden where you can sunbathe in private.

Planning your patio

A patio needs to be sited on reasonably flat ground; otherwise you will have to invest a lot of time and labor building retaining walls, steps and terraces. You also need to consider how your patio will integrate into the rest of the garden's design, particularly in a small garden where the paved area will take up a higher proportion of the available space. Useful techniques, such as echoing the paving materials elsewhere in the garden or softening the edges of the paved area with plants (as described on the opposite page), both work well.

You can also use the paving stones to create interesting shapes—don't feel that you have to stick to square or rectangular paving stones. Another useful design idea to consider is to lay a path that curves away from the patio area and into the garden so that it disappears behind a border or another feature in the distance. This not only leads your eye away from the patio, but entices the casual observer to explore the rest of your garden.

If you decide that the best place for your patio is away from the house, make sure that you include a reasonably direct all-weather path between the two, so that your patio is easy to reach and will, therefore, be used on regular occasions (see page 54 for ideas).

Avoid positioning your patio under overhanging trees with large leaves that tend to drip for a long time after a rain shower or under lime and maple trees, which attract sap-sucking insects that will shower the area with sticky honeydew, making it unpleasant to use.

Concrete paver finishes

Brushed A finish that looks like yard broom brush marks in wet concrete.
Cobbled A multi-block finish to look like cobbles, bricks or other small unit paving.
Exposed aggregate The surface of the concrete slab is studded with exposed pieces of gravel.
Riven A weathered appearance that looks like natural flag stones.
Stippled The surface is covered by a series of raised lines or spots for a non-slip finish. This is ideal for shady areas where algae can make smooth paving slippery.

Adding texture to a paved area

Sow seeds of flowering plants such as aubrieta in the cracks between paving slabs to provide color and interest. Wide crevices can be planted with small plug plants for a more instant effect.

- Use a screwdriver to remove the weeds, complete with their roots, then clear the soil and other debris from the crack to a depth of at least 3 inches (see picture, left), deeper if possible. Fill the crack with loam-based compost, pushing it into place with a piece of wood or a bamboo cane.

- Level and firm the surface, then scatter seed thinly on the crack. Cover with a dusting of sieved soil, then water using a watering can with a fine rose attached.

- When seedlings emerge, thin any overcrowded ones by removing the weakest. Once established, trickle a layer of fine gravel between the plants.

Once you have decided on the position and design of your patio, you could think about temporary or permanent screens, which can provide privacy from neighbors and shelter from cool breezes.

Choosing materials

A patio can be made of either a hard surface such as pavers or bricks, or a loose material such as gravel. Gravel can also be laid to form a solid surface if mixed with a bonding agent, such as resin. In general, hard surfaces require the most ground preparation and are hard work to lay, but are practically maintenance free. Loose materials tend to be less expensive and easy to install, but are less convenient to use and need seasonal maintenance such as weeding and raking.

When choosing a material, match it if you can to those already used in other parts of your house or garden. To make large expanses of paving appear less imposing, break them up with another type of material that contrasts in shape, texture and color—gravel, lava rock or rounded stones are ideal. Try to avoid using more than three materials in any one area; otherwise the effect will look too busy. To make the laying easier, make sure that the different materials are all of the same thickness.

There is a wide range of paving materials on the market. Concrete pavers are the most common and available in a wide range of sizes, shapes, colors and finishes to suit most situations (see the list above left). Some are available in several sizes which neatly fit together to form a more interesting paved pattern. Frost-proof bricks, glazed tiles and flagstone are other, more expensive options. They can be more difficult to lay evenly, however, so you may prefer to hire professional help.

Creating planting pockets

Add interest and a splash of color to your patio by using a variety of low-growing plants within the patio area. Plants can soften and break up large areas of stark concrete and prevent your patio appearing bleak and bare.

The best plants to intersperse among paved areas are dianthus, hens-and-chicks (*Echeveria* spp.), smaller sedums, and fine-textured ornamental grasses such as blue fescues. In cracks or along edges, use mat-forming, aromatic plants such as creeping or wooly thyme, and Roman chamomile, which can stand up to occasional foot traffic and which will release a delightful scent when stepped upon.

1 Using a spade, pry up the slab and set to one side. Push a strip of old carpet under the spade to prevent it from damaging the surrounding paving.

2 Remove any gravel under the slab and then loosen the soil underneath. Dig out the soil to a depth of 12 inches and replace it with fresh soil. While the plants are still in their pots, water them and allow to drain. Place the plants, while still in their pots, on the planting area and adjust the arrangement until you achieve a pleasing result.

3 Plant the largest specimens first, then fill in the gaps with the smaller plants. (If you are using bulbs, see page 60 for instructions on planting.)

4 Water the plants thoroughly and then mulch with gravel, lava rock or pebbles that either contrast with or complement the colors of the paving.

Flower borders

No garden is complete without a generous selection of flowers. They herald the changes from one month to the next, providing seasonal variation in hue, form and texture. Some, such as early spring bulbs, produce wonderful blooms for a few short weeks; while others, such as reliable summer annuals, last for several months, creating an unbroken succession of color and interest.

Flowers can be classified according to how long they live and the way they grow. The annuals and biennial types bloom for one season only, but perennial flowers and bulbs can last for many years. Flowers come in all shapes and sizes, too, from the most delicate alpines that eke out their existence in cracks between paving stones, to monster border plants that throw up rocket-like flower spikes or produce flamboyant blooms the size of a saucer.

The selection on offer is huge and constantly growing, with even an average garden center offering several hundred varieties as seed, seedlings, small plants and flowering specimens in spring and early summer. For the Virgin Gardener, however, such an unlimited choice may seem overwhelming. Your choice of flowers should depend on whether you want them to last for one season or more, the time of the year you want them to bloom, what the growing conditions are like in your garden, and how they will blend in with your color scheme.

Although there are many flowering gems to be found, there also are quite a few duds that you should avoid. Use the guide on the following pages to help you make the right choice.

spring flowers

Spring bulbs herald the coming of the growing season in colder regions and are an easy and reliable way of adding much needed color at the beginning of the year. Spring annuals follow soon after, while certain perennials are in flower even earlier than this.

Making use of bulbs

Bulbs can be used all around the garden: in beds and borders, naturalized in grass, planted under deciduous trees and shrubs, and even in containers (see page 114).

Plant spring-flowering bulbs as soon as they become available (see FAQs, opposite). Wait until the soil temperature starts to cool in mild areas. You may have to give some bulbs a winter chilling in the salad crisper of your refrigerator for six weeks before planting in areas that have warm winters (check with your local garden center or bulb supplier if you are not sure).

To get the best results, you need to plant the right bulb in the right place—taking into account the bulb's soil and sunlight requirements as well as its flowering height and color. Spring bulbs offer many different, often bright, colors that when used effectively can make eye-catching features in their own right.

However, a poor combination of heights and colors can be disappointing or even garish. To help you combine different types effectively, use the color photographs and heights detailed on the packets of pre-packed bulbs as a useful reference.

To achieve a natural appearance, bulbs should be planted in irregular shaped groups or drifts (see FAQs, opposite). Plant odd numbers of bulbs to avoid creating unnatural-looking symmetrical plantings. Large bulbs, such as tulips, can be planted in small groups of five or so, but smaller bulbs, such as crocuses and anemones, need to be planted in larger drifts of twenty or more to have an impact. Perhaps the easiest and most reliable bulb for the Virgin Gardener to start with is the daffodil. Given a sunny site, it will flower reliably in cold and mild climates, producing its bright yellow trumpets year after year.

If you have problems with squirrels or other wildlife digging up the bulbs for food in winter, try burying a piece of chicken wire over the bulbs at planting time.

After flowering, the plants should be allowed to die naturally, so that they can build up enough reserves to flower the following

Spring carpet of flowers
Tulip 'China Pink' and the spring bedding double daisy 'Red Pomponette' combine to form a brilliant spring ground covering in a mixed border.

PLANTING DEPTHS FOR BULBS

BULB TYPE	PLANTING DEPTH	BULB TYPE	PLANTING DEPTH	BULB TYPE	PLANTING DEPTH
Anemone	1–2 inches	Fritillary, snake's–head	2 inches	Lily, enchantment	5–7 inches
Cyclamen	½ inch	Large daffodil	5–8 inches	Ranunculus	3–4 inches
Crocus	2–3 inches	Grape hyacinth	3 inches	Squill	3–4 inches
Chionodoxa	2–3 inches	Gladiolus	4–5 inches	Snowdrop	2–3 inches
Dwarf daffodil	4–5 inches	Hyacinth	4–6 inches	Species tulip	4–5 inches
Freesia	3 inches	Iris (bulb)	3–5 inches	Tulip	6–8 inches

(see plant label). Spring annuals should be planted during mid-fall in mild winter areas, or in early spring in colder regions. Plant them between 6 and 12 inches apart, depending on the type of plant.

Color choice is largely a matter of personal taste, but combinations of pastel colors always work well, as does planting compatible colors such as blues and pinks, or yellows and reds in the same scheme. Another reliable pairing worth a try is to plant a single color bulb, such as yellow tulips, with a planting of single-color annuals, such as blue forget-me-nots.

Early perennial interest

Evergreen perennials such as bergenia, hellebores and lungworts (*Pulmonaria*) provide the flowering link between winter and early spring. The saucer-shaped flowers of the Lenten rose (*Helleborus orientalis*) are borne in shades from white to deep maroon, while the stinking hellebore (*H. foetidus*) offers both attractive foliage and flowers, so is double value in early spring. Another good foliage plant is lords and ladies (*Arum italicum*), which produces arrow-shaped dark green leaves marbled with cream.

Although most herbaceous perennials don't come into leaf until early summer, a few useful plants provide attractive foliage in mid- to late spring. The new growth of some hostas, for example, is particularly attractive as they unfurl in mid- to late spring. Euphorbias, such as *Euphorbia amygdaloides* 'Purpurea', produce striking foliage. Ferns supply delicate greenery.

year. For this reason, it is important not to remove foliage until at least six weeks after flowering; for the same reason, don't tie the plant into bundles as is often recommended.

Spring annuals

Plants such as forget-me-nots and pansies combine well with spring flowering bulbs to create bold splashes of early color, and help extend the flowering period right through to summer.

Annuals come in a wide range of bright colors as well as pastel shades. Most will grow in sun or shade and will tolerate all types of soil, although they will perform better if given the ideal conditions

FAQs – BULBS

Q What kind of soil conditions do bulbs need?

A In general, most bulbs prefer a well-drained but moisture-retentive soil in full sun. Several bulbs, such as glory-of-the-snow (*Chionodoxa*), autumn crocus, lily-of-the-valley (*Convallaria*), hardy cyclamen, winter aconite, dog's-tooth violet (*Erythronium*), and snowdrops (*Galanthus*), however, thrive in areas of dappled shade.

Q When should I plant spring-flowering bulbs?

A The best advice is to plant them as soon as they are available, provided the soil conditions allow. This means late summer for daffodils and early to mid-fall for the rest. Tulips can be planted as late as early winter in milder areas without affecting the following season's flowering display.

Q What's the best way to plant bulbs?

A Bulbs can be planted individually using a trowel or special cylindrical bulb planter, but for larger drifts they are easier to plant in a trench scooped out using a shovel. Space bulbs out in an irregular pattern for the most natural effect.

Q Which way up should a bulb be planted?

A If there are no roots showing around the flat bottom of a bulb, plant it with the pointed side facing upward. Crown imperials (*Fritillaria imperialis*), however, should be planted on their sides to prevent the hollow bulb from filling with water and rotting.

Q How deep should I plant them?

A As a general rule, a bulb should be planted in a hole about three times as deep as the bulb is high. So, a 2-inch bulb should be planted in a 6-inch deep hole. Use the chart opposite as a guide.

colorful summer flowers

Although a temporary addition, summer bedding plants, commonly called annuals, can provide wonderful color displays during the summer months. They can be used all around the garden, as individual specimens in small groups or in massed displays. You can find a dazzling variety of summer annuals at garden centers, or you can grow your own from seed.

Creating displays

There is a huge range of summer bedding varieties, but for reliable long-lasting displays look no further than ageratum, alyssum, begonia, calendula, dahlia, dianthus, geraniums, impatiens, lobelia, marigold, petunia, salvia and verbena, which will all flower continuously from early summer. Bachelor's-buttons, cleome, cosmos, sunflowers and zinnias are easy annuals to grow from seed planted directly in the garden. Most will flower best if planted in full sun and kept well watered, but some can tolerate shade and drought (see opposite).

Summer bedding plants are tender and usually raised in a heated environment indoors, so they cannot be planted out before the threat of frosts has passed in frost-prone areas, otherwise they will be killed. You must make sure that any summer bedding plants have been acclimatized to the harsher weather conditions outside before you buy them (ask the garden center for advice). This process is known as hardening off (see page 114). The exceptions to this rule, however, are snapdragons and alyssum which can tolerate a light frost, so they can be planted a week or so before the other plants—useful if you have a lot to plant. If frost threatens after planting, cover the displays with a protective double layer of spun row cover. If disaster strikes and plants do get a light frost, cover them with sheets of newspaper early in the morning to slow the rate of thawing, as this is when most of the damage is caused. Don't allow the soil to dry out before planting.

If you want massed displays of annuals, use the chart below to calculate how many plants you will need. Combine plants with complementary colors and a range of

HOW MANY PLANTS

ANNUALS	NUMBER OF PLANTS (per square yard)	PLANTING DISTANCE	ANNUALS	NUMBER OF PLANTS (per square yard)	PLANTING DISTANCE
Ageratum	15	10 inches	Lobelia	45	6 inches
Alyssum	45	6 inches	Marigold	25	8 inches
Begonia (fibrous-rooted)	45	6 inches	Mesembryanthemum	45	6 inches
Calendula	45	6 inches	Nasturtium	10	12 inches
Cineraria	25	8 inches	Nemesia	25	8 inches
Coleus	45	6 inches	Nicotiana	10	12 inches
Dahlia (dwarf)	10	12 inches	Pansy	25	8 inches
Dianthus	25	8 inches	Petunia	15	10 inches
Echium	10	12 inches	Phlox	45	6 inches
Echeveria	45	6 inches	Salvia	25	8 inches
Gazania	25	8 inches	Snapdragon	20	9 inches
Geranium	10	12 inches	Stocks	25	8 inches
Helichrysum (dwarf)	25	8 inches	Verbena	15	10 inches
Impatiens	25	8 inches	Zinnia	15	10 inches

Puddling in for a perfect start
If the soil is dry, fill the planting hole with water before planting so that the roots get plenty of water.

heights to create attractive displays. Plant taller plants in the center and smaller ones toward the edge of the scheme, so that all the plants can be seen. Also try to include individual plants which contrast in height, form and color to the annuals. Foliage plants such as phormiums or dusty miller work particularly well, as do tall flowers such as amaranthus, canna, nicotiana or fuchsias.

Reliable perennials

There is a wide variety of garden perennials. Some are saints and some are sinners, so it is essential you choose the right varieties.

Several perennials, such as bee-balm, gooseneck loosestrife and Maximilian sunflower, are invasive, spreading by underground roots. Avoid these in a small garden; they are better in a naturalistic planting where they can spread at will. Control is difficult because pieces of root left in the ground will sprout into new plants.

A few perennials (such as perennial sunflowers, purple loosestrife and *Centaurea montana*) invade by dropping seeds, which germinate into new plants. These can become a weed problem in hospitable garden soil unless you root out young seedlings as soon as you see them.

Some taller perennials, such as peonies and tall fall asters, tend to flop over as soon as the flowers start to open. To avoid the need to stake plants, use tall perennials that can stand on their own, such as foxglove, rudbeckia and red-hot poker.

Perennials should be considered permanent additions to your garden. Plant them in spring or fall into weed-free soil that has been improved with well-rotted organic matter. Try to plant taller varieties among shrubs to give them natural support. If this is not possible, push bamboo canes into the soil next to the plants and link them with string or use special linking stakes. The plants will grow up through the support so that it cannot be seen by the time the plant is in flower.

Exotic summer bulbs

You can add an exotic touch to your summer displays by planting certain summer flowering bulbs. Allium, iris, Asiatic lilies and other hybrid lilies are among the hardiest summer-blooming bulbs, and can be left in the ground over winter in most areas. Agapanthus, acidanthera, cannas, gladioli, and tigridia are more tender and usually will not survive outdoors over winter in frost-prone areas. All summer bulbs require a sunny, sheltered site and well-drained soil. Plant them in mid-spring after the threat of frost has passed. Stake individual flower stalks with a bamboo cane to prevent them from flopping in bloom.

VIRGIN GARDENER'S BEST BETS

Annuals for shade
Begonia, fuchsia, impatiens, ornamental sweet potato vines and pansy.

Trouble-free perennials
Agapanthus, ajuga, artemisia, asters (especially 'Purple Dome'), catmint, columbine, daylily, dianthus, *Eryngium alpinum* (pictured at right), hosta, irises, Japanese anemone, obedient plant (*Physostegia*), penstemon 'Husker Red', peony, phlox 'David', Russian sage (*Perovskia atriplicifolia*) and verbena 'Homestead Purple'.

Drought-tolerant bedding
African daisy, dianthus, dusty miller, marigold, geranium, petunia and verbena.

Weather-resistant bedding
Alyssum, calendula, dianthus, geranium, lobelia, salvia, snapdragon and verbena.

fall and winter blooms for gardens

Many gardens suffer from a lack of flower power during early fall as the summer displays wane. Often the only color is provided by seasonal leaf tints, bark and eye-catching crops of berries. Yet there are a number of reliable fall-blooming flowers that can add color to your garden even at this late date. In mild-winter areas, the garden flower season continues right through the winter.

Bulbs in the fall

A few bulbs, including tender nerine, the hardier colchicums and *Sternbergia lutea*, will add a splash of color to the garden during the fall. The spidery pink blooms of nerines are, perhaps, the most distinctive and like a warm sheltered spot, such as the base of a sunny wall. The pink- or white-flowering colchicums, which have large crocus-like flowers, and hardy cyclamens both do well in sun or partial shade found under leafless deciduous trees at this time of the year. Like other colchicums, the double variety 'Waterlily' **(1)** produces its flowers before the leaves, making them

particularly striking set against the bare earth. However, the flowers can be ruined by splashing mud in heavy rain. The strap-shaped foliage also has to be left until early summer when it dies down. The fall daffodil, *Sternbergia lutea*, produces lots of bright yellow flowers and dark green strap-shaped leaves, but likes a sunny spot and well-drained soil.

Fall and winter perennials

You can create wonderful fall and winter colors by encouraging several early and mid-summer flowers to give repeat performances later in the year (see page 66).

For the best displays, however, it is worth planting a few flowers that naturally bloom at this time. Fill your borders with fantastic blocks of purple by planting fall asters, available in heights to fit any garden niche. Search out the 'Purple Dome' for rich color, or try *Aster* x *frikartii* 'Monch' for a more graceful look. All fall asters give a blockbuster show that can last for weeks. These plants grow happily in sun to light shade in most soils.

Russian sage (*Perovskia atriplicifolia*) continues its show of airy, pale blue flowers from summer right through frost, attracting the last of the butterflies to its blossoms. For a sunny splash of yellow in fall, try heliopsis.

In the West and Southwest, many native salvias come into bloom in late summer through winter, just in time to nourish migrating and over-wintering hummingbirds. One of the most striking species is pineapple-scented sage (*Salvia rutilans*, also sold as *S. elegans*), which grows to shrub size and has aromatic foliage and myriad red-flowered spikes. In cold-winter areas, it may not bloom before frost; protect with a sheet when early frost threatens. In milder regions it will continue blooming through winter.

Sedum 'Autumn Joy' is another popular fall perennial. Its long-lasting flat, reddish pink flowers attract many butterflies. Sedums are drought-tolerant and prefer full sun and well-drained soil.

Perennial sunflowers are also valuable for very late season color, adding a splash of golden yellow. Maximilian sunflower is one of the

---

VIRGIN GARDENER'S BEST BETS

 Flowers in the fall
Chinese lantern (*Physalis alkekengi*), chrysanthemums, colchicums, fall asters (*Aster* spp.), fall-blooming salvias (*Salvia* spp.), Japanese anemone (*Anemone japonica*), obedient plant (*Physostegia virginiana*), plumbago (*Ceratostigma plumbaginoides*), red-hot poker (*Kniphofia* spp., pictured at left), Russian sage (*Perovskia atriplicifolia*), perennial sunflowers (*Helianthus* spp.), *Sedum* 'Autumn Joy'.

 Winter flowers
Christmas rose (*Helleborus niger*), dwarf bamboos, elephant's ears (*Bergenia* x *schmidtii*), hardy ferns, *Helleborus lividus*, *Iris foetidissima* 'Variegata', hardy cyclamen (*Cyclamen coum*) and ornamental grasses.

 Seedheads for winter interest
Agapanthus, bear's breeches (*Acanthus* spp.), coneflowers (*Echinacea* and *Ratabida* spp.), *Crocosmia*, honesty (*Lunaria annua*), ornamental grasses, *Penstemon*, *Rudbeckia*, and sea holly (*Eryngium* spp.).

most widely available; it stretches to 6 feet or more and bears bouquets of yellow daisies. Beware, though: these sunflowers can run rampant (see page 63). Partner with other aggressive perennials, such as obedient plant (*Physostegia virginiana*).

An old reliable fall border plant is chrysanthemum, which is available in many cultivars, both tender and cold-hardy. Mums in bloom are sold in fall at garden centers, all ready to slip out of the pot and into your garden. In cold-winter areas, the plants won't have time to get established before the ground freezes, so mulch with a deep layer of leaves when they are done blooming to protect the plants until spring. Plant in a sunny position in well-drained soil.

Rudbeckia fulgida 'Goldsturm' **(2)** is a superb late summer and early fall flower for the border. It is very easy to grow and bears an abundance of large yellow daisy-like blooms with a pronounced brown central cone. It forms a compact 2-foot high plant with glossy green foliage. For a taller version at the back of a border, try 'Autumn Sun' which can reach 6 feet high. Both like any fertile soil and full sun.

The Kaffir lily, *Schizostylis*, is an excellent choice in mild-winter areas because it is fantastic looking and easy to grow. The different varieties flower at slightly different times, producing blooms of various shades of red, pink and white. So, by growing two or three varieties you could get a succession of blooms from late summer through to mid-winter in mild areas. Good varieties include 'Viscountess Byng' (pink) and 'Sunrise' **(3)**.

Flowers for frosty weather

A few hardy evergreen perennials are able to brave the winter weather. You can choose from a variety of plants. One of the earliest flowering

is *Helleborus lividus* which can be in bloom from mid-winter, bearing its pink-tinted white flowers until mid-spring. The better known Christmas rose flowers a little earlier, but it can be temperamental unless you can give it a shady spot with a rich alkaline soil. These should be planted close to the house so they can be appreciated from the warmth and comfort of indoors.

A couple of irises are also worth including in your winter borders. *Iris foetidissima* is usually grown for its seedpods that split to display bright orange seeds over the winter months, while the variegated form offers bright evergreen cream-striped foliage.

Bergenias add lovely glossy foliage and winter flowers in milder areas. The earliest bergenia to flower is *Bergenia* x *schmidtii*, producing contorted sprays of pink flowers at the turn of the year. Other varieties, such as *B. purpurascens*, offer rich, red, purple or bronze foliage that cloaks the ground all winter long. All bergenias are tough plants that can survive in sun or shade, but can be prone to frost damage in especially cold regions.

leave flowers to frost

Don't be in a hurry to clear herbaceous borders when the flowers fade, since many dead blooms have an architectural quality that will provide interest throughout the winter months, especially after a heavy frost. Ornamental grasses look wonderful all winter so should be kept in the garden, but other plants such as a spiky sea holly, the dark, rounded seedheads of rudbeckia, the papery seedheads of honesty and bright orange Chinese lantern, as well as the distinctive flat seedheads of 'Autumn Joy' sedum, are also worth saving.

bigger and better displays

Many garden flowers can be encouraged to bloom longer or produce a second flush later in the season. The trick is to make sure that the plants put all their energy into producing more flowers rather than seedpods and seed. To achieve this, remove the seedpods regularly so they don't have a chance to develop. With some flowers the effect this has can be significant. Zinnias, for example, stop flowering once they have lots of seedpods forming on their stems. By picking the plants over regularly you will stop this from happening, making the plant go on producing flowers longer.

Getting more flowers
Pinch off or remove faded blooms from roses with pruners to improve the overall display and encourage them to flower longer.

Pruning and deadheading
The best time to remove old flowers, known as deadheading, is as soon as the flowers start to fade. Not only does this prevent the plant from wasting its energy producing seed, but the seedpods are easier to spot if the petals are still attached. Indeed, with some plants, such as petunias and pansies, the seedpods can be a bit difficult to find because they tend to hide among the foliage.

Deadheading should be carried out regularly, perhaps once a week if you have the time. For plants with soft stems, old flowers can be pinched out between finger and thumb, but with others you might find it easier to use an old pair of scissors or pruners. The only practical way to deadhead plants that produce a lot of tiny flowers, such as alyssum, is to use scissors.

A few garden flowering plants, such as foxgloves and delphiniums, produce their blooms on tall spikes. Once the last flower is over, these too can be removed to encourage a second flush later in the season. Use a pair of pruners to cut the old flower spike back to the first sideshoot, which will bare the flowers later in the season.

Foliage plants such as coleus, dusty miller, and ornamental sweet potatoes, which are grown for their attractive leaves benefit from having their flower buds, if any, removed. In this case, the buds should be cut off before they open so the leaves stay healthy and vigorous longer.

Many perennial plants can look a bit worse for wear by the middle of summer as the old foliage gets attacked by disease or is scorched in the sun. A few plants, notably hardy geraniums and violas, will respond to being trimmed back hard by producing a bright new mound of foliage and sometimes a second flush of flowers. This can be traumatic for the plant, so keep it well watered and give it a boost of fertilizer. Use a pair of shears to trim off the old foliage. Other perennials, such as aquilegias, pulmonarias and alstroemerias, can be cut back hard after flowering in early summer;

Longer-lasting displays
You can get a second flush of blooms from many popular flowers by cutting them back after flowering.

VIRGIN GARDENER'S BEST BETS

 Flowerspikes to remove
Delphinium, foxglove, hollyhock, lupines, monkshood (*Aconitum*), penstemon, *Salvia* x *superba* and snapdragons.

 Flowers to cut back hard after bloom
Catmint (*Nepeta*), *Centaurea montana*, geum, hardy geraniums, lamium and violas.

 Flowers to deadhead
Ageratum, alyssum, African daisy (*Arctotis* spp.), California poppy (*Eschscholzia* spp.), bachelor's-buttons, cosmos, cleome, dahlia, dianthus, fleabane (*Erigeron* spp.), marguerite daisies, monkeyflowers (*Mimulus* spp.), *Osteospermum*, pansy, geraniums, annual poppies (pictured at right), *Scabiosa,* and sweet peas.

they won't flower again, but will produce attractive new foliage, adding to the overall display.

Self-sowing flowers

If you like a casual look in your flower garden, choose plants that self-sow by dropping their seeds at the end of the season. Alliums, annual poppies, bachelor's-buttons, calendula, cleome, columbines, cosmos, feverfew, foxgloves, forget-me-nots, and larkspur are some of the most generous self-sowers, producing a crop of seedlings to add to the display the following season.

The Virgin Gardener can turn this habit to good advantage, by shaking seedheads into crevices between paving or on any bare soil. If you prefer not to let your plants decide where to plant themselves, most seedlings are easy to transplant when young into a more suitable location. Or you can smother seedlings under a layer of grass clippings, compost, or other mulch.

Watering and feeding

Water plants well after cutting back and give them a high-potash liquid feed such as tomato fertilizer to encourage a second flush of blooms in late summer. Plants that have been deadheaded are also worth feeding during early summer. Flowers that like poor soil conditions, such as nasturtiums, canary creeper and godetias, however, should not be fertilized because this will encourage leafy growth at the expense of flowers.

expert tips   **Delayed flowering**

If you have large clumps of plants, such as coreopsis, helenium, phlox and fall asters, you can extend the overall period of the display by selective trimming. Simply cut back about one-third of the stems before the flower buds appear. New branched growth will be produced from further down the plant on the trimmed stems, and the flowerbuds carried on this new growth will appear later than the flowers borne on the stems that were not cut back, spreading the flowering display over a longer period.

a shady perennial paradise

Judy and Chris Barnes bought a dilapidated house in the city which needed a lot of restoration work. The garden, too, was full of challenges. It was a narrow garden that was kept in deep shade for most of the day because of a large tree in a neighbor's garden. The soil appeared dry and impoverished. Despite being an enthusiastic gardener, Judy found it very difficult to get anything established. The Barnes would like their garden to be an oasis full of flowers and lush foliage, with plenty of space for sitting out on warm days. However, they didn't want to spend all their available time on garden maintenance.

Ground raising

Restoring this garden was not going to be easy. The neighbor's tree had spread its roots just below the surface of the soil, right across the garden, removing most of the available moisture and nutrients. Its branches stretched just as far overhead, cutting out most of the sunlight during the day. Clearly some drastic measures were needed. The Barnes decided to raise the level of their garden to create a root-free environment for their new garden plants. They opted to create a series of planting beds between areas of decking at various levels.

Steps and decking

The garden is accessible from both the first floor and the kitchen on the second floor. It was from the latter that Judy and Chris would view and access their garden, so the design needed to look good from this point. The existing series of steps from the kitchen door were rotten and unsafe so needed replacing. Judy and Chris decided to base their garden design around a combination of small decks made from pressure-treated lumber with a wood preservative. Planting would be confined to perimeter beds and pots. They employed a professional team to build the deck structure with linking walkways and a new set of steps to the most elevated area outside the kitchen door. This was the only deck to receive a lot of direct sunlight.

Bamboo boundaries

The existing boundary wall around the garden was in very poor shape, so needed to be brushed down and re-pointed. To create the jungle effect that Judy wanted, and to raise the height of the boundary without cutting out too much light, Chris attached 6-foot-high split bamboo screens along each wall. Shade-tolerant vines such as hydrangea, jasmine and honeysuckle were then added to scramble over the screens.

Creating the beds

Most shade-tolerant plants with lush foliage prefer a moist soil, so the quality of their remaining soil between and around the decks needed to be improved. To do this,

Chris used good quality topsoil enriched with heaps of well-rotted organic matter. This helps to increase the soil's water-holding capacity. Over 600 bags of soil and manure had to be carried through the house to the back garden to fill all of the beds.

Lush planting

A range of foliage perennials were used to create a jungle effect in their garden. Judy bought a huge *Gunnera manicata* which has huge rhubarb-like leaves. This she placed at center stage and then surrounded it with a variety of hostas, angelica, euphorbia, rogersia and dragon arum (*Dracunculus vulgaris*). For foliage contrast, many ornamental grasses were added, including white and cream-variegated species.

At the back of the borders, trees such as ginkgo and a Japanese maple were planted, the former for its unusual fan-shaped leaves and the latter for its deep red fall foliage. To complete the jungle atmosphere, a mature evergreen *Ensete*, with its long paddle-shaped leaves reminiscent of a banana plant, was placed in the deepest border at the bottom of the garden. If you decide to plant an *Ensete* in your garden, you should be aware that it is not a very hardy plant, so it requires protection during the winter in frost-prone areas.

Flowering interest

To add seasonal focal points in any garden, it is a good idea to plant flowers. Judy used flowers to edge many of the borders. Dramatic spikes of foxglove, ligularia and lilies are used to good effect with ground-cover flowers, such as bugle (*Ajuga*), lysimachia, and lilyturf (*Liriope*).

She also used other perennials including the red masterwort (*Astrantia*) and toadlily (*Tricytris*) to help fill the gaps, and combined them with seasonal additions of potted shade-tolerant summer bedding plants, such as impatiens and nicotiana. Around the seating area, tender palms completed the exotic scene.

Jungle atmosphere

Rustic furniture and bamboo screens add the finishing touches to this jungle of lush foliage plants under the canopy of a large tree. The summer display is supplemented by beautiful pots of colorful shade-tolerant annuals (below). From the raised deck outside the kitchen, the garden can be seen in all its glory (right).

revitalizing old flower borders

After ten years of wonderful summer displays, the herbaceous borders in Anna and Steven Donovan's leafy suburban garden have lost their appeal. This is a common problem in well-established gardens. The plants produce fewer flowers, and the blooms that do appear tend to be smaller and don't last as long as they once did. Many of the Donovan's favorite varieties disappeared altogether. They want to revamp the borders and recapture the glories of past years without starting all over again and buying new plants.

Problem borders

Long-established herbaceous borders are prone to several problems. The more vigorous plants tend to spread out and swamp their less vigorous neighbors, and the center of large clumps die out as they spread. The soil also becomes depleted of nutrients. In addition, older plants are more prone to pest and disease attacks, which spoil their displays, and perennial weeds can become established throughout the bed, ruining the overall appearance of the borders. Fortunately, all of these problems can be overcome by digging up the whole border, enriching the soil and reinvigorating the displays.

Anna and Steve's first job was to decide which plants they wanted to keep and which they were happy to dispose of. The best time to do this is in the summer when the plants are in flower; you should clearly tag with a label all the plants you have chosen to keep.

Digging up the border

Anna and Steve chose a fine mild day in the fall to dig up the border. If you live in a cold-winter area, it's best to tackle this type of task in spring, because plants will need time to

get established in the soil. Before you start removing any of the plants from the soil, the first job is to cut off any old foliage which has started to die down for the winter. This will make access easier and you will be able to clearly see what you are doing. It took Anna just half an hour to trim back all the selected plants.

The next step is carefully to remove the selected plants from the soil. Anna and Steve used a shovel to cut around each plant to loosen the solid rootball. They then cut through the roots under each plant and levered the rootball carefully from the soil using a shovel or digging fork. Very large clumps of roots had to be cut into sections with a shovel before they could be moved.

Steve laid out a black plastic sheet on the ground in a shady spot to hold all the selected perennials, and folded one end of the sheet over the top to prevent the roots from drying out. Finally, they dug up all the old plants they didn't wish to keep.

Improving the soil

Anna and Steve then set about clearing the weeds from the soil and digging in lots of well-rotted organic matter. This helps to improve the structure and water-holding capacity of the impoverished soil. A general-purpose fertilizer was also scattered on the surface and forked into the soil at the rate of 2-ounces per square yard.

Preparing the plants

As they grow, many perennials develop into larger and larger clumps, each with many growth buds. By separating a clump into smaller sections, each with several healthy buds and plenty of roots, you can invigorate an old plant. This easy technique is known as division. The sections taken from around the edge of an old clump will provide the most

expert tips **Dealing with weeds**

The roots of many troublesome perennial weeds, such as bindweed, can become tightly enmeshed with flowers' roots. This not only means that they are competing for soil moisture and nutrients, but also makes them impossible to clear from the beds by pulling them out by hand, since any small piece of the weed's root left in the ground will resprout and start colonizing the bed all over again. The only way to deal with this problem for good is to dig up the affected plants and painstakingly pull out all the weed roots from the roots of the flowers. This may seem laborious, but it will save a lot of time in the long run.

vigorous new plants. These will establish quickly, produce the best flowers and be able to shrug off pest and disease attacks more effectively. The old woody central sections of each rootball should be discarded.

To begin the process of dividing their selected plants, Steve placed another sheet of plastic on the wide path to give them plenty of room to move around. All clump-forming perennials are divided in the same way. The best tools for the job will depend on the size of plants being dealt with. For the large solid rootballs, such as the rudbeckia, Steve used a sharp shovel to slice through the dense and woody core. To separate smaller clumps, such as the sedum, he used a sharp knife and a pair of old pruners.

Many of the flowers he and Anna saved, including asters, formed loose clumps that were easy to divide by hand, simply by gently teasing the roots apart. Those clumps that were tangled tightly together were pulled apart using a pair of garden forks held back to back. Anna found that herbaceous plants, including the bergenias, which had loose fleshy underground stems (called rhizomes), were easy to chop up using long-handled pruners. Finally, the Donovans checked over all the sections they intended to replant to remove any weed roots (see the expert tip, on the page opposite).

A few herbaceous plants flower better when the roots are congested, so should not be divided unless they have outgrown their allotted space. In the Donovan's garden, clumps of *Agapanthus* and peony, which were still flowering well, were not divided.

Replanting the new bed
The new sections were planted carefully at the same depth as before. The soil around the plants was pressed down gently to firm it and watered thoroughly. All bare soil was covered with a 2-inch layer of well-rotted manure to keep the ground weed-free. The new herbaceous border was then kept well watered throughout the following season until all the plants were well established.

Drastic improvement
The fiery displays in this herbaceous border have been transformed by a thorough overhaul. Summer displays of penstemon, crocosmia and *Echinops* are complemented by nasturtiums and potted geraniums (pictured left). The addition of *Schizostylis* and *Rudbeckia* with *Nerines* extend the color theme into the fall (picture above).

When the going gets tough
Shade-tolerant hostas, ferns and foxgloves cover the ground in this shady corner **(1)**; under a high pine canopy, tough shrubs such as hebe and eucalyptus thrive **(2)**; dianthus and other drought-tolerant plants have found their niche **(3)**; seaside plantings of lavender and crocosmia brave the bright sunlight and the salt-laden winds **(4)**.

Tough customers
for difficult situations

Every garden contains at least one border where plants are reluctant to grow.

Fortunately, there are flowers to suit every situation, even dry soil under trees,

provided you give them a helping hand to get established.

Some plants are well adapted for growing in difficult conditions where other plants would fail to thrive. The key to success is to choose the right plants for the particular conditions, but you must also prepare the soil thoroughly before planting (see page 166). If all else fails, you can always grow plants in containers (see page 110).

Windy tunnels and exposed gardens
Long, straight passages between buildings are usually heavily shaded and dry. The buildings also can act as a wind-tunnel, producing buffeting currents of air even on quite still days. To cope with these conditions, a plant needs to be very resilient. To maximize the conditions, paint the walls a pale color to increase the chances of growth in these light levels and use bamboos and tough shrubs, such as aucuba, to act as a windbreak at both ends of the passage. Suitable flowers for windy, shady spots include hellebores, *Heuchera*, hosta, *Pulmonaria*, annual lobelia and perennial ajuga.

In coastal gardens, the exposure is made worse by salt-laden winds—scorching the foliage of all but the toughest plants. In this situation try perennials such as *Eryngium*, crocosmia, *Senecio* and yucca or bedding plants such as snapdragon, *Arctotis* and *Dimorphotheca*.

Dry soil under trees
The soil under established trees and alongside hedges is usually filled with roots that draw out all the available moisture and nutrients. This makes the ground difficult to cultivate and prevents new plants from becoming established. To make matters worse, the area will be in shade for much of the year. To add a splash of color under the shade of deciduous trees, such as white birch and hawthorn, try planting foxgloves, impatiens, honesty, forget-me-nots, nicotiana or pansies, or bulbs such as dwarf daffodils.

For a permanent underplanting of perennial flowers, try barrenwort (*Epimedium*), euphorbias, hardy geraniums, and *Heuchera*. If the trees produce a dense canopy of foliage but don't come into leaf until mid-spring, you could underplant them with drifts of bulbs that are in flower earlier in the year—try snowdrops and bluebells or carpet the floor with cyclamens.

Damp and shady areas
Soil that remains constantly moist causes many plants to rot, particularly over the winter months. This usually occurs where the water table is high and the soil is heavy, containing a lot of clay. If your soil remains waterlogged for long periods, choose moisture-loving flowers such as astilbe, cardinal flower (*Lobelia cardinalis*) and Japanese iris. If your soil drains but remains moist after rain, you could create a woodland effect by using plants that thrive in moist soil, such as bleeding heart, ferns, hostas, primroses, Virginia bluebells or any other woodland wildflowers native to your area. If you have problems with slugs and snails in damp, shady areas, install copper barrier strips or apply a border of diatomaceous earth, which may discourage them from entering the bed; if all else fails, you could try commercial slug and snail products.

Exposed dry borders
Borders in full sun require plants that can take bright light and often high temperatures. Your local garden center will stock many suitable sun-lovers, such as African daisies, artemisias, and zinnias. Sunny borders at the base of a wall are particularly tough because the wall may absorb soil moisture and also radiate heat, making it a real hot spot. Here, turn to plants with silvery, hairy, or waxy leaves—adaptations that prevent moisture loss through the foliage. Try artemisias, cacti, euphorbia, lamb's ears, lavender, mulleins and yucca.

Climbing plants

Vines and other climbers are an asset to the Virgin Gardener because they can be used to enhance the appearance of every garden. They are easy to grow and most require little maintenance, provided you choose the right plant for the position.

Climbing plants can be used all around the garden to provide vertical interest to flat borders, create screens to cover eyesores and break up the stark appearance of walls and fences, as well as provide shade when trained over arches and pergolas. Many vines, notably evergreen ivies, can also be used to cover the ground, providing a foliage carpet that decorates the floor and helps keep weeds at bay. Vines are of particular value in small gardens that have high walls or fences because they can be used to add living color and interest without taking up a lot of ground area. Every vertical surface can be covered, because there are climbers suited to growing in sun or shade and types that will tolerate most soils. They even can be grown successfully in containers on a patio or balcony.

Every style of garden suits climbing plants. Most climbers can be trained easily into any shape or form to suit a formal setting. When tied against the bars of trellis or along wires attached to a wall or fence, for example, a perfectly symmetrical design can be achieved. Climbing plants look wonderful in informal gardens, too, where they can be left to their own devices—new growth can cascade from a support or fence to produce a billowing froth of flowers and foliage.

Many vines, such as clematis, are grown for their spectacular flowers, which are produced in abundance for many months. A few, such as jasmines, have a delicious fragrance, while others, such as ivies and vines, can be grown for their attractive and bold foliage, which is often strikingly variegated and takes on dramatic tints and hues in the fall. There are also vines that produce attractive seedheads and colorful berries, which can decorate your garden throughout the winter.

adding interest using climbers

An essential element of any garden, climbing plants can be used to cover fences and other structures to hide eyesores or provide a colorful backdrop to other plants. If you choose the right plant for the position and plant it correctly, a vine will look after itself and need less maintenance than most other garden plants.

Many vines originate from the tropical rainforests so are not hardy in temperate areas, but there are still plenty of hardy types to choose from if your garden is prone to frost.

In nature, climbers use other plants as a means of support; growing quickly up toward the sun and spreading out over the supporting plant's canopy. For this reason, many climbers are so vigorous they can be used to quickly cover large or unsightly areas—an expanse of stark wall or a dilapidated shed, for example. On the other hand, climbers quickly outgrow small spaces, so it is important to match the vigor of your climber to the growing space available; otherwise you will spend a lot of time keeping it in check.

Choosing a good plant

There are climbers to suit both sun and shade as well as most types of soil from light, sandy soil to heavy clay. Climbers also can be grown successfully in containers. Small pots can be used to grow annual vines such as sweet peas and black-eyed Susan vine (*Thunbergia alata*), whereas large tubs placed against a wall or other sturdy support can accommodate the largest of climbing specimens. Small ever-green vines such as ivies or vinca are also useful for planting around the edge of a container to trail over the edge. (See page 110 for details about growing plants in containers.)

Although most climbing plants flower in the summer, there also are excellent varieties that put on their display at other times. If you choose

Natural support
This majestic scented rambling rose has been trained to scramble through the canopy of an old apple tree to give it another season of interest.

Steps to success with climbers

3

- Decide the size of structure you want to cover.

- Choose an appropriate climbing plant to cover the area involved.

- Construct supports and tie the climbers to them securely.

carefully you can combine different climbers to create a year-round display of fabulous foliage and berries. Use the plant lists on the following pages to help you choose the best climbers for your garden.

Buying tips

Look for healthy specimens with well-balanced frameworks of stems and no physical damage or signs of pests and diseases.

Avoid plants with rootballs covered in weeds or tightly coiled roots around their bases. Some plants, particularly roses, are sold as bare-rooted plants, and these should have moist, fibrous root systems.

Container-grown climbing plants should be bought in the spring. The soil is moist and the weather is becoming warmer at this time of year, so the plants are easier to establish. You will also find the best selection of plants during spring.

The natural climbers

Many climbing plants are self-clinging, which means once they are established they can hold on to the support without the need for tying in shoots as they grow.

Clematis and honeysuckle, for example, produce twining stems or leaf stalks that tangle themselves into the support; while sweet peas and passion flowers produce coiling tendrils that spiral around the support and hold on tight. Some plants, such as Virginia creeper, produce tiny suckers that stick fast onto any surface, and ivy produces a fringe of aerial roots from its stem that provide a firm anchor.

Other climbers, such as roses, are not self-clinging; they need to be tied onto the support (see page 78).

Color contrasts
A cerise-pink climbing rose makes the most of a bright blue obelisk support to stand out from the crowd in this informal border display.

FAQs - CLIMBERS

Q Are climbers difficult to prune?

A Most require little or no pruning. Simply trim once a year to keep them within bounds. Some flowering climbers, particularly clematis, wisteria and roses, however, require special pruning if you want them to bloom to their full potential (see page 184 for details).

Q Will climbers damage my house?

A While it is true that some climbers can speed the deterioration of unsound walls with crumbling mortar, sound brick walls will not be damaged. If you allow a vine to scramble over guttering and a tiled roof, it will grow under the tiles and the foliage can block gutters. By giving the plant a trim at the end of the growing season you can prevent this from happening.

Q Do you have to have a wall or fence to support climbers?

A No, but it is essential that you match the growing vigor of the climbing plant to the size and strength of the support. A solid wall can support a vigorous vine that produces lots of heavy growth, while trellises, bamboo canes or even a string tepee can support a slow-growing or more delicate climber.

Q How do you cover a bare fence quickly ?

A Climbers naturally grow toward the light, so if you spread out the stems horizontally, they will produce shoots from each leaf joint to produce more upward growth that will quickly clothe the support.

Q Are all climbers tender?

A No, although many originate from the tropical regions of the world and are not hardy enough for growing outdoors in colder regions. Others are perfectly hardy or are at least hardy enough to survive when trained against a sheltered, south-facing wall.

planting and supporting

All climbers need support. You can use wires or trellis fixed to a sturdy wall or fence, or provide them with their own free-standing support such as an obelisk, arch or screen. Many garden structures, such as arches and arbors, are available in kit form from garden centers (see page 92) or mail order.

All climbing plants enhance the appearance of your garden, but you can extend the flowering period of your climbers and create some eye-catching displays by combining two or three climbing plants onto one support using the methods described below. Choose varieties that have the same cultural requirements so that pruning and other maintenance tasks can be carried out at the same time.

Attaching climbers to walls and fences

Before planting your climber, fix the trellis or wires onto the wall or fence about 12 inches above the ground, making sure they are strong and firmly attached.

Using trellis Choose sturdy well-made trellis that will last many years. Avoid the cheap expanding-style trellis for all but the lightest of climbing plants.

Mark out the position of the trellis on the wall or fence. Then, screw the spacing battens onto the vertical surface to help maintain the airflow between the climber and its support—this helps prevent disease and damp problems. Screw the trellis directly to the battens to form a permanent feature.

Alternatively, hinge the trellis to the bottom batten and then attach it to the top one using a hook and eye mechanism. This allows easy access to the supporting fence or wall to carry out periodical maintenance. A section of wire fence, attached to wooden supports or a wall, makes a quick trellis for annual vines.

Using wires Strong, plastic-coated or galvanized wire is attached to a wall or fence using special hooks called vine-eyes (available from garden centers or mail order). These can be screwed directly into wooden fences. On walls, however, you need to use a different method. About 12 to 18 inches above the ground, mark out holes 1 yard apart across the wall. Drill these holes in sound mortar using a ¼-inch bit, then push in the wall plugs and screw in the vine-eyes. Attach the wire to the end vine eye using a pair of pliers. Then thread the wire through the intermediate vine eyes. Once through the

Putting up trellis
Securely fix the trellis to the wall using corrosion-resistant screws. Use spacers between the wall and the trellis to increase air flow and reduce the incidence of disease.

final vine-eye, pull the wire taut before securing with pliers. Repeat this process with the other parallel wires, spacing them 12 to 18 inches apart up the wall.

Double-value climbers

Climbers that naturally clamber through other plants are an ideal way of brightening up dull shrubs or hedges, or providing a second season of interest to a large flowering shrub. Bear in mind, however, that the climbing plant will be

Planting a climber near a wall

The soil alongside walls is often dry and lacking in nutrients, so good soil preparation is essential before planting. To do this, dig the soil to a full shovel's depth and remove any weeds, large stones and other debris. Incorporate plenty of well-rotted garden compost or planting mixture to improve moisture retention. If you have heavy soil, add a bucketful of grit to improve drainage. Then, fork in a slow-release general fertilizer before planting.

Dig a large hole at least twice the size of the plant's rootball 18 inches away from the wall or fence. Add some more planting mixture into the base of the hole.

1 Position the plant in the hole at a 45 degree angle to the wall so that it leans toward the wall and reaches the bottom of the trellis or wire support (which should be at a height of 12 to 18 inches up the wall or fence). Use a cane placed across the hole to check that the top of the rootball is level with the surrounding soil.

expert tips **Plant clematis deep**

Clematis are susceptible to wilt disease so are best planted deeper than other climbers. Position the top of the rootball 3 inches below the soil surface so that if the top-growth is killed by wilt there are plenty of buds underground to regrow the following year. After planting, take care not to damage stems when cultivating or hoeing the soil.

competing with the supporting plant for food and moisture. The climber should be planted in a spot level with the edge of the supporting plant's foliage. This area is known as the drip zone because it is where rainwater runs off the shrub's canopy. Prepare the planting area by digging a hole and removing roots, weeds and other debris. Add some manure and a slow-release general fertilizer. Line the sides of the hole with old boards to prevent root invasion from the supporting plant. Place more planting mixture into the hole, then attach one end of a rope to the shrub and lay the other end underneath the rootball of the climber in its planting hole. Check that the top of the rootball is level with the surrounding soil and fill the hole. Firm and water well and apply a layer of well-rotted manure or bark chips as a mulch to reduce moisture loss and prevent weed competition. Tie the climber to the rope and entwine any long stems into the shrub support.

2 Fill in the hole with soil, firming it down periodically with the heel of your foot to remove any air pockets. Water well and cover the surrounding soil with a 2 or 3-inch layer of well-rotted manure or bark chips to reduce water loss and prevent weed competition. Keep the mulch clear of the climbers' stems to prevent rotting.

3 Now, tie the plant's support cane (this comes with the climber when bought) to the bottom of the trellis using string or a wire tie so that it is firmly anchored.

4 Finally, train a few of the longer climber stems onto the bottom of the trellis, tying them to the support if necessary.

spring climbers

In mild winter areas, many perennial or woody vines bloom all through winter and into spring. In colder areas, however, vines that bloom in spring are a welcome sight after the sparseness of winter. Select plants from a local garden center, which will stock plants that thrive in your hardiness zone.

Fragrant jasmines

Jasmines are tender and can't take much cold, although a few species will survive an occasional dip to single-digit temperatures. If the top growth is killed by frost or cold, cut back the plant to the ground and, if the roots haven't been harmed, they will quickly send up new shoots.

Several species of jasmine begin blooming in winter in mild areas, and continue during early spring. Others come into bloom in early spring, even in areas with some winter cold. Sublimely fragrant, white-flowered wax jasmine (*J. volubile*) blooms throughout the year in mild areas. Winter jasmine (*J. nudiflorum*) produces yellow, unscented flowers in winter to spring. Downy jasmine (*J. multiflorum*) has a slight sweetness and flowers from late winter to early spring.

A little later in the season, these early bloomers are joined by star or Confederate jasmine (*Trachelospermum jasminoides*), which attracts bees to its clusters of small white flowers from spring to early summer.

Another jasminelike vine is reliable Carolina jessamine (*Gelsemium sempervirens*), an evergreen climber with scented yellow flowers from late winter to early spring.

A pretty partner for jasmine-type vines is Cape plumbago (*Plumbago auriculata*), which has beautiful blue flowers that bloom throughout the year in frost-free areas, and from spring to fall in chillier climes.

1

VIRGIN GARDENER'S BEST BETS

Hardy climbers for spring interest
Carolina jessamine (*Gelsemium sempervirens*), clematis, Chinese wisteria (*W. floribunda*), hardy kiwi (*Actinidia kolomikta*), ivy, (*Hedera helix*), Japanese wisteria (*W. sinensis*).

Tender climbers for spring interest
Blood-red trumpet vine (*Distictis buccinatoria*), bougainvillea, Cape plumbago (*Plumbago auriculata*), Confederate jasmine (*Trachelospermum jasminoides*), downy jasmine (*J. multiflorum*), royal trumpet vine (*Distictis* ' Mrs Rivers'), vanilla trumpet vine (*D. laxiflora*), violet trumpet vine (*Clytostoma callistegioides*), wax jasmine (*J. volubile*), winter jasmine (*J. nudiflorum*).

Early-flowering clematis

Clematis vines are more cold-hardy than jasmines. They flourish where soil moisture levels stay even year-round, but suffer in drought. Be aware, though, that they may take two years or more to become settled and begin growing with vigor.

Spring-flowering clematis produce flowers on growth of previous seasons. *Clematis armandii* (1) bears scented white blooms in early spring. The dainty, nodding flowers of *C. alpina* (2) add an interesting touch from mid-spring to early summer. *Clematis macropetala* is another early-blooming species. For vigorous growth, look for *C. montana*, which can quickly cover a fence or an arbor with color in late spring. C. 'Doctor Ruppel' puts on a spectacular show in late spring to early summer, with cascades of rose-colored flowers, and often reblooms in fall.

Wisteria for vigor

Wisteria is the quintessential spring-flowering vine, blooming at tulip time in cold-winter areas with its lovely, hanging clusters of lavender

2

Bright-colored bougainvillea also bloom for months. The flowers are hardly noticeable; the flashy color of this vine comes from colored leaf-like bracts below the flowers. 'San Diego Red' is high-climbing and very vigorous; 'Crimson Jewel' is good for covering banks; 'Brilliant Variegated' has green and white leaves; 'Hawaii' is one of the least tender. Virgin Gardeners in colder areas, take heart: you too can enjoy bougainvillea as a hanging basket plant or for seasonal color, after the danger of frost has passed.

Experiment with ivy

Ivy offers the benefit of year-round greenery for walls, fences, and ground cover. It is tough and easy to grow, but can become invasive. As a general rule, the larger the distance between the leaves on the stem, the more vigorous the ivy.

If you want to cover the ground with ivy **(3)**, choose whatever cultivar appeals to you. *Hedera helix* is a classic groundcover, and the ivy most commonly sold in garden centers, but you can find many other interesting cultivars in the houseplant section. Cold-hardiness varies. Try variegated or golden-foliaged varieties to brighten up shady areas.

(or white) blooms and heady fragrance. It is easy to grow, cold-hardy and vigorous. Give wisteria a strong arbor or pergola for support. You can also buy wisteria vines that have been trained as a tree-shape, with a single trunk and a head of bloom.

Grafted plants will bloom sooner after transplanting than ones grown from seed. If your vine doesn't flower after three years of good growth, prune it back severely in late winter to jump-start it.

Tender spring bloomers

In mild-winter areas, you have a wide selection to choose from. *Distictis* vines, which bear flowers like small, flared trumpets, can bloom for eight months straight. Try blood-red trumpet vine (*Distictis buccinatoria*), or royal trumpet vine (D. 'Mrs Rivers'), which offers flowers that are purple outside, orange inside. Vanilla trumpet vine (*D. laxiflora*), named for its scent, has purplish flowers fading to white.

3

covering tree stumps

Evergreen climbers, including ivy, are ideal for disguising tree stumps. Choose a vigorous ivy with dense, attractive leaves for the most appealing cover. Ivies are evergreen, so you will have year-round camouflage for the stump.

summer scent and color

Summer gives you a chance to enjoy some wonderfully aromatic roses, exotic passion flowers, and other perennial and woody climbers. It is also the time to revel in fast-growing annual vines, such as cypress vine, colorful sweet peas, and old-fashioned morning glories and their nocturnal counterpart, the lovely white moonflower.

Roses and clematis

Roses begin the summer season of climbers in many gardens, lending their romantic touch and perfume to the peak display of perennial beds. Some cultivars bloom in a week's-long burst, while others continue right through the first frost.

You will find a vast variety of roses available, from diminutive types that thrive even in containers to climbers that can cover an arbor.

Roses thrive in full sun in well-drained soil. Many roses are susceptible to black spot, mildew and other diseases, so seek out those described as disease-resistant.

Many climbing and rambling roses are highly scented. 'Paul's Himalayan Musk' and 'Treasure Trove' have a fruity smell; 'Zépherine Drouhin' and 'Mermaid' **(2)** have a sweet, floral perfume. For something different, try 'Gloire de Dijon', which has a rich tea-like scent. All are ideal for covering arbors and other open structures, which allow breezes to circulate and pick up the fragrance. To cover a fence or shed, try the large 'New Dawn' **(1)**, which has pink blooms.

Hardy clematis vines are the perfect companion for roses. Their vines can weave up a support right alongside a rose. The classic deep

purple *Clematis* x *jackmanii* is a reliable choice, as are the large-flowered clematis hybrids. All bloom in early summer. 'Nelly Moser', pink with darker pink stripes, and regal purple 'The President' are perennial favorites. Rosy pink 'Hagley Hybrid' has an unusually long flowering season, producing another round of buds after the initial flush of blooms.

Heavenly honeysuckles

When selecting a honeysuckle, try to track down a species native to your area to avoid the possibility of introducing another plant thug like the Japanese honeysuckle (*Lonicera japonica*)—a sublimely scented vine that escaped from gardens to run rampant in American wildlands.

Better choices for honeysuckles include several vines with bright-colored flowers in orange, red, salmon or pink. All are manna to hummingbirds, so plant them where you will be able to watch the birds. *Lonicera sempervirens* has orange-yellow to scarlet flowers that begin in late spring or early summer. Hall's honeysuckle (*L. japonica* 'Halliana') and gold-flame honeysuckle (*L.* x *heckrotti*) follow the same schedule, with bloom going into fall. Vivid red *L.* x *brownii* 'Dropmore Scarlet' blooms from early summer to frost.

Exotic interest

One of the most spectacular vines is the passion flower (*Passiflora spp.*), a

Scented double act
You can combine climbers with complementary or contrasting colors if they flower at the same time. Here a scented honeysuckle and a rambling rose make perfect partners against a sunny wall.

complicated beauty with its wide-open flower that was named for its symbolic representation of the Passion of Christ: a crown of thorns decorates its center, and its petals represent the apostles. Several species are available, and are much easier to grow than they appear. Purple passion flower (*P. incarnata*) is one of the most cold hardy.

Dutchman's pipe (*Aristolochia spp.*) hides reddish-brown pipe-shaped flowers beneath its leaves. Pipevine swallowtail butterflies use the vine as food for their caterpillars; it's also ideal for shading a porch. Hummingbirds flock to the red-orange flowers of *Campsis radicans*, a fast-growing vine that needs frequent pruning. Silver fleece vine (*Polygonum aubertii*), a beautiful vine for covering an arbor or pergola, is transformed into a frothy mass of tiny white flowers from summer until fall.

Tender vines

Virgin Gardeners in mild-winter areas can experiment with heat-loving vines that stay in the garden all year. In colder areas, many of these vines are available at garden centers for a spot of summer color; winter them over as houseplants.

Brilliant pink 'Alice du Pont' mandevilla (*Mandevilla* x *amoena* 'Alice du Pont') is eyecatching on a trellis or in a container. Chilean jasmine (*M. laxa*) bears white flowers that smell like gardenias. Evergreen bower vine (*Pandorea*

jasminoides) offers pink-throated white flowers from early summer through fall.

In Florida, Texas, and the Southwest, coral vine or Queen's wreath (*Antigonon leptopus*) provides a good display, with leafy stems decorated with sprays of small, rose-pink flowers from midsummer to fall. Hot 'Baja Red' lives up to its name.

Annual vines

You can use these to decorate fences, trellis, porch posts or arbors. All are easy to grow from seed planted directly in the garden.

Among the most vigorous annaul vines is purple-flowered hyacinth bean, as simple to grow as a garden stringbean. Red-flowered scarlet runner bean is another super-easy annual vine.

In cool-summer areas, annual sweetpeas **(3)** are a delightfully old-fashioned choice. Scented varieties like 'Old Spice' smell wonderful. Perennial sweetpeas can be invasive, but they are are good for covering steep banks.

Morning glories grow quickly in warm soil, and their tendrils soon cover any support you offer. Look for ethereal 'Heavenly Blue', or choose pink, purple or mixed colors. For a nighttime show, plant moon-flower vine, a white morning glory that unfurls its saucer-size blooms at dusk. Cypress vine and cardinal creeper, relatives of the larger morning glories, offer tiny red trumpet flowers.

Exotic climbers

The passion flower (*Passiflora caerulea*), grown for its striking white and blue flowers during summer, sometimes produces edible orange fruit. Another exotic summer climber is the trumpet vine (*Campsis radicans*), which sparkles with orange flowers and has a backdrop of feathery foliage. The related and similar looking variety 'Madame Galen' is more reliable, so ideal for the Virgin Gardener. Both need good soil and warm sunny walls in a sheltered spot.

fall and winter climbers

In warm weather gardens, many vines keep blooming through fall and winter. But in colder areas, you should turn to bright berries and colorful foliage to keep vines interesting through the fall and winter.

Vines for fall foliage

One of the best vines for fall foliage color is Virginia creeper (*Parthenocissus quinquefolia*). The rich green leaves transform into fiery hues in fall, setting the whole garden ablaze with crimson. Even when the foliage

falls, the slender stems are attractive throughout winter. Give this vigorous vine a large wall or fence; it also grows well up a house wall, but its suckers will leave marks when the vine is removed. It does wonders at dressing up a chainlink fence. Virginia creeper also makes a beautiful fall ground cover in naturalistic shaded gardens, where it can wander among shrubs and fallen leaves. Boston ivy (*P. tricuspidata*) is a relative of Virginia creeper with similar brilliance in fall. These vines are self-clinging, so they need no training, other than cutting back wayward shoots. Wire them to fences or trellis to get them started when they are young; after that, they will climb on their own.

Another interesting vine for fall is porcelain berry (*Ampelopsis brevipedunculata*). The leaves turn red in fall, but the vine's berries are even more striking, as they ripen from green to pink and finally to metallic blue. The fruit will attract songbirds to your garden.

American bittersweet (*Celastrus scandens*) is a vigorous hardy vine that bears clusters of orange berries which split open to reveal gleaming red fruit. It is less widely available than Chinese or Oriental bittersweet (*C. orbiculatus*), which has escaped from gardens and crowded out the native bittersweet vine in some areas. Both are high climbers that need a strong support and frequent pruning. Provide bittersweet with a sturdy arbor or pergola that will remain secure under the heavy weight of an established plant.

Tunnel of purple foliage
Climbing over an arbor, the ornamental vine, *Vitis vinifera* 'Purpurea', transforms the garden as it changes to a deep shade of purple in the fall.

Ornamental grapevines (*Vitis vinifera*) may be difficult to find at mass-market garden centers, but they are well worth asking your local nursery to order. They have stunning tints in the fall, turning copper, yellow, orange, red and purple. 'Purpurea' turns an eyecatching shade of deep purple in the fall. Ornamental grapevines do produce fruit, which is suitable for winemaking, in areas with a long, warm summer. But their fall foliage and quick-climbing growth during the year are even more valuable. They are moderately vigorous, and thus ideal for covering an arbor or disguising an eyesore such as an old shed. Their stems will also sprawl if not given a support to climb, making an attractive ground-covering under shrubs and trees.

Don't overlook the pleasures of seedpods on vines for fall interest. Spring-flowering wisteria and the summer-blooming *Campsis radicans* offer dangling pods that make these two vines interesting even after the leaves have dropped.

Fall-flowering clematis

Several species of clematis continue to flower well into fall and a few will brave the winter months. A second flush of bloom is often produced by popular large-flowered clematis hybrids in autumn. These blossoms are often smaller than the main summer crop, but they are just as welcome for a splash of late color.

Autumn-flowering clematis (*C. terniflora*) is a reliable choice in colder regions as well as milder climes. It bears a cloud of tiny white fragrant flowers in early fall, which last for weeks. They are beautiful in arrangements as well as covering an arbor or fence. This vigorous vine is ideal for cloaking a chainlink fence,

Frosty reception
Evergreen variegated ivy covered in spiders' webs make a striking point of interest in the early morning sunlight after a heavy frost.

(*Pandorea pandorana*) is also worth considering. Plant it near to the house so that you can admire and smell its fragrant creamy and red trumpets, which are held above glossy leaves throughout the winter.

In coastal gardens, as well as those in more favorable conditions, Cape honeysuckle (*Tecoma capensis*) is a good choice. Its orange-red tubular flowers bloom from fall through winter, offering nectar to wintering hummingbirds. It copes well with salt air and wind.

If you live in a mild-winter region, visit your garden center to find fall-blooming vines ready to pop into the ground. Or plant them in spring, so they can cover ground in the garden before it's time for the fall and winter show to begin.

and the foliage often stays green through much of the winter. Autumn-flowering clematis thrives in light shade as well as sun.

Another particularly easy clematis for autumn interest is virgin's bower (*C. virginiana*), which is as valuable for its fuzzy seedheads as as it is for its small white flowers. The long-haired seeds are held together in tight clusters of light-catching fuzz. A clematis vine bedecked with seedheads is beautiful when backlit by winter sun.

It is best to plant fall-interest vines in spring in cold-winter areas, so that they have time to become established before the soil freezes. This also ensures that the vines will have time to grow enough to put on a decent show, even in their first year in the garden.

Tender fall and winter vines
Blooms continue in mild regions in fall on such vines as bougainvillea, and many jasmines and other tender species come into flower in fall. The winter jasmine (*Jasminum nudiflorum*) bears its bright yellow blooms through early spring, on attractive

bright green stems. Although it is treated as a vine, winter jasmine is actually a sprawling shrub that will need to be tied onto its support.

The Chilean bellflower (*Lapageria rosea*) offers waxy red bells that last until fall. The wonga-wonga vine

---

VIRGIN GARDENER'S BEST BETS

Flowers
Autumn-flowering clematis (*Clematis terniflora*), Cape honeysuckle (*Tecoma capensis*), Cape plumbago (*Plumbago auriculata*), Chilean bellflower (*Lapageria rosea*), *Mandevilla laxa*, trumpet vine (*Campsis radicans*), winter jasmine (*Jasminum polyanthum*), wonga-wonga vine (*Pandorea pandorana*).

Foliage
Boston ivy (*Parthenocissus tricuspidata*), ornamental grapevine (*Vitis vinifera* 'Purpurea'), ornamental kiwi (*Actinidia kolomitka*), porcelain berry vine (*Ampelopsis* spp.), Virginia creeper (*Parthenocissus quinquefolia*).

Seedheads or berries
Autumn-flowering clematis (*Clematis terniflora*), bittersweet (*Celastrus* spp.), Boston ivy (*Parthenocissus tricuspidata*), ornamental grapevine (*Vitis vinifera* 'Purpurea'), ornamental kiwi (*Actinidia kolomitka*), porcelain berry vine (*Ampelopsis* spp.), Virginia creeper (*Parthenocissus quinquefolia*), virgin's bower (*Clematis virginiana*).

vertical gardening with climbers

Roger and Jill Sherman bought a converted brick-built schoolhouse with a yard that is a sun-trap in summer. The yard was heavily dominated by old brick walls that, although attractive, made the garden seem very confined. They wanted to make maximum use of all the vertical growing space as well as the changes in level the garden provided. They particularly liked the idea of dividing the garden into different "rooms."

Improving the soil

The main problem the Shermans faced was the very poor free-draining soil, which needed improving before they could start planting. The soil at the base of the walls was very dry and little rain reached these areas. To improve the situation, the existing soil was dug out to a depth of 18 inches and replaced with a good quality topsoil enriched with plenty of well-rotted farmyard manure.

When deciding on plants for this sort of position, it is not worth planting clematis because it needs a soil that remains moist with its top-growth in the sun. Instead, choose drought-tolerant, sun-loving climbers. Jill planted passion flower (*Passiflora caerulea*) and *Solanum crispum,* which appreciate a warm sheltered position. After planting, the soil was covered with a thick layer of well-rotted organic matter to help reduce moisture loss. However, a 6-inch-wide space was left around each climber to prevent the organic matter from touching the plants' stems.

Clearing the walls

Like most old walls, these were in need of repair before they could be used to support vines, especially the self-clinging types such as Virginia creeper and ivies. All loose material was cleared from the walls using a wire brush. The loose mortar was picked from the cracks and then the walls were re-pointed. Jill didn't want to spoil the appearance of the walls with trellis, so she opted to use long galvanized screw-in vine-eyes to attach parallel heavy-duty galvanized wires 12-inches apart up the wall. The vine-eyes were spaced every 3 feet along the wall for vigorous climbers and every 5 feet elsewhere. The advantage of wires and vine-eyes is that they are virtually invisible even on areas where there are no vines.

Dividing the garden

A good way to split a garden into pretty and secluded "rooms" without cutting down on the sense of space is to install a series of plastic-coated metal arches. These are available in kit form and slot and bolt together very easily. In Roger and Jill's garden, the end sections of the arches were concreted into the ground and, where possible, bolted to an upright wall using expansion bolts. This made the structure very secure and stable and suitable for long-term vigorous climbers. Roger and Jill decided to plant several wisterias that would cover the frame quickly and eventually merge to look like one plant.

To the north side of the garden, a pair of climbing roses were planted against the metal arch. They chose two good varieties: 'Albertine', which bears pink flowers during early summer, and 'Madame Alfred Carriere', which blooms on and off until early fall—both are reliable and free-flowering.

Quick cover

To help camouflage the large expanse of brick building to one side of the courtyard, Roger and Jill decided to plant a quick-growing honeysuckle and a jasmine. These needed to be planted in well-prepared soil and trained up a series of wires as before. If you wish to create a delightfully natural effect, you should allow the plants to sprawl at will in some areas. Quick-growing annual vines, such as morning glory, black-eyed Susan vine and canary creeper, were also planted to ensure a mixture of colorful vines throughout the first year.

Climbers in trees

To brighten up the evergreen foliage of the tree in the center of the middle courtyard, the climbing *Bomarea caldasii* has been added. Distinctive, bright-orange blooms stand out against the evergreen backdrop and will be borne more or less continually from late spring to fall. The wiry growth of this vine makes it particularly suitable for this purpose because it will not swamp the growth of the tree.

Plants for all seasons

To ensure that you have plenty of colorful interest throughout the year, it is important to select a range of different climbers. The following would provide a display in all seasons.

In spring the clematis variety 'Balearica' and the scented chocolate vine (*Akebia quinata*) would be good choices, followed by *Clematis montana* and *Actinidia kolomikta* in early summer. Mid-summer favorites, such as scented summer jasmine and the Chilean potato vine (*Solanum*), are also worth including, with *Clematis tangutica* and ornamental grape vine. To fill the winter gap, winter-flowering jasmine and evergreen variegated ivies are always welcome.

Climbing out of adversity

A range of vines were chosen to cope with the difficult conditions. Sun-loving passion flower and *Solanum* were used in the sunny courtyard, while shade-tolerant ivies and hoya covered some of the north-facing walls.

reviving old climbers

Oliver owns a property on the outskirts of a small town. Over the past year, he has lovingly restored it, which has taken up most of his free time. Now that he has finished the house, he wants to spend time restoring the garden and wishes to create an outside area filled with summer color. The old garden contained a number of interesting climbers which Oliver would like to incorporate into his new garden design. Most of the existing climbing plants, however, are overgrown and in need of serious renovation work. His aim is to use the climbers to hide or disguise much of the boundary fence as possible in his long, narrow plot, to make the garden seem larger than it really is.

Time for drastic pruning

All the climbers in Oliver's garden have been left unpruned for many years. When this happens, vines tend to turn woody at their bases and produce very few flowers. Any blooms that do appear often grow out of sight on new growth, which is produced at the top of the plant. Most climbers respond well to heavy pruning, although you may lose the flowering display for a year or two until the plant produces new growth. The best time to carry out drastic pruning of climbers is while they are dormant between fall and early spring. It is also an ideal time to make repairs or replace supports that need it while they are easily accessible.

Reinvigorating clematis

One of the attractions of Oliver's garden was the variety of clematis used to clothe the fences on both sides, but they were very overgrown and in need of a drastic trim. Before you can prune clematis, you need to know whether they produce their flowers on growth produced the previous year (early-flowering), during the current year (late-flowering) or both. To find this out, Oliver had carefully kept a record of each vine's flowering habit the previous year, to make sure he used the correct pruning method (see page 184). However, with the help of reference books and a neighborly experienced gardener who lived down the road, he was able to identify all but one of his clematis. He did, however, know that this mystery clematis flowered on new growth so needed to be cut back in early spring.

He pruned back the spring-flowering *Clematis montana* 'Elizabeth' after it had flowered. The other two clematis in his garden were 'Lasurstern' and 'The President' which are mid-summer flowering, producing their blooms on both old and new wood, so Oliver pruned them by cutting selected shoots back to a pair of plump buds near ground level. Other stems were simply trimmed to fit the support. He then securely tied all unpruned stems on the clematis to their supports **(1)**.

1

Chopping back honeysuckles

There were two honeysuckles in the Oliver's garden. The first covered part of a panel fence near to his house. This plant was so top heavy that it practically doubled over with the weight of its stems that had grown beyond the support. Before any detailed pruning could be done, Oliver used a pair of shears to cut back the massed tangled growth to reveal the main stems. When most of the tangle had been removed, he changed to a pair of pruners to selectively remove or shorten alternate sideshoots to create a basic structure of evenly spaced shoots. He then tied these onto their supports. The second honeysuckle, further down the garden, still had new shoots growing from its base, so this climber didn't need to be cut back so drastically. Oliver removed all the top-heavy growth as before, but only pruned the stems back to a new shoot low on the plant. He then thinned out congested stems by removing the largest and oldest first and leaving the newest growth.

Ornamental vines

Vigorous vitis respond well to cutting back hard, which is just as well because the pair of climbers at the end of Oliver's garden were starting to take over. It is important to prune ornamental vines before the end of winter; otherwise the cuts can bleed badly as the sap starts to rise in spring. Oliver started regaining control of his monster vine by tracing the wayward stems back to the main stem while still attached to the support. He then cut back the stems cleanly, using a pair of loppers for the large stems and pruners for smaller ones. Once he identified a framework of main stems, Oliver tied those stems in the best position and removed the rest completely, using a special pruning saw. New shoots produced from the base were also tied to the support during the following year.

Curbing rambling and climbing roses

A thicket of overgrown rambler rose stems battled with the ornamental vines and dominated a bottom corner of Oliver's garden. To tackle this beast, Oliver decked himself out with thick leather gloves, goggles and a thick coat. He also found a piece of old carpet to act as a thorn-proof shield when gaining access to the middle of the thicket. His aim was to cut out all the oldest shoots back to ground level, but this was easier said than done as the thicket was very overgrown. With a little perseverance, however, he managed to cut back all but a handful of vigorous new shoots, which were gingerly tied to the new support.

Unlike rambler roses, climbing roses don't respond well to drastic pruning. There was one gnarled old specimen that was prone to diseases, however, which Oliver wanted to keep because it produced a constant trickle of pretty flowers all summer. So, he decided to give it the kill-or-cure treatment by cutting it back hard with a pruning saw to leave just a couple of shoots near ground level. This he hoped would help reduce the disease problem and encourage the plant regrow healthily.

Good company

Revitalized climbers filled the new garden design with color. Next to the house, Oliver added a new climbing rose to make a perfect partner for the clematis 'Lasurstern'. The rose neatly filled the color gap between the clematis' early and late blooms.

A YEAR LATER. . . NEW FLOWERS FROM OLD

Nearly all the climbers responded well to the cull of unproductive growth, producing vigorous new stems near the base, and many added a splash of color to the new garden with a display of flowers in the first year. All the new growth was trained into the supports and used to replace older stems that were pruned out. Unfortunately, the old climbing rose didn't survive, so Oliver decided to replace it with a new plant the following year.

Adding interest
to borders with climbers

Arches, arbors, trellis and posts are ideal ways of adding height to your garden quickly. Garden structures also offer the opportunities to grow climbers if you do not have a suitable wall or fence.

Climber-clad structures not only look great but are easy to construct (see page 92). They can be used to draw the eye to certain parts of the garden or create the illusion of depth and provide a tempting glimpse of the partially hidden areas beyond.

Providing a backdrop
Use painted trellis or posts linked by stout colored rope to create an elevated support at the back of a large border. Alternatively, try rustic poles and posts to make a series of A-frames on legs that will provide an attractive geometric pattern at the back of the border that can be clothed in a curtain of flowers and foliage. A vigorous clematis, climbing rose or the perennial golden hop would make effective seasonal backdrops, as would the fiery fall hues of the ornamental grape vine, *Vitis vinifera* 'Purpurea'.

Framing a view
An arch or arbor, made from a simple do-it-yourself kit or constructed out of rustic poles, is an ideal way of framing a point of focus, such as a birdbath, or drawing the eye to a distant feature, such as a statue at the end of a path. In the picture opposite (4), for example, the shady arch covered by the delicately fragrant 'Iceberg' rose effectively brings the garden beyond into focus.

An arch can be placed over a path to allow close scrutiny of foliage and flowers, or positioned mid-border where it can be viewed from a distance. To ensure that the arch doesn't fight for attention, its size should be in proportion with the rest of the garden and the vigor of the climber to complement its surroundings. A broad path, for example, would look best if bridged by a heavy-weight arch and covered with a variety of colorful climbers that provide interest through the seasons, while a simple statue would be complemented by an elegant metal arch clad in a colorful small-leaved ivy that framed the focal point all year round. Be prepared to experiment with color for an eye-catching feature. For instance, try growing a climber that bears contrasting bright-yellow flowers over a blue painted arch.

Secluded seating
Arbors are also an effective way of creating a secluded seating area in a small garden. Again it is important to maintain a sense of proportion and choose a seat that fits within the arch comfortably. Also make sure that the position you choose has an attractive outlook; otherwise you'll be less tempted to stop and rest each time you pass by. You can then cover the arch with perfumed rambling roses such as 'Alberic Barbier', 'Albertine', 'Emily Gray', 'Sander's White Rambler' and 'Seagull'. Alternatively, make a cool and shady retreat by covering the arch with an ornamental vine or the ferny foliage of summer jasmine. On a large arch or arbor, combine several climbers including clematis and honeysuckles for a succession of color and scent throughout the summer. For example, in the picture opposite (1), the two scented climbing roses have been planted alongside wisteria and jasmine to form a striking feature and fragrant arbor.

Adding a focal point
A simple climber-clad post can make an attractive focal point in its own right. A formal atmosphere is easy to create using metal obelisks, which look especially effective when used in pairs either side of a path. Less formal structures can look just as good in the right setting and cost next to nothing to make. A tripod of bamboo canes or a handful of long twiggy prunings, bundled together at one end with string and stuck in the ground, can be covered in annual vines, such as sweet peas or morning glories.

Floral frames
Scented roses, jasmine and wisteria cover a white-painted trellis arbor **(1)**; clematis partners a wall-trained ceanothus **(2)**; a rose-clad arch focuses the eye ahead **(3)**; and golden hop covers a rustic twig arch **(4)**.

constructing arches and pergolas

The design and material from which an arch or pergola is made should complement the style of the rest of the garden. Wooden structures, for example, are chunky and can have an angular feel, so they look most effective in a traditional garden design. This is particularly the case with rustic poles, which look best covered in billowing scented climbers in a cottage-garden setting. Arches and pergolas made from slim timbers and colored with wood stain or coated in paint, however, can look effective in a contemporary garden design, especially when covered in a climber with a contrasting flower color. In a larger garden, pergolas with brick or stone piers and a timber overhead frame are worth considering.

Metal-framed pergolas and arches offer a sleek and clean appearance that complements most modern garden designs. If you have the space, you could try to incorporate attractive circular structures or

shady arbors. These look decorative and can be used to create a shady, cool place to eat. You should also remember that arches and pergolas must be strong enough to take the weight of the climber you have in mind, as well as being sufficiently well anchored so that they don't collapse in high winds.

Kits or special orders

Many easy-to-assemble flat-packed kits in wood and metal are now available and the range of designs is growing. To help you choose which style to opt for, many larger garden retailers and home supply stores have assembled kits on display. (Manufacturers of the various kits may also be able to tell you where you can go locally to see one of their structures assembled.)

Local fencing specialists often produce designs of their own, so it's worth checking out what outlets there are in your area before you buy. Make sure that wooden frames

VIRGIN GARDENER'S BEST BETS

Plants for scent
Clematis armandii, C. montana, climbing roses, honeysuckle (*Lonicera* spp.), jasmine (*Jasminum* spp.) and wisteria (*Wisteria* spp.).

Plants for arches
Less vigorous clematis, jasmines (*Jasminum* spp.) and honeysuckles (*Lonicera* spp.); also cardinal creeper (*Ipomoea coccinea*), morning glories (*Ipomoea nil, I. hedera, I. purpurea, I. tricolor*), moonflower vine (*Ipomoea alba*) and thornless rose 'Zéphirine Drouhin'.

Plants for arbors and pergolas
Autumn-flowering clematis (*Clematis terniflora*), blue dawn flower (*Ipomoea indica*), Cape honeysuckle (*Tecoma capensis*), Dutchman's pipe (*Aristolochia* spp.), honeysuckle (*Lonicera* spp.), jasmine (*Jasminum* spp.), moonflower vine (*Ipomoea alba*), ornamental grapevine (*Vitis vinifera*), passion flower (*Passiflora* spp.), trumpet vine (*Campsis radicans*) and wisteria.

Plants for pillars and posts
Less vigorous clematis, jasmines (*Jasminum* spp.), and honeysuckles (*Lonicera* spp.); also black-eyed Susan vine (*Thunbergia alata*), canary creeper (*Tropaeolum peregrinum*), cardinal creeper (*Ipomoea coccinea*), Chilean glory flower (*Eccremocarpus* spp.), cup-and-saucer vine (*Cobaea scandens*), morning glories (*Ipomoea nil, I. hedera, I. purpurea, I. tricolor*) and climbing roses such as 'New Dawn'.

are made from pressure-treated wood or wood with natural durability, such as western red cedar, redwood, or cypress.

If you want a structure to fit a specific space in your garden, you may have to have it specially designed and built by a contractor; alternatively, you can make it yourself from the component parts. You should ask for advice at your local building supply store or fencing specialist if you want a wooden structure, or contact manufacturers of metal ones to get a catalog and price list. Metal structures should have a thick plastic coating without cracks or chips. Also, check that the frame slots together easily and the pre-drilled holes for bolts line up to make it easy to assemble the kit.

Putting them together

Well-made metal structures are probably the easiest and quickest to put together—expect to spend about half a day for a pergola and half an hour for an arch. The sections simply slot together and, once constructed, the whole structure is rigid and quite lightweight so it can be easily moved around.

Wood structures require more do-it-yourself skill to construct, though are still well within the scope of a Virgin Gardener. Wood arches are usually supplied with extra-long vertical posts so they can be concreted directly into the ground.

When building a wood pergola, it is very important to get the posts in the right position at the outset, so measure the position accurately and mark it out with pegs and string or with spray paint **(1)**. You then need to dig holes for the main post anchors, which should be concreted in place. Use a spirit level to check that the posts are upright before adding concrete to the holes **(2)**. You should be aware that the wood may rot if concreted directly into the ground, so you may prefer to trim each of the posts and bolt them to metal fence-post spikes that are driven into the ground with a sledgehammer.

Choose a suitable climber for the site and size of the structure (see box, opposite). At the base of each upright post, plant single specimens or pairs of climbers with complementary flowering times **(3)**. Wood pergolas are quite heavy once assembled, so make sure you have at least one extra pair of hands available during the final stages of construction.

Shrubs and trees

Perhaps the most important plants in the garden, shrubs and trees are the backbone that brings a permanent sense of structure to the design as a whole as well as to individual borders. Many change dramatically throughout the year, giving a variety of seasonal interest. In short, shrubs and trees represent a wealth of color and diversity that no garden should be without.

Shrubs are woody perennial plants, smaller than trees, usually with several stems or trunks. Some varieties, such as camellia, produce spectacular displays of flowers that rival the floral shows of summer annuals, while others, such as maple trees, offer a stunning array of intensely colored leaves in the fall. Many shrubs and trees bear berries in the winter while others fill the air with heady fragrance all summer.

Shrubs and trees need the right growing conditions to thrive, so check the plant label before you buy. Many are adaptable to a variety of conditions, while some will thrive in heavy clay soil or other difficult areas. They will even grow in exposed seaside gardens and alongside heavily polluted roads. Although most shrubs prefer a sunny site, there are some that will do well even in heavy shade. Use the lists of recommended shrubs and trees to help you make the right choice.

Deciduous plants drop their leaves at the end of the growing season, while evergreens hold onto their leaves. The latter can provide year-round structure, but if you have too many, the garden will seem static, changing little throughout the year. The secret to success is to have a balance: one evergreen to every two deciduous plants. You also need to decide how big you want the specimen to grow and how quickly. This can vary a great deal between seemingly close relatives. The dwarf mugho pine, for example, grows to just a few feet tall whereas the Scotch pine can reach well over 100 feet. Finally, consider what function you want the shrub or tree to perform, so you can decide upon its shape (see also page 16).

spring selection

Spring-flowering shrubs and trees herald the new season with a burst of bloom **(3)**. No matter where you live, the garden center will be loaded with flowering shrubs at this time. Always ensure your soil and light conditions match the plant's requirements.

Classic choices

Forsythia (*Forsythia* x *intermedia*) is a classic spring-flowering shrub, and it is ultra-easy to grow. For the best effect, frame forsythia against a wall or let it drape over a fence.

Azaleas and rhododendrons are also a garden standard, thanks to their abundant bright flowers. Many shades of red, pink, white and purple are available, in sizes from dwarf to head-high or taller. One of the very earliest to bloom is *Rhododendron mucronulatum* 'Cornell Pink', which bears a cloud of blossoms before the leaves appear.

Camellias offer stunning flowers that look best against dark glossy foliage **(1)**. Plant them in a sheltered spot protected from cold winds and strong sun.

Magnolias are another spring favorite. Star magnolia (*Magnolia stellata*) is an early bloomer, its white flowers accompanying spring bulbs. Saucer magnolia (*M. soulangiana*) is an attractive small to midsized tree, with most cultivars, such as 'Lennei' **(2)**, growing to about 25 feet tall. The pink, white, or rosy purple flowers usually bloom early, and may be damaged by a late spring frost in colder areas. *M. grandiflora* 'Majestic Beauty' has flowers of up to an astounding 12 inches across.

Spring fragrance

Fragrance is a welcome attribute in the spring garden, whether the plant is at nose height along a path or wafting its aroma from a hidden corner of the garden. Mexican orange (*Choisya ternata*) has heavenly citrus-scented white flowers that bloom for several weeks.

Highly fragrant *Viburnum burkwoodii* is a shrub for extremely cold areas as well as milder regions. Its white flowers open in clusters from pink buds, very early in spring or even in late winter. Several other viburnums offer sweet scent, such as Korean spice (*V. carlesii*) and fragrant snowball (*V.* x *carlcephalum*), both white-flowered shrubs.

An small early blooming shrub which is beautiful with spring bulbs is flowering almond (*Prunus glandulosa*). Its branches are bedecked with fluffy pink pompom flowers.

Lilacs are an excellent choice because they are easy to grow and reliable bloomers. Best-known is

Syringa vulgaris, with its deliciously fragrant purple or white blossoms. Other lilac species and hybrids, including vigorous, ultra-cold-hardy *S. x hyacinthiflora* 'Blanche Sweet' and *S. microphylla* 'Superba', which reblooms in late summer, are also worth investigating.

In mild-winter areas, gardenias are legendary for their heavy scent. 'Veitchii' is a dependable performer. 'August Beauty' and 'First Love' are two of the larger cultivars, reaching several feet tall.

Small flowering trees

Elegant white flowering dogwood (*Cornus florida*) is an elegant choice as a specimen or in a perennial border, but it is unfortunately affected by blight in some regions, particularly the East. Flowering crabapple trees (*Malus* spp.) in vivid pinks, purples and white, and flowering cherries (*Prunus* spp.) in pastel pink

and white are widely available. Rose-pink or white redbuds (*Cercis* spp.) also add a splash of early spring color. Silverbell (*Halesia* spp.), a moderately sized tree, offers clusters of snow-white bells in mid-spring. Underplant spring-flowering trees with daffodils, tulips, or small bulbs for a beautiful effect.

In mild areas, many trees, such as acacias, bloom from winter through spring or begin blooming in spring. Bauhinia trees are easy to grow, because they thrive in almost any well-drained soil. Spectacular red bauhinia (*Bauhinia galpinii*) has vivid flowers as eyecatching as those of bougainvillea. Brazilian butterfly tree (*Bauhinia forficata*) has an interesting twisting trunk and creamy white flowers.

Foliage interest

Many trees and shrubs have colorful spring leaves that can be used to

add interest to the garden. Perhaps the best shrub for this purpose is *Pieris* 'Forest Flame' because it is a dark-leafed evergreen that produces strings of tiny white, bell-shaped, scented flowers and bright red new growth that slowly darkens as it matures. Pieris prefers semi-shade and an acid soil.

Trees with bright spring foliage need to be viewed both from a distance and close up to be appreciated to the full, so plant them at the end of a path or near the boundary in your front garden. This way they are easily accessible, but you can still view them from the house. In a small garden try *Acer pseudoplatanus* 'Brilliantissimum' or *A. negundo* 'Flamingo' which both grow to only 15 feet or so when mature. They both bear pink foliage in spring and yellow hues in the fall, with the latter having the added attraction of variegated foliage all summer.

VIRGIN GARDENER'S BEST BETS

Hardy shrubs
All spring-flowering species of azalea, *Deutzia*, *Kerria*, lilac (*Syringa*), magnolia, mock orange (*Philadelphus*), rhododendron, smoke tree (*Cotinus*), *Spiraea*, viburnum and *Weigela*.

Hardy trees
All species of flowering cherries (*Prunus*), flowering crabapple (*Malus*), flowering dogwood (*Cornus florida*), hawthorn (*Crataegus*), redbud (*Cercis*), shadblow (*Amelanchier*) and silverbell (*Halesia*).

Tender shrubs
All spring-blooming species of broom (*Genista*), camellia, gardenia, golden trumpet tree (*Tabebuia chrysotricha*), jasmine (*Jasminum*), Mexican orange (*Choisya ternata*), fuchsia (pictured right), *Hebe*, *Olearia*, *Pittosporum* and rosemary.

best summer choices

Several of the best garden shrubs not only produce spectacular displays during the summer, but also scent the air with their delightful perfume. Roses are perhaps the best example, but there are other shrubs that also will help perfume your garden display.

Aromatic plants

Botanists consider lavender (*Lavandula* spp.) a shrub, and in hospitable climates, certain species can reach 6 feet tall. It prefers well-drained soil and a sunny spot. If your soil is heavy, grow lavender on a mound filled with a mixture of rubble and sand, covered with a 6-inch layer of topsoil mixed with grit to improve drainage in the winter. To really appreciate the scent, grow lavender next to a path as a low hedge or edging plant. For these situations, the best choices are dwarf varieties such as 'Hidcote' (purple), or 'Munstead' (purple). French lavender (*L. stoechas*) has distinctive "wings" that protrude from the top of each flower, making it particularly decorative and worth giving a prominent position.

For a sweet honeysuckle-like scent, try growing the moderately tender *Abelia chinensis* which bears its pale pink blooms in mid- to late summer. It grows in most soils but likes the sun and shelter from the wind, so would be ideal at the base of a south-facing wall or fence.

The butterfly bush, *Buddleia davidii*, will grow almost anywhere provided the soil drains freely. Its musk-scented, conical flowers act like a magnet to pollinating insects and butterflies. Look for a named variety to get the best display of flowers: 'Lochinch' (lavender-blue), 'Royal Red' (purple-red), 'Black Knight' (deep purple) and 'White Profusion' (white). All buddleias require hard pruning in spring to get the best displays (see page 182).

Cold-hardy Carolina allspice or sweet-shrub (*Calycanthus floridus*) has dark red-brown ribbony-petaled flowers with a scent that reminds some of strawberry, others of chocolate. Its relative, California allspice or spice bush (*C. occidentalis*), is also strongly aromatic with both purple-brown flowers and foliage having a winey scent when crushed.

In moderately mild areas, hebes are an ideal choice. Most are tough, fast-growing plants. Showy hebe (*Hebe speciosa*) boasts glossy, dark green foliage and reddish-purple flowers. Its cultivar 'Imperialis' has foliage flushed with red and spiked with magenta flowers. Hebes can also thrive in coastal gardens.

Foliage for color and texture

In the heat of summer, the cooling effect of variegated leaves is particularly welcome. Shrubby variegated dogwood (*Cornus alba* 'Argenteo-marginata') is a hardy choice for brightening summer scenery with its white-edged leaves. Its red stems are a bonus in wintertime. Creamy white marbling gives an interesting effect to the foliage of the variegated Cornelian cherry (*Cornus mas* 'Variegata').

VIRGIN GARDENER'S BEST BETS

 Flowering shrubs for hummingbirds
Abelia, Acacia, beautybush (*Kolkwitzia amabilis*), *Bouvardia terniflora*, butterfly bush (*Buddleia*), *Calliandra*, flowering maple (*Abutilon*), flowering quince (*Chaenomeles*), fuchsia, hibiscus, lavender (*Lavandula*), lemon bottlebrush (*Callistemon citrinus*), pineapple guava (*Feijoa sellowiana*), red flowering currant (*Ribes sanguineum*), rosemary, Texas ranger (*Leucophyllum*), *Weigela*, yellow bells (*Tecoma stans*).

 Shrubs for fragrance
Abelia chinensis, Atlas broom (*Cytisus battandieri*), butterfly bush (*Buddleia davidii*), lilacs (*Syringa*), lavender (*Lavandula*), magnolia, *Osmanthus*, red flowering currant (*Ribes sanguineum*), roses and viburnum.

 Disease-resistant roses
'Auguste Renoir', 'Abbaye de Cluny', 'Brandy', 'Carefree Wonder', 'China Doll', 'Dr. Van Fleet', 'Eden', 'Frederic Mistral', 'Leonardo da Vinci', 'New Dawn', 'Paris d'Yves St. Laurent', 'Pascali', 'Polka', 'Red Fairy', 'Zéphirine Drouhin'; all Rugosa roses, such as 'Blanc Double de Coubert', 'Henry Kelsey', 'Martin Frobisher' and 'Topaz Jewel'; all cultivars of the David Austin's English roses strain, such as 'Cottage Rose', 'Fair Bianca', 'Gertrude Jekyll', 'Graham Thomas', 'Mary Rose', 'Tamara', and 'Glamis Castle'; all cultivars of the Meidiland strain, such as 'Alba Meidiland', 'Royal Bonica', and 'Sevillana'.

For more bright color, try golden barberry (*Berberis* 'Bonanza Gold'), 'Goldflame' spiraea (*Spiraea bumalda* 'Goldflame'), or a yellow-tinged cultivar of mock orange (*Philadelphus* 'Aureus'). All are attractive with blue perennials or as accents in a mixed hedge.

Purpleleaf plum (*Prunus x cistena*), some cultivars of smoke tree (*Cotinus coggyria* 'Royal Purple' and 'Velvet Cloak'), and red-leaf barberry (*Berberis thunbergii* 'Crimson Pygmy' and 'Atropurpurea') provide deep red-purple foliage, an excellent contrast to pale pink roses and pastel perennials, or a good partner to yellow flowers.

Ferny foliage is the most attractive feature of the lemon bottlebrush tree (*Callistemon citrinus*). Tender and sun-loving, this plant does best in the shelter of a south-facing wall or fence. Tolerant of heat and poor soil, it is particularly worth growing in the milder conditions often found near a coast. Hummingbirds are attracted to the red bristle-like flowers, which are produced off and on throughout the entire year. For the best flowers, look for the cultivars 'Splendens' and 'Improved', which are propagated by cuttings for reliable larger-size flowers.

Trouble-free roses

Roses have a lot to offer the Virgin Gardener—for sheer flower power there isn't a plant that can beat them. There are literally thousands of varieties so you won't be short of choice, and many offer a delicious scent, too. Roses are, however, renowned for their susceptibility to the diseases of blackspot, mildew and rust, so it is important that you choose with care to be sure of buying a disease-resistant varieties. Always be sure to read catalog descriptions and labels carefully. In general, rugosa roses are an excellent choice for trouble-free plants. For all roses, practise good garden hygiene to minimize disease outbreaks: rake up and dispose of all dropped foliage; snip off affected stems if possible; and be sure your roses get good air circulation to reduce fungal problems. If all else fails, you can turn to chemical solutions which are widely available at garden centers.

If you want scented roses, search out the yellow 'Arthur Bell' or 'Mountbatten', the salmon-pink 'Fragrant Delight' or 'Silver Jubilee', orange-red 'Lovers' Meeting' or 'Matangi', or the deep red 'Royal William'. If your local garden center doesn't sell them, try contacting a rose specialist.

Sensual planting
Colorful roses, aromatic French lavender and furry lamb's ears (*Stachys*) are combined with other sun-loving plants such as red valerian (*Centranthus*), catmint (*Nepeta*) and hardy geranium in this sunny border.

fall and winter color

When nearly all other garden interest is winding down for the winter, certain shrubs and trees can provide brilliant color. Because most new trees and shrubs can be planted in the fall, this is a good time to plan a fall display. But the danger for the Virgin Gardener is to be tempted by startling bright scarlets, oranges and yellows only to find the plant chosen is lackluster for the rest of the year. Fortunately, there are plenty of examples which have more to offer than just a rainbow of shades in the fall.

Fall favorites

Valued for their striking fall foliage colors, maples like this sugar maple **(1)** are a common sight in many gardens. Where space is limited, the Japanese maple (*Acer palmatum* 'Dissectum') is ideal for a sheltered position in light shade. Forming a neat mound of ferny leaves, the intricately divided foliage is bright green as it unfurls in spring, but still looks great all summer. In the fall, the leaves turn brilliant shades of pink, red and orange. For extra summer color, try one of the named varieties such as 'Dissectum Atropurpureum', 'Dissectum Garnet' and 'Dissectum Crimson Queen', all of which have wonderful purple leaves. If your soil is heavy, it is best to grow these plants in containers.

Another purple-leafed shrub with added value is the deciduous barberry, *Berberis thunbergii* 'Atropurpurea'. Its richly colored foliage takes on vivid red hues in the fall before dropping from the plant to reveal a hidden treasure of red berries in the winter. Although a really versatile shrub that can cope with almost any soil in sun or shade, it produces its best leaf colors in full sun. For a really tight corner try the dwarf variety 'Atropurpurea Nana' which grows to just 24 inches tall.

In a woodland setting, consider *Fothergilla major* for its brilliant fall foliage in shades of orange, red and scarlet. It has the bonus of scented flowers in late spring. Another option is the winged euonymus or burning bush (*Euonymus alatus*) which is slow growing, reaching about 6 feet high in ten years. Leaves turn an attractive pink shade in the fall and drop to reveal the decorative corky ridged bark on the stems. The small fruits, revealed when the leaves fall, are relished by songbirds.

If you have space, the smoke tree, *Cotinus coggygria*, is worth planting as a focal point in the middle of a lawn, for example. Apart from its bright fall tints of orange and yellow, in summer it is covered in a

haze of pinkish flowers that turn to a smoky gray. Purple-leafed cultivars such as 'Royal Purple' and 'Velvet Cloak' are also available, with foliage that provides an unusual deep color during spring and summer, then turns yellow to orange-red in fall.

Viburnums **(3)** are an excellent choice for fall color. Most are trouble-free and adaptable to a variety of conditions. They also bear colorful berries that may be orange, red, black, white or even metallic blue. Arrowwood (*Viburnum dentatum*) turns yellow, orange or red in fall, with blue-black fruit.

Berries for winter wonder

A bonus in any garden, berry-producing plants can be included to give added interest to the coldest months. The decorative value of berries tends to be short-lived, however, because they are usually eaten by birds and other wildlife, but the following shrubs and trees produce an abundant harvest that will last at least until the coldest weather sets in.

Barberry (*Berberis*), burning bush (*Euonymus alatus*), pyracantha, viburnums and ornamental crabapple trees (*Malus*) **(2)** are the usual fall-fruiting plants offered at garden centers. All offer plenty of decorative interest in the autumn garden, plus the bright fleshy seedpods, or hips, of roses. Also look for *Mahonia*, a shrub that has so much to offer that its eyecatching strings of blue berries are almost forgotten. Its upright architectural shape and distinctive horizontal evergreen holly-like foliage are reasons enough to include it in your garden. Before the berries appear, they also produce attractive, scented flowers.

Evergreen hollies are always popular in fall and winter gardens, thanks to their glossy foliage and

---

VIRGIN GARDENER'S BEST BETS

 For autumn foliage color
Barberry (*Berberis*), birch (*Betula*), chokeberry (*Aronia*), *Euonymus alatus*, *Fothergilla*, fringetree (*Chionanthus*), Katsura tree (*Cercidiphyllum japonicum*), maple (*Acer*), mountain ash (*Sorbus*), ornamental pear, viburnum, Zelkova (*Zelkova serrata*).

 For interesting bark and branch form
Blood-twig dogwood (*Cornus sanguinea*), birches (*Betula*), broom (*Cytisus*), coralbark maple (*Acer palmatum* 'Sango Kaku'), Harry Lauder's walking stick (*Corylus avellana* 'Contorta'), Japanese tree lilac (*Syringa reticulata*), lacebark pine (*Pinus bungeana*), paperbark maple (*Acer griseum*), red-twig dogwood (*Cornus stolonifera*), *Stewartia* and winged euonymus (*Euonymus alatus*).

 For fall and winter berries
Chokeberry, cotoneaster, euonymus, flowering crabapple (*Malus*), hawthorn (*Crataegus*), hollies, Kousa dogwood, mahonia, mountain ash , *Photinia*, pyracantha, *Skimmia*, viburnum.

---

colorful berries, which are attractive to songbirds. Adaptable American holly (*Ilex opaca*) and the more tender English holly (*I. aquifolium*), which does not flourish in the East, Midwest, or humid South, grow into large trees. For shrubby evergreen hollies, look to cultivars of Chinese holly (*I. cornuta*), Japanese holly (*I. crenata*), and highly popular 'Blue Girl', 'Blue Boy' and other cultivars of *I. meserveae*. Deciduous hollies (*I. decidua, I. verticillata*), which drop their leaves in fall to reveal bare branches studded with bright berries, are even more striking, at least until the birds strip the heavily laden branches. All hollies need both a pollinating male and female plant for a good crop of berries.

Year-round color

Evergreen conifers are the stalwart of winter displays. They range from ground-hugging prostrate types, for covering the ground, to narrow vertical columns that can be used

like exclamation marks at the end of a border planting. Most provide a static display of constant color throughout the year, with different varieties offering subtly different colors—from bright yellow to deep bronze, from the palest green through steely blues to almost blackish-green shades. The variety you choose should depend on the function you want it to perform; for example, choose a prostrate variety for weed-smothering ground cover. Growth rates and ultimate sizes vary enormously, however, from miniature plants that grow less than an inch a year, to giant specimens that reach well over 100 feet tall. They also vary in their hardiness.

Visit a garden center to find excellent evergreen shrubs and trees to add year-round color to your garden. Junipers, hemlocks, spruces, arborvitae, and many other species —and their dozens of cultivars—are sure to provide just the right architecture, texture and color for your garden.

planting trees and shrubs

It is important to plant trees at the correct spacing if they are going to fulfill their potential. If you plant them too close to one another, you will either have to move them later on, which is hard work and not always successful, or you will have to prune them regularly to keep them in check. With the exception of very slow-growing species, don't be tempted to buy semi-mature plants to create an instant border. These are not only expensive, but take far longer to get established than smaller, less mature plants.

If you do buy small plants, however, your planting scheme can look somewhat barren for the first few years. There are two ways of overcoming this. First, you could plant quick-growing but short-lived "filler" shrubs in between your main shrubs. Many inexpensive shrubs such as forsythia, butterfly bush, mock orange and rose-of-Sharon can be used. These establish quickly and provide a good display during the early years, but they will need to be removed once the main shrubs grow and need more space. The second option is to fill the gaps between the main shrubs with a mixture of bulbs, ground-covering perennials and hardy annuals. These give instant color to the border and will slowly die out over the years as the main shrubs use up the light, moisture and nutrients.

Getting the best from new shrubs and trees

It is essential that new shrubs and trees don't run short of moisture around their roots or suffer from competition from weeds and other plants. The easiest way to achieve this is to water thoroughly after planting and to cover the soil with a 3-inch-deep layer of organic matter,

Correct planting distances

There is a very simple formula for calculating the planting distances between shrubs or trees. First, you will need to find out the mature height of the shrubs or trees you are buying. This information is often given on the label but it is also worth looking up the varieties in a good plant encyclopedia. Once you have found out this information, add together the mature height of the two specimens you are planting adjacent to one another. Now, divide this number by either three, to get the correct planting distance for shrubs, or divide it by two to get the correct planting distance for trees.

such as bark chips, or a 3-foot-diameter sheet of landscape fabric (available from garden centers).

In drought-prone areas, make watering easier by ridging up the soil about 12 inches from the tree to form a small reservoir around the base of the trunk. Any water will remain in the reservoir until the roots have soaked it up **(1)**.

Alternatively, hammer a plastic pipe into the ground near the plant and fill it with gravel, then pour the water down the pipe **(2)**. The gravel holds the water, while the pipe directs the water to the roots.

To keep weeds at bay between shrubs and trees, turn to mulch. A generous layer of wood chips, chopped leaves, or other organic

Planting shrubs and trees

To ensure that shrubs and trees establish quickly, they should be planted carefully. Container-grown plants can be planted at any time of the year but establish far quicker if planted in the spring or fall. Specimens sold with no soil around the roots, known as bare-root, should be planted while dormant. Evergreens and conifers are best planted in spring. Always water the plants thoroughly before you plant them.

1 Dig the soil thoroughly and remove any weeds and large stones. Now, dig a large planting hole, about twice as wide as the rootball and a little deeper. Prick over the bottom and sides of the hole with a fork to allow the roots to spread out easily—this

material will smother weeds and make it easy to hand-pull any weeds that sprout later. Renew the mulch as necessary as it decomposes.

Most shrubs benefit from the occasional pruning (see page 182), but a few can be left to their own devices—*Aucuba japonica* varieties, *Acer palmatum* 'Dissectum', *Berberis thunbergii* varieties and *Yucca filamentosa*, to name but a few. It is usually impractical to remove the dead flower heads from garden shrubs and trees, but a few will benefit. Roses, azaleas, camellias, lilacs and rhododendrons are all worth deadheading as their flowers fade. Leave the old flowers on hydrangeas until spring to provide winter interest and help protect the new flower buds.

Some popular shrubs are prone to producing vigorous shoots from the roots, known as suckers. These need to be removed by excavating the soil

from around the root and tearing the sucker from the root. Don't just cut off the sucker because this will encourage more to be produced. Some variegated shrubs also produce vigorous and less decorative all-green shoots which should be removed using pruners.

Several shrubs need winter protection in colder areas, such as bay, choisya, *Jasminum officinale*, myrtle and ceanothus. Wrap up evergreen shrubs, such as bay and myrtle, with an insulating double layer of spun row cover or a quilt made from a double layer of netting stuffed with straw or dry leaves. Protect any conifers and choisya from cold winds by wrapping them in windbreak netting (available from garden centers). Protect the roots of semitender plants by covering the soil with a thick layer of evergreen prunings, bark chips or dead leaves held in position with netting.

is particularly important in heavy clay soil. Then, incorporate some well-rotted manure or proprietary planting mixture into the bottom of the planting hole.

2 Place the plant in the hole and lay a bamboo cane across it to check that the hole is deep enough. Adjust the depth, if needed, so that the plant is at the same depth as it was in the pot (look for a change in bark color to indicate the soil depth for bare-root trees and shrubs). Check over the rootball and remove any weeds and loose soil, then gently tease out the roots using your fingers. Place the plant in the hole then add about 6 inches of soil around the edge, before firming with your heel. Repeat this process until the hole is filled. Water thoroughly (see above).

3 If a tree is in a very windy site, a stake will add stability until the roots can maintain a good grip. To stake a tree, hammer a sturdy wooden post into the soil at a 45-degree angle to the tree trunk so that it avoids the rootball (hammer the stake in vertically for bare-rooted trees, carefully avoiding the roots). Loosely tie the trunk to the post using a special tree tie (available from garden centers) or a piece of strong wire threaded through a section of discarded garden hose, to prevent the tie from damaging the bark. Cover the surface of the soil in a 3-foot-diameter circle around the tree with a 3-inch-deep layer of an organic mulch, such as bark or wood chips, to suppress weeds and help retain soil moisture. But prevent the mulch from touching the tree.

planning a year-round border

Debbie and Tom had neglected their garden while renovating their house. Apart from a formal walled area nearest the house, they wanted to create a formal structure to the rest of their garden design, but were also keen to include lots of informal borders full of fragrant flowers. Although they wanted the planting scheme to peak during the summer months, they also liked the idea of including several plants that offered lots of interest at other times of the year too.

Formal structure

If you want your garden to have year-round appeal, you need to include both deciduous and evergreen plants. Too many evergreens may make your garden uninteresting for much of the year; too few and your garden will lack continuity and look bleak in winter. As a rule of thumb, it is best to aim for about one evergreen for every two deciduous plants.

Debbie and Tom's garden design was based around a symmetrical series of beds separated by simple straight grass paths. A central, wider paved walkway ran down the middle of the area forming a natural focal point out of an arched gateway that leads to the walled garden nearest the house. They wanted to add height and color to this formal design that would last all year round. They opted to use a series of semi-mature upright conifers rescued from elsewhere in the garden to form an evergreen parade. Standing like sentinels down each main border, the junipers' columnar shapes added a real sense of drama to the scene.

Several other evergreens, including sweet olive, viburnum and myrtle, were incorporated into the border's planting plan to provide a backbone structure throughout the year. Tom wanted to include a series of boxwood clipped into

spheres and conical shapes. As an unusual finishing touch, he added a bird bath water feature that became the envy of all his friends. He made it from a salvaged feeding trough that he bought at the local flea market. He positioned it in the center of the main walkway and raised it up on bricks to give it more height and presence.

Flowering informality

To contrast with the formal plantings of static evergreens, Debbie wanted to fill the borders with a combination of deciduous shrubs and perennials with airy or relaxed habit and plenty of summer flowers. Her aim was to transform the formal borders by overwhelming them with informal growth during the summer months.

She decided to give the polyantha rose, 'Little White Pet', center stage because she liked its huge trusses of mini pompon-like flowers that last all summer long. Grown in groups of threes and fives along the main borders, the plants spilled out into the paths so that passers-by could fully appreciate the fragrant white blooms, giving the whole garden a fairy-tale atmosphere. These roses are not large or vigorous; they grow to a height and width of between 2 and 3 feet, so they would suit even a small garden.

At the back of the borders, Debbie planted the taller pink-flowering rugosa rose 'Frau Dagmar Hartopp', for its highly fragrant blooms and repeat flowering performance. As an added bonus, it produces a crop of tomato-shaped deep red hips in the fall.

Spring interest

Most people buy plants for their garden in spring and this can lead to gardens looking great at that time of year, but rather lackluster at other times. A well-designed planting scheme has lots of color and interest throughout the year. To achieve this, Debbie and Tom chose plants that bloom at different times to offer more than one season of interest as well as plants which produced berries, fall leaves or colored winter bark.

Under the roses they planted shade-tolerant snowdrops and winter aconites which brightened up the borders before the roses came into leaf. The dainty white snowdrops are the first to emerge, followed by the bright yellow blooms of the winter aconites. Elsewhere, other bulbs, including crocus, scillas, chionodoxas and muscari, plus later-flowering dwarf tulips, were planted in irregular blocks to give a succession of color during the spring months.

Summer scenes

Apart from the roses, which bloom more or less all summer long, Debbie and Tom added a range of herbaceous perennials which added to the light and airy feel of the summer border. At the back of the border, large frothy plants, such as *Crambe cordifolia* and baby's breath, were included for their clouds of summer flowers. Tall spires of foxgloves, hollyhocks and mullein as well as the attractive globes of alliums were also added. Toward the front, they chose lady's mantle (*Alchemilla mollis*), catmint (*Nepeta* x

faassenii) and hardy geranium, *G. sanguineum* and its variety *G. sanguineum* 'Striatum'. A few hardy annuals were scattered here and there to fill any unsightly gaps. Plants such as love-in-a-mist (*Nigella*), night-scented stock and candytuft were particular favorites.

Flowers in the fall

Many of the summer blooms lasted well into the fall, but to add more interest to the border at this time of the year, Tom planted late flowering herbaceous perennials including aster, sedum and rudbeckia. He chose *A. x frikartii* 'Mönch' for the back of the border—a clump-forming plant that bears lavender blue flowers from mid-summer to mid-fall on 36-inch stems; *Sedum* 'Autumn Joy' toward the front for its flattened pink flowerheads in late summer that darken to bronze by the end of the fall; and *Rudbeckia fulgida* 'Goldsturm' for a mid-border position where it bears a succession of brilliant yellow brown-eyed daisies from mid-summer to mid-fall.

Winter wonderland

The clearing of borders and any pruning was left until after the worst of the winter weather. This meant the old stems provided some protection to the crowns of less hardy plants in the border during the coldest months and helped decorate the scene, creating an interesting winter landscape, especially after a heavy frost.

A border for all seasons
The formality of neat borders, upright conifers and colorful bulbs in the spring gives way to the billowing summer displays of roses and herbaceous plants (left); in the eerie light of winter, the skeletal remains of the herbaceous flowers (above) reveal the ghostly dark shadows of the evergreen shrubs as the sun rises on a frosty morning.

controlling overgrown shrubs

Agarden can seem extremely small when it becomes overgrown after it has been neglected over a period of time. Meg and Paul realized this when they bought their first home—a detached colonial-style house in the suburbs. Although the house was less than 20 years old, its previous owners, a retired couple who were dedicated gardeners, had planted a range of interesting but vigorous shrubs that had filled all the available space in the garden. Meg and Paul wanted their garden to have a more structured design, but hoped to use as many of the existing shrubs as possible. They were also keen to add a sitting area that would not detract from the rest of the garden's design.

Treasure hunt

When you renovate a neglected garden, preserve existing plants particularly if they are healthy and flowering, because it is expensive to replace them with mature specimens. With this in mind, Meg and Paul decided to research the plants in their garden for a year before clearing out the old and bringing in the new. During this period they kept a record of what plants were in their garden, and when they flowered, and tried to identify as many species as possible. In the meantime, they drew up plans for a garden overhaul.

Regaining control

If you know when a shrub flowers, you can be sure to prune it correctly without losing all the blooms during the following year. The records that Meg and Paul had collected enabled them to decide the best time to prune most of the shrubs in their garden. With those shrubs on which they lacked information, they opted to prune using the one-stem-in-three method during early spring. This is where one-third of the shrub's oldest and largest stems are cut back hard to within a few inches of ground level each year (see page 182).

Dieback and disease

Meg's priority was to remove dead and diseased stems or branches from the existing plants. She sterilized the cutting blades of her pruning tools with a garden disinfectant after removing every diseased branch, to prevent disease from spreading to healthy branches and shrubs.

Lopsided growth

Some of the shrubs had been heavily shaded and developed a lopsided shape, with weak growth on one side and vigorous growth on the other. These shrubs required a different pruning treatment. Paul used the one-stem-in-three method for the majority of each shrub, but cut back the weak sides very hard—pruning each stem back to a plump bud near to the ground. The vigorous growth, on the other side of the shrub, he simply trimmed lightly. This is because the more you prune off a plant, the greater the response you will get from the plant when it puts out new shoots. So, by pruning weak shoots heavily you encourage new vigorous growth, whereas the light pruning of the vigorous side has the opposite effect.

All-green shoots

Several of Meg and Paul's variegated shrubs had developed all-green shoots that were more vigorous than their desired ornamental form, spoiling the appearance of the shrub. Meg checked each shrub over and pruned the all-green shoots she found back to the main stem. The resulting new growth was all variegated.

Hard pruning

Shrubs that flower in summer produce their flowers on new growth produced during the current season. This means they can be cut back hard without losing flowering display the following year. These shrubs are best pruned in early spring before new growth starts. Using a pair of long-handled loppers and a pruning saw, Meg tackled the large butterfly bush and lavatera, cutting all stems back to within a couple of inches of the ground. They also discovered several dogwoods that produce brightly colored winter stems and a mock orange (*Philadelphus coronarius* 'Aureus') normally grown for its colorful golden foliage. To improve the performance of these shrubs, Meg cut all the stems back hard to near ground level during early spring.

Evergreen shrubs

During late spring, after the threat of frost had passed, Paul pruned back the evergreens, which included overgrown *Elaeagnus*, *Photinia*, and *Viburnum tinus*, to remove leggy growth. He made sure that any vigorous shoots were cut back to another shoot lower down, rather than leaving a bare stub. This is because evergreens are generally less likely to produce new shoots from old woody stubs.

Light and space

One bonus of cutting back all the shrubs hard was all the extra light and space this created. Meg took the opportunity to underplant these areas with colorful geraniums, iris and euphorbias in sunny spots, and dwarf bamboos, hostas and hardy ferns in the shady corners. In the largest open space, near to the house, they had an area of decking installed.

A shrub-filled haven

The area of decking located in a sunny spot by the house was an ideal vantage point for Meg and Paul to relax and appreciate their new colorful, plant-filled garden.

Good boundaries
for a modern garden

A boundary wall or fence can have a huge impact on the atmosphere of a garden. It is important to select a style that will reinforce the overall look and feel of your garden design, but also bear in mind its practical function when choosing the type.

A boundary wall, fence or hedge can perform several functions in a garden, depending on its size and the type of materials you choose. At its most basic, a boundary simply denotes the borderline between one garden and another. This can be a line marked out on the ground with paving stones, for example, or a simple hedge reaching just knee high. This form of boundary is often used in front gardens where privacy is not a major issue. White-painted picket fences are another popular option at the front of a house, and in rural areas, ranch-style post-and-rail fencing can be appropriate.

Walls, fences and hedges also can provide shelter in exposed gardens, a backdrop for planting schemes, and privacy and security if this is desired. Solid, high boundaries offer more security and privacy and are often favored for the back yard. In a small garden, however, high boundaries tend to overwhelm the whole design.

Permanent walls
Walls last a lifetime if well built, but are expensive and take a lot of skill and labor to erect. They can be made from a wide range of materials including bricks, natural stone and concrete blocks, and can be adapted in design to suit any style of garden or effectively combined with other materials such as wooden trellis. The appearance of old walls can be improved easily by first rendering and then painting them to add light or a splash of color to the garden.

Feature fences
By far the most popular type of boundary, fences are relatively quick and easy to erect. On the other hand, fences do need good foundations for the supporting posts and require occasional maintenance to keep in good order. Since they can be made from an enormous range of materials, including various woods, metals and even plastic in almost any style, there is a fence to suit every garden design. The materials can be combined to good effect, too. In the Japanese-style garden at right, for example, there is a solid wood barrier on the outside providing security that looks imposing. But on the inside, the simple split-bamboo screen erected against it has a much softer appearance and fits in well with the Eastern style of the garden.

In a situation where a high boundary is needed but light and a feeling of space are important, a see-through boundary such as trellis can be effective. Add height for privacy and make the fence solid if security is your priority. It is often best to compromise, combining both solid and see-through sections.

Living boundaries

Hedges have a soft natural appearance that changes to a formal look when kept neatly trimmed. They are cheap, too, but take a long time to grow. Even quick-growing hedges such as Lawson's cypress can take many years to provide a dense cover. They also need to be trimmed regularly and take up more space than fences or walls.

You must take into account your local climate and soil conditions when selecting plants for a hedge. Dense-growing compact shrubs such as boxwood and lavender make perfect small hedges; evergreen shrubs and conifers are best for larger ones. If you live in a windy seaside location, escallonia and griselinia are good sturdy choices.

On the border line
Blue-stained poles provide support and a stylish backdrop to the foreground plants (1); wood and split bamboo join forces to create a sympathetic yet secure boundary (2); a metal fence is softened by covering it with trellis (3); and brick with wrought-iron are a good mix (4).

Potted plants

Growing plants in containers offers many exciting opportunities for the Virgin Gardener, however big or small your garden. Scent and vibrancy can be added to paved areas, doorways can be brightened and inhospitable corners can be given a seasonal boost of color.

Containers produce better displays by raising the plants off the ground, making them easier to view and to care for. Plants with intricate flowers or foliage can be brought closer to the eye, and those which fill the air with a heady scent can be grown in areas where they will be most appreciated. Common pests, such as slugs and snails, also are less of a problem.

A further advantage of growing plants in pots is that you are not reliant on the quality of the soil in your garden. Indeed, you can grow plants which require a totally different type of soil—acid-loving plants such as camellias or rhododendrons, for example, can be grown successfully in tubs even if your garden soil is alkaline. Pots and tubs also allow you to correct gardening mistakes more easily. If you inadvertently combine two incompatible plants in the same pot, one or both can be removed and replaced very quickly.

Finally, plants in containers can be moved. This means that they can provide instant solutions to problem areas in and around your garden or be shifted to sheltered spots during the winter where they will be protected from harsh elements.

choosing pots and plants

Anything that can hold a reasonable amount of soil can be used as a container for plants. Old sinks, large pots and wash tubs can be successful. In fact, even leaky containers, such as log baskets, can be lined with perforated black plastic before planting to produce unusual and stylish planters.

Your choice should both complement the look of your garden and be suitable for the type of plants you wish to grow. For example, you will need large sturdy pots (frost-proof in cold areas) for permanently planted trees and shrubs.

Terra cotta pots

These are perhaps the most versatile of all containers because they can be used in almost any garden. They are widely available and you can choose from a variety of designs. If you live in a cold-winter area, make sure you buy pots that are guaranteed frost-proof if you intend to leave them out during the winter.

Urn-shaped terra cotta pots, which narrow at the neck, may look wonderfully appealing, but you will find them difficult to plant and maintain.

Terra cotta is a porous material, which means water is lost through the sides of a pot via evaporation. However, you can help to prevent

evaporation by lining the inside of the pot with plastic before adding the potting soil and plants (see page 114). You also can buy specially glazed pots that are non-porous and come in many attractive styles and designs. Make sure you buy pots with drainage holes.

Wood containers

Half-barrels and other tubs have a rustic appeal and are large enough to plant permanently with a shrub or small tree. Their wide bases make them very stable. Genuine half-barrels, used for wine- or beer-making, are hand crafted and self-sealing. Mock barrels, on the other hand, and square and rectangular planters, may need to be lined with plastic to prevent water from leaking out.

Good combinations
Galvanized pails set off the natural tones of terra cotta pots to good effect as they ascend a series of steps (pictured top). To add emphasis, each container is filled with contrasting spring-flowering displays of daffodils or hyacinths. In a hot spot in summer (right), an assortment of containers, filled with drought-tolerant plants of strikingly different foliage, are grouped.

Steps to success with potted plants

- Select the largest container possible and fill it with special potting soil formulated to retain water.

- Choose drought-tolerant plants that flower continuously or look good without flowers.

- Water the container as often as needed and add a slow-release fertilizer at planting time so the plants never go short of food during the growing season.

Square or rectangular wood planters are popular for entrances and formal settings. The most durable ones are made of a strong wood, pressure-treated with preservative.

Modern materials

It is possible to buy convincing terra cotta and wood lookalike plastic pots in a range of sizes and designs. They are lighter than the genuine article, so easier to move around, and often less expensive. Although frost-proof, plastic pots can become hard and brittle over time, especially if exposed to bright sunshine for long periods.

If you want to create a traditional-looking garden, a stone urn or trough is an ideal addition, but can be extremely expensive. A good alternative is to buy a container made from reconstituted stone—these look as good, are as heavy and nearly as frost-resistant as the real thing. Alternatively, you could buy concrete pots. These take longer to weather, but you can speed up the process by painting the surface of the pot with a liquid manure or yogurt—this will encourage the growth of algae and mosses.

Similarly, instead of buying a heavy and expensive lead trough for a traditional garden setting, choose a fiberglass lookalike, which is equally strong but a fraction of the weight and cost. Fiberglass containers also come in a range of bright colors, such as burnished bronze and copper, which look fantastic in a modern garden. So, too, will shiny metal containers made from galvanized steel.

Which plants?

Most garden plants will grow perfectly well in containers, so choose your favorites. Bear in mind, however, they should look good from a distance as well as up close.

Plants that produce compact, neat growth, have attractive foliage and flower over many months are ideal. If choosing plants for a sunny patio, select ones that are drought-tolerant—look for those with thick waxy leaves such as *Echeveria*, gray hairy leaves such as *Helichrysum petiolare*, or spiky foliage like yucca or agave. Such plants are more likely to be able to survive short periods without water.

For areas in light shade, choose shade-tolerant plants, such as hostas and fuchsias. Moisture-loving plants such as impatiens can be grown successfully in pots provided they are well watered.

Don't use plants that are prone to pest or disease attack, or those which suffer badly when they run short of water. Campanulas and mimulus, for example, don't recover well if they are allowed to dry out. Avoid, too, permanent plants that produce a spectacular show for a few weeks, but are dull for the rest of the year. Fast-growing plants, such as climbing roses also should be avoided; they will get too big and need a lot of training and support.

VIRGIN GARDENER'S BEST BETS

 Scented plants for containers *Cheiranthus*, cosmos, herbs such as thyme (pictured below), hyacinth, honeysuckle, *Houttuynia*, jasmine, lilies, scented-leaf pelargoniums, old-fashioned pinks, sweet pea, sweet William and tobacco plant.

 Shrubs *Aucuba japonica* 'Crotonifolia', boxwood, *Euonymus*, hebe, laurel, lavender, *Mahonia* x *media* 'Charity', *Nandina domestica* 'Firepower', *Pernettya mucronata*, pieris, pittosporum, skimmia, *Viburnum tinus* 'Eve Price' and vinca.

 Perennials Agapanthus, bergenia, diascia, *Dicentra spectabilis*, *Euphorbia characias* 'Wulfenii', *E. myrsinites*, erigeron, hosta, hellebore, *Ophiopogon planiscapus* 'Nigrescens', *Sedum spectabile*, *Zantedeschia aethiopica* 'Crowborough'.

 Trees *Acer palmatum* 'Atropurpureum' or 'Bloodgood', *Betula pendula*, dwarf conifers, holly (variegated varieties), *Laburnum alpinum* 'Pendulum', *Salix caprea* 'Pendula', *Pinus mugo* 'Gnom'.

 Grasses *Carex morrowii* 'Evergold', *C. riparia* 'Variegata', *C. stricta* 'Bowles' Golden', *Festuca glauca*, *Hakonechloa macra* 'Alboaurea', *Milium effusum* 'Aureum', *Miscanthus sinensis* 'Variegatus' or 'Zebrinus', *Molinia caerulea* 'Variegata', *Phalaris arundinacea* 'Picta', *Stipa gigantea*, *S. pennata*.

planting containers

Most of the new containers you buy will be ready for planting immediately, but some new pots don't have any drainage holes. Before adding any plants, check to see if you will need to drill the base. This is a fairly straightforward if the containers are made from soft plastic or wood. Simply drill three or four equally spaced ½-inch holes through the base. If they are fiberglass, terra cotta or hard plastic, however, before drilling you need to attach some adhesive tape to both the inside and outside surface to prevent cracking or chipping the material. Use a variable speed drill set at a low speed to make neat holes. Start with a small carbide-tipped drill bit, then gradually use

Acclimatizing new plants

In frost-prone areas in spring, certain tender plants, such as summer annuals and tender vegetables, which have been raised indoors, should be acclimatized to the growing conditions outside before they are planted. This means slowly exposing them to the harsher conditions over a period of time. Make sure that the garden center has done this before you buy your plants.

larger ones until the holes are the required size.

You can use pots year after year. Once the display is over, carefully empty out the old plants and soil—saving as many plants as you can (see page 121) and reusing the potting soil in your garden. Clear as much debris from inside the pot as possible, then wash it thoroughly

inside and out with soapy water using a scrub brush to remove stubborn roots, stains and algae. This will help prevent any carryover of pests and diseases. Rinse and allow container to dry before use.

Before planting, gather all the materials you need. Set out the new plants, in their pots, in formation on the ground. If you are planting seasonal displays, such as summer annuals, you could use a soil-less mixture made up of peat moss plus perlite or vermiculite. For long-term or permanent planting schemes, use a loam-based potting soil; this will maintain its structure longer and is heavier so it will provide extra stability for any top-heavy plants. If you want to grow acid-loving plants (see plant label), use a special acid compost (known as *ericaceous compost*) instead. Bear in mind that large containers are very heavy once planted, so it is a good idea to position them before planting.

Planting a simple container

To prepare the pot for planting, cover the drainage holes with one or two large pot shards or stones **(1)** or a piece of window screen to prevent compost from falling out. Fill the container with soil, breaking up any lumps with your fingers. Keeping the rootball intact, add each plant in turn, making sure each is upright and planted at the same depth as in its original pot **(2)**.

Firm soil lightly around each plant and push slow-release fertilizer tablets into the soil to feed the plants for the first growing season. As a finishing touch, cover the surface of the compost with layer of fine gravel or pebbles. This will help prevent weeds, reduce water-loss through evaporation and provide an attractive finish. Water thoroughly and let it drip dry.

Planting windowboxes or troughs

The easiest way to create attractive windowbox displays is to plant a series of removable plastic trough-shaped containers (called liners) that fit snugly inside. This will save you having to lift or detach a heavy stone trough or wooden window-box each time it needs replanting. A windowbox should be fixed securely in position on a ledge using

special brackets and rust-proof screws, and you can then slot in your plastic liners once they have been planted. This system also allows you to create a continuous year-round display of color using successive selections of potted plants in a series of liners.

To prepare a liner or windowbox for planting, cover the drainage holes with a couple of pot shards or large stones to prevent the soil falling through. Change the display to fit in with the time of year:

Spring Half-fill your windowbox with fresh potting soil and position bulbs, such as dwarf tulips or daffodils in small groups so they are planted at the correct depth (see page 60). Top up with soil, then plant bedding plants, such as brightly colored polyanthus, double daisies or forget-me-nots with trails of ivy cascading over the edges.

Summer For long-lasting, easy-care displays in sunny spots, choose drought-tolerant plants such as

trailing verbena, *Helichrysum*, gazania, upright and ivy-leaved pelargoniums and petunia. In light shade, try impatiens, spider plants, fuchsia and *Lamium*.

Fall and winter Combine winter-flowering pansies, with red-berried skimmia, silver-leaved curry plant and variegated vinca. If you have a large planter, add ornamental cabbage or kale for a dramatic foliage contrast.

Planting a layered container

Using both bulbs and plants in a container can enable you to extend the season of the display. You will need a variety of bulbs, one large potted plant and a few small filler and trailing plants.

1 Prepare your planter as for the simple container, opposite. Place your first set of bulbs in groups toward the side of the container, then cover with a layer of potting soil. Now add the second set of bulbs and cover them with a layer

of soil. Ensure that each type of bulb is planted at the correct depth and the right way up (see page 60). Once the second layer of bulbs has been planted, add more potting soil to your container, leaving a few inches of space at the top.

2 Now, add your largest plant, making sure it is upright and planted at the same depth as it was in its original pot. Tease out any circling roots around the

rootball to encourage them to grow into the new soil. Next, position the small filler and trailing plants around the large one.

3 Firm soil lightly around the roots of each plant and push slow-release fertilizer tablets into the soil to feed the plants for the first growing season. Cover the surface with a layer of pebbles or fine gravel and water thoroughly.

planting hanging baskets

Q What size basket should I buy?

A Choose the largest basket you can because it will hold more potting soil and so there will be more space for plant roots to grow—a 16-inch diameter basket holds twice as much soil as a 12-inch basket and over three times as much as a 10-inch basket. Larger baskets also require less watering.

Q What sort of soil is best?

A Choose a specially formulated bagged potting mixture for containers. Such soil will absorb more moisture and so require watering less frequently.

Q When is the best time to plant a summer hanging basket?

A If you can keep it somewhere frost free, plant it several weeks before the last predicted frost date in your area. Then place it in its final position after this date. Otherwise, plant and position the basket after the threat of frost has passed.

Q How often do baskets need watering?

A Hanging baskets require watering more often than other containers because they hold a lot of plants in a relatively small amount of potting soil. Water requirements vary depending on what kind of plants are in the basket; in general, water two times a week, or more if needed, while plants are getting established, and then increase the frequency to once a day. If plants show signs of wilting, increase watering as needed. Twice a day may be necessary for a hanging basket in full sun.

For splashes of summer color, nothing beats hanging baskets. They can have a dramatic effect all around the garden but perhaps are most effective when sited around the patio or when used to brighten up fences or walls. If you choose the right plants and keep them well fed and watered, the glorious displays can last for several months.

Choosing a basket

There are two main types of hanging basket—open-mesh wire baskets and solid-sided plastic baskets, both of which are available in various shapes and sizes. Wall-mounted baskets of both types are also available.

Most Virgin Gardeners will find conventional wire frame baskets very easy to plant. They can look decorative when the plants are positioned along the sides as well as in the top. Wire baskets do, however, need to be lined with moss, plastic or other liner (see right) and need frequent watering, often as much as twice a day during hot weather. This is because the liner is exposed to the air which causes the soil to dry out.

Water evaporates very quickly through a wire frame basket. To reduce the need for watering, you can incorportate water-holding granules, available at garden centers, in the soil mix. Or you can create a water reservoir in the base of your chosen container to retain water so that roots can absorb it before it runs off. Keep in mind that baskets will be heavy when the reservoir is full, so make sure they are firmly secured.

Basket liners

To hold in the soil in a wire basket, you will need a liner between the frame and the soil. You can buy readymade mats for lining, made of natural or synthetic materials. Coconut fiber mats are widely available. Even a matted plastic-fiber furnace filter will do, but be sure to choose an unobtrusive color. Or you can make your own liner from moss or pine needles. Any material that doesn't detract from the plants, and which will resist decay when wet, will do the trick.

Buying a preplanted basket

Hanging baskets brimming with beautiful plants are widely available at garden centers, discount stores, and nurseries in spring and summer. They are usually planted with a single kind of plant—all petunias, say, or all impatiens—but they are generally reasonably priced and ready to take home for an instant accent. Sometimes the baskets appear for sale before the last danger of a late spring frost has passed. If you buy a basket of tender annuals early in the season, protect it by bringing it indoors when cold weather is forecast.

Green tip

Efficient watering
Baskets need to be kept moist at all times if the displays are to last throughout the summer. Stop water running off the edges when you water by sinking a small pot rim-deep in the center of the basket and fill this each time you water. The water will then remain in place long enough to be absorbed by the soil, reducing run-off.

VIRGIN GARDENER'S BEST BETS

Plants for full sun
African daisy (*Osteospermum*), alyssum, begonia, cascading snapdragon, blue marguerites, (*Felicia*), geraniums, lavender, marigolds, gazania, heliotrope, nasturtium, petunia, rose moss (*Portulaca*), thyme and verbena.

Plants for light shade
Coleus, fuchsia, torenia, impatiens, ivy, ornamental sweet potato vines, *Plectranthus* and vinca.

Trailing plants
Alyssum, Australian fan flower (*Scaevola*), begonia, cascading snapdragon, catmint, diascia, nasturtium, parrot's beak, Martha Washington geraniums, petunia, ornamental sweet potato vines, verbena and vinca.

Planting a wire basket

Planting your own hanging basket allows you to choose a combination of plants that may not be available in preplanted baskets. For small baskets, it is a good idea to choose one large central plant and a selection of trailing plants (see plant lists, above). Plant winter baskets densely because they will not put on much growth after planting.

1 Line your basket with your chosen material (see left). Loose lining material, such as conifer clippings, will need to be lined with a piece of perforated black plastic to prevent the soil falling through. It is also worth placing a small piece of plastic or an old saucer on top of other types of liner to act as a water reservoir.

2 With larger baskets, half fill the basket with potting soil and then make holes in the liner so that you can plant the sides. To make planting easier, wrap the top-growth of the plant in a strip of plastic to protect it as it is pushed through the mesh.

3 Insert the plant from the inside through the hole in the liner until the top of the rootball butts against the liner and the top-growth of plant is sticking outside. Remove the plastic and untangle the stems of the plant. Repeat with your other plants until the sides are full. Then plant the top of the basket, starting with the main specimen plants and finishing off with the edging and trailing plants.

4 Add potting soil around the rootball of each plant and firm gently. Top up with soil and push pellets of a slow-release fertilizer into it—this prevents having to feed the plants regularly during the growing season.

caring for container plants

Plants in containers are completely dependent on your care. They are crammed together in a small space with a very limited amount of potting soil in which to root. This means they are in competition with one another for the available water, nutrients and growing space. It is important, therefore, to choose plants that grow at similar rates and require similar amounts of water and nutrients so they all have an equal chance of thriving. Check the plant label for this information when you buy. Plants which grow at similar rates will also produce more balanced displays that will remain looking good longer.

Feeding and watering

If plants run short of nutrients or water, they will be put under stress; growth and flower production will slow down and they will become more susceptible to attacks from pests and diseases.

After about six weeks in fresh potting soil, plants will start to run short of nutrients. To ensure sufficient nutrients, insert slow-release fertilizer tablets into the potting soil at the time of planting or later. These tablets provide all the nutrients the plants need over a set period of time—anything from a few weeks to several months, depending on the type used (refer to the packet for details). Fertilizer tablets are coated in a resin that releases more nutrients as the temperature and moisture levels increase. This means that the plants get exactly the amount of feed they need all the time. An alternative solution is to use a high-potash liquid fertilizer, every other time you water.

Watering is more of a challenge to get right. It can be very time-consuming to water a lot of containers. During hot spells in summer, containers may require watering more than once a day. One way to cut out the guesswork when watering and to make the task easier is to

Easy-care patio collection
This drought-tolerant combination of potted succulents and cacti make an easy-care permanent feature on a sun-drenched patio. The hand-painted containers add a primitive art theme, which is particularly striking.

Five ways to cut down on watering

- Plant large containers, if possible —oversized pots and baskets hold a much larger volume of potting soil, which means your plants will require watering less often.

- Combine plants that have the same watering requirement in each container.

- Choose drought-tolerant plants that that are well adapted to surviving long periods without water (see page 117).

- Line the sides of porous terra cotta pots with plastic to prevent moisture from evaporating away.

- Use moisture-retaining granules which absorb water that plants can draw from when they need it.

invest in an automatic watering system that supplies a regular amount of water to each container via a series of small plastic pipes (see photo at right).

The best time to water

The amount of water a container needs depends on its size and material, the number and type of plants it contains, where it is positioned, the time of year and the prevailing weather conditions. The best way of checking to see if a container needs watering is to push your finger into the potting soil about an inch below the surface to check whether the soil is moist. If it feels dry, the container needs watering; if not, test it again the following day. You also can get special moisture meters from garden retailers that will test the water content of potting soil.

When you water a container, it is important to water it thoroughly so the whole rootball is soaked—not just the surface. Try to apply water slowly, so that it has time to soak into the potting soil. Stop when the water starts to trickle from the drainage holes at the bottom of the container.

If the surface soil of a container dries out completely, it can be hard to get the water to soak in. Stop water from running off by breaking up the surface with a hand cultivator tool, or add a drop of dishwashing liquid to the watering can before you begin.

If the entire rootball has dried out, it can shrink away from the pot so that water runs down the insides of the pot and out of the drainage holes, without ever wetting the soil. If this is the case, stand the container in a bowl of water until the roots are thoroughly soaked.

Watering equipment

The type of equipment you need depends on the number of containers you have to water. If you have just a few pots, you can water by hand using a watering can or garden hose. Spending time watering gives you the opportunity to inspect the plants on a regular basis, so you can spot and deal with any pests or diseases early. For hanging baskets, consider investing in a hose wand, which will extend your reach, saving a lot of bending and stretching.

If you have many containers, an automatic watering system will save you lots of time. The water is delivered via a network of tubing that is attached to the water supply. You can regulate the amount of water each container receives by adjusting the nozzle at the end of

Watering made easy
Install an automatic watering system with adjustable nozzles that can be set to deliver exactly the right amount of water to each container of plants. Check nozzles from time to time to make sure they are still working properly.

each tube. The water supply can be switched on and off by hand or made completely automatic by attaching the tubing to a timer that has been fitted to the outside faucet. Bear in mind, however, that you still have to check the soil in each container from time to time to ensure there are no blockages in the system.

getting better displays

The plants recommended in this book will generally perform well if you keep them properly watered and fed. However, displays can still be improved with a bit of occasional care. If, for example, a plant starts to overwhelm its neighbors or is getting overgrown and messy, trim it back using a pair of scissors or pruners. Cutting back lanky growth also encourages a plant to become more bushy.

Bedding and border plants

Check plants regularly and pick off fading flowers to keep the display neat and to encourage the plant to produce more blooms; this technique is known as *deadheading*. Even annuals that continue to flower when old blooms are left on the plant will waste energy producing seeds at the expense of future displays. To deadhead

More flowers
Remove fading blooms from annuals to tidy up the plants and promote flower production. Pick off large, fading blooms individually.

Caring for your plants during vacations
If you cannot find a willing neighbor to water your plants, use the following tips to get your plants through the vacation period unscathed. If you are away for just a few days, move your containers into a sheltered spot in the shade and water them well. For longer trips, lay out a plastic sheet on a level surface and raise the edges to create a large water reservoir. Cut 2-inch-wide strips of capillary matting (available from garden retailers) and poke these through the drainage holes of each pot so that they are in contact with the compost. Then stand the containers on bricks on top of the plastic sheet so their capillary matting wicks stick out out like short tails. Water each container thoroughly until water trickles out the bottom and then fill the reservoir with water. Each pot will then draw water from the reservoir via the wick.

annuals, simply pinch off the fading flowers between your finger and thumb just above the next bud or leaf. If a plant produces a lot of tiny flowers, deadheading may be impractical, but it might be worth trimming the whole plant lightly with shears when it begins to look tattered. It is also worth tidying displays of flowers to remove unsightly yellowing foliage.

When watering and deadheading, keep an eye open for early signs of attacks by pests and diseases. Sickly looking leaves, unusual holes or spots and colonies of tiny insects on new growth or the undersides of leaves are common signs. If the problem is not severe, pick off and dispose of affected leaves and rub off colonies of insects using your fingers. If the problem is severe, use chemical control.

Later in the season, slow-release fertilizer tablets may start to run out of nutrients, reducing flowering and slowing the overall growth of plants. If the performance of your plants starts to fade in late summer, give them a boost by applying a high-potash liquid fertilizer every couple of weeks until the end of the growing season.

Permanent container plants

Trees, shrubs and other permanent plants will need watering throughout the year. During the winter, give the soil a thorough soaking about once a month. It also is worth turning these containers occasionally to prevent lopsided growth. This is particularly important if the container stands next to a wall or fence. Turn the pot by about 90 degrees once every two weeks from spring to the fall. Some permanent shrubs benefit from an annual light pruning to keep their shape well balanced. Do this during the dormant season (from fall to spring) for deciduous plants and in spring for evergreens.

As plants grow, you will need to repot them into larger containers using fresh loam-based potting soil. Carefully tip the plant from its old pot and remove any loose soil, then repot it into a slightly larger container, making sure that the plant is planted at the same level in the soil as it was before. If it is impractical to repot a large permanent display, simply remove the top 2 inches of soil from the container and replace it with fresh loam-based potting soil instead.

Patio clean up

Keep your paving looking good by giving it a thorough annual clean. Sweep up accumulations of dirt and clean stubborn stains and slippery algae (you can rent a pressure washer to make the job easier). If algae is severe, especially near steps, use an algaecide to control it.

Remove weed seedlings by hand or apply a patio or path weed-killer to deal with large areas. However, make sure you cover up nearby ornamental plants with a plastic sheet before you spray and leave the sheet in place until the spray has dried completely.

Overwintering containers

Potted plants are more susceptible to winter cold and wind than those grown in the garden. Plants that are too tender to survive outdoors in winter will need to be moved to a frost-free place, such as a cool porch. Even hardy plants will need some protection in severe weather.

Roots Protect roots from freezing by wrapping containers in layers of bubblewrap. Alternatively, sink your pots rim-deep in border soil and cover the rim and soil surface with an insulating layer of soil or shredded bark.

Plants Protect the top-growth from cold by wrapping with a double layer of Remay or other spun row covering (available from garden retailers) tied into position with string. Even when conditions are above freezing, some evergreens, such as conifers, are susceptible to damage from cold winds. Move such plants to a sheltered spot or protect as described above.

During cold winter weather, protect climbers and shrubs trained against a wall. Make an insulating blanket of dry leaves or straw and keep it in place with netting. Remove all protection in spring.

Re-using container plants

Don't be in a hurry at the end of summer to throw away old plants from your containers. You will find that many can be used for next season's display.

Hardy perennials and shrubs can be planted out in your garden, unless you want to use them in a new container scheme. Sift through the potting soil for bulbs and plant any that are firm to the touch. Trim any tattered leaves from plants and vines such as ivy and vinca before transplanting to the garden.

In cold winter areas you can save tender perennials such as geraniums over the winter to include in displays the following year. Cut back the stems to about a couple of inches using a pair of pruners (1). Then, place the root of the plant in a box of moist potting soil (2). Repeat this procedure with the other plants and pack them into the box (3). Store in a frost-free place until spring .

creating a private terrace

In the heart of the city, Scott's shady garden is overlooked by neighboring properties. He wants to create an intimate garden in a contemporary design that will reflect its urban setting. He is looking to provide a quiet sanctuary for restful contemplation as well as be somewhere he can entertain his friends, but he does not want to feel boxed-in by high fences. The soil is very poor so he will either have to spend a lot of time and effort improving it or grow plants in containers and raised beds filled with fresh topsoil. He likes plants, particularly those which stimulate the senses with attractive fragrance and interesting textures, but his busy lifestyle means that he has little time to look after them.

A simple patio

The northwest-facing backyard receives sun for a few hours in the afternoon and early evening, and less during the winter months. Due to this, Scott decided that he wanted to base his design around a paved patio to make maximum use of the available space, bordered by a selection of delicately scented and textural plants that require little maintenance. Raised beds take far less time to look after than lots of potted plants.

Mediterranean-style

Scott liked the idea of a simple Mediterranean-style patio area and opted to cover it with frost-proof tiles in a split-level design. He decided to choose light-colored tiles to reflect as much of the available light as possible, making the garden brighter. In order to soften the appearance of stark tiles, it is best to employ a variety of shades. Scott selected small terra cotta tiles and mixed them with large pale yellow-colored ones to create a clean, contemporary feel in his garden. If you are buying garden tiles for your patio, it is important to ensure that they are of the same thickness to make laying easier.

Scott cleared the site of the existing vegetation and then he leveled the area. He then marked out the patio area and covered it with a 6-inch-deep foundation of dry concrete mix. This was carefully leveled and then consolidated with a plate vibrator (available from tool-rental shops) and allowed to harden. Scott then laid the tiles on top. As a functional detail, he decided to leave the terra cotta tile in the middle of the patio loose. Beneath the tile, Scott installed a hidden slot that he could use to anchor his garden umbrella or his wash line.

Planting pockets

Scott wanted to include plants to soften and add interest to his patio, so he decided to include random planting pockets. To do this, he removed several of the smaller tiles along with their foundations underneath and replaced the area with topsoil. He then planted the pockets with aromatic ground-hugging thymes which, when walked on, filled the air with a pungent scent. He also left a planting strip between the two levels of his terrace, which was filled with aromatic plants and topped up with gravel.

Raised boundaries and borders

To create a quiet and secluded atmosphere and to prevent the terrace from being overlooked by neighbors, Scott extended the boundary walls upward. He did this by fixing

buying wood for use outdoors, you must make sure that it has been pressure-treated with a wood preservative to prevent rotting, or is naturally rot-resistant.

To make the raised beds, Scott constructed a series of sturdy box-like structures and bolted them to the walls along each boundary. The wooden frames were supported at each corner by 3-inch-square fencing posts that were concreted into the ground; the sides were then clad in 1-inch thick boards. Once complete, Scott lined the inside of the boxes with heavy-duty black plastic to prevent soil from washing out between the boards. Next he filled them with good-quality topsoil and allowed them to settle. He then topped them up again with soil and added some plants. After planting, Scott covered all the raised beds with a 1-inch thick layer of gravel to reduce the need for watering and to suppress weed growth.

Sensual planting

Scott chose a range of aromatic herbs including sage, rosemary, thyme and mint to plant in the raised beds, combined with plants that have textural foliage such as furry lamb's ears, artemisia and mullein as well as silvery santolina. He trained scented climbers, such as jasmine and clematis, to cover the trellis and added a backbone planting of compact evergreens such as clipped boxwood. Architectural plants such as phormium and globe artichoke were also included.

Patio full of plants

An intimate yet spacious patio was created in a very small space using deep raised beds overflowing with flowers and foliage. By covering the surface of the soil with a 1-inch layer of gravel mulch, watering and weeding were kept to a minimum.

6-foot posts to the low brick walls using expansion bolts and screwing a 3-foot-high trellis to the posts. As a finishing touch, he topped each post with a matching finial.

Scott was worried about the patio feeling enclosed, so he raised the beds along the three boundaries. The raised beds on either side were 3-feet high and deep. To add interest and increase the sense of space in his small garden, Scott cut the section along the end of the garden, farthest from the house, lower and set it back further than the others. This created an illusion of depth as well as a stepped effect to the raised beds, which were emphasized by the featured posts at each corner.

He then created another step on the sunny side of the garden where part of the raised bed was converted into an intimate double seat. All the beds were built from rough-sawn wood bought from the local fencing specialist. When

using containers in the garden

Jenny enjoys growing plants in containers, but wants to try something different. She would like to use containers more creatively, so that they add interest to all parts of her garden. Jenny already owns a lot of different sizes and styles of container which she wants to incorporate. She would also like to make the most of an existing raised terrace situated next to the house.

Using containers effectively

The great thing about containers is that they can be moved around. This means you can alter the appearance of your garden by simply substituting one style of container for another or mixing and matching containers in different parts of the garden. To create effective displays, it is important to develop a theme, as an uncoordinated group of different pots made from a variety of materials and containing completely different plants will not rest easily on the eye.

Jenny liked natural materials so she decided to create a collection of different sized containers made from wood and terra cotta and placed them beside a seat on a sunny path. She filled them with a range of sun-loving Mediterranean plants to complete the effect. Jenny is not afraid to experiment; she coordinated a selection of varied containers placed outside the back door by planting them with annuals of similar flower colors and foliage textures.

Mix and match

In a formal setting, matching containers can be very striking. A pair of terra cotta urns, for example, filled with an identical planting scheme, standing on either side of a

doorway or garden gate, can be dramatic. Similarly, a series of identical pots filled with the same flowering plants running up one side of a series of steps helps accentuate the change of level. Jenny tried this with two pairs of matching but different-sized containers, to create the illusion of space in her small front garden. Each of the large containers was planted with two identical conifers and placed in the foreground, while the smaller ones were filled with similar looking, but smaller, conifers and placed further away. This created the illusion of depth when viewed from the road outside her house.

Using the same-sized containers in an informal setting can look a bit regimented. However, you can break up the uniform appearance by standing some on upturned pots or bricks to create a change in level and scattering pebbles in front to provide a contrasting shape and texture.

Containers to catch the eye

In common with many gardens, Jenny's plot lacked focal points for attracting the eye. Containers, both planted and empty, are ideal for this purpose if used in moderation. Choosing the right pot for the setting is important if it is to be effective, and you must decide whether it is the plants or the pot that will be the focus of attention. Jenny had a beautifully ornate container that she wanted to accentuate. She planted it with a simple unassuming scheme of white marguerite daisies so that the container and not the plants it contained remained the point of focus. Further down the

garden, she grouped a collection of elegant urns with a bright green backdrop of leafy hardy geraniums and colorful roses to good effect (pictured below).

The surroundings can have a significant impact on whether a container display has the desired effect. As a rule, displays of vibrant colors need a light-colored or plain background to have the most impact, while pastel shades often look most effective if given darker surroundings. Jenny made the most of all her left-over containers by filling them with colorful bedding plants and grouping them together to create a virtual border along the edge of her raised terrace. The brilliant flowers contrasted well against the pale stone wall and paving.

Plant selection

When choosing plants, look for ones that offer more than just flowering interest. Keep the color scheme simple and stick to a theme. Jenny chose plants to suit the style of her containers. In decorated Oriental-style pots she stuck to a simple single-subject planting of bamboo—Japanese maple also would have looked effective. In terra cotta containers, fiery displays of geraniums and gazania worked well.

Jenny also used plants to provide a seasonal change to her scheme. She moved containers into prominent positions while they were looking their best, and changed her display regularly. She did this by planting plastic liners that fitted snugly inside a decorative container. She then regularly swapped the liners to keep the display consistently good. A simpler option for a large container is to plant the rim with permanent edging plants and to slip in different flowering interest for every season. You could start with a camellia and spring-flowering bulbs, for example, and follow with lilies in early summer and then cannas when the lilies fade. Try adding an aster for a splash of autumn color and a flowering evergreen over the winter months to complete the year-round display.

Backing winners
Pale stone walls and paving provide a neutral setting for the vibrant colors of summer annuals (left); an all-green backdrop of hardy geranium foliage (below) is a good contrast for the elegant lines of terra cotta urns.

Setting the scene
Collections of pots look most effective when linked by a common theme. Alongside a garden bench on a sunny path, Jenny arranged wood and terra cotta containers planted with drought-tolerant bedding, such as geraniums, gazania and curry plant, to good effect (left).

Bountiful harvest

Choose dwarf-growing forms of fruit trees to grow in containers **(1)**; mix flowers and food crops to create stylish displays **(2)**; cherry tomatoes and strawberries provide summer color and wonderful eating **(3)**; given a sunny spot and well-drained potting soil, many herbs will thrive in containers **(4)**.

A kitchen garden
in and around the patio

You don't need a vegetable patch or a large backyard to grow fruit, vegetables and herbs in your garden. Many popular foods can be raised successfully in containers of all shapes and sizes on the patio or elsewhere in the garden.

Nothing can beat the flavor of freshly picked fruit and vegetables. It also is highly satisfying to be able to grow and harvest your favorite foods. The best crops for the Virgin Gardener to start with are those that are easy to grow, don't take up much space and will give reliable yields—many herbs and salad crops, such as radishes, lettuce and tomatoes, give excellent results in containers.

Growing your own herbs

Many popular herbs thrive in containers on the patio because they like well-drained soil and sun (see page 128). A few, such as mint and parsley, prefer moisture around their roots in a lightly shaded spot, so are best grown in the border. A word of warning, however. Mint is invasive and can become a weed problem unless its roots are restricted. The easiest way to do this is to plant it in a bottomless bucket sunk into the border. Leave a couple of inches of the rim showing above the ground to prevent the runners from spreading into the surrounding border.

Vegetables in containers

On the patio, choose varieties of vegetables with attractive foliage or flowers. Ruby chard, for example, with its bright red stems and glossy green foliage, is as striking as any flowering plant. Runner beans are also easy to grow, but will need a supporting teepee of canes or trellis. Their flowers are either red or white: both are very attractive.

To produce tasty baby vegetables, grow salad crops and root vegetables such as carrots and beets about 1 to 2 inches apart either in a border or a container. Harvest carrots when they are about ½ inch across and baby beets at about twice this size.

To get good results with vegetables in containers, you will have to pay careful attention to watering and feeding. This may mean watering more than once a day in warm weather. Give leafy vegetables a balanced liquid fertilizer with every watering. Throughout the growing season, fruit- and pod-bearing vegetables, such as tomatoes and beans, should be given a weekly liquid high-potash fertilizer, such as tomato fertilizer, which promotes flower and fruit production.

Among the tastiest crops from the garden are new potatoes, and these are fairly easy to grow in containers. Choose an early variety such as 'Dark Red Norland', 'Yukon Gold', or 'Superior', and grow the plants in a large tub or plastic trash basket half-filled with potting soil. Top up the potting soil as the shoots grow, making sure that at least 2 inches of shoot remain above the soil. Repeat until the container is full of potting soil. When the potatoes reach about the size of a chicken's egg (put your hand in the soil to check), tip out the container and harvest the new potatoes.

Patio fruits

Most fruit trees require sunlight to flourish and can be grown successfully on and around a sunny patio. Dwarf forms of fruit trees can be grown in large tubs, but must be kept well watered from the time they blossom in spring until the crop is harvested in the fall. Sun-loving patio peaches and nectarines are particularly worth trying. It is also possible to grow vining crops in containers, but they do need a sturdy support and careful pruning. Use a stable container with a wide base, as tree fruits and vines become top heavy when the fruits swell.

Strawberries are well-suited for being grown in containers, even hanging baskets. By selecting varieties that fruit at different times you can get crops from early summer to mid-fall. The season can be extended if you can provide protection early in the year, with the first crop in mid-spring (see page 128).

growing herbs in containers

Herbs vary in color, shape and texture, so they can be combined to make very attractive container displays. On the patio, shrubby herbs such as rosemary and bay look effective trained into decorative shapes. Bay in particular lends itself to being pruned and trained into various conical or pyramid shapes or even grown as a mini-tree with a clear trunk and a ball-shaped head of foliage.

Remember, large containers will be very heavy once they are filled with compost and plants, so position them in your garden before planting. Wood containers, such as rectangular boxes or half barrels, can be fitted with outdoor casters that make moving them around the patio a lot easier.

In a large tub, surround the base of the shrubby herb with variegated sages and thymes, which will cascade over and soften the edges. Another herb worth growing in a large container is lemon verbena, which produces a wonderfully fresh scent and flavor.

Keep herbs growing well

Most sun-loving herbs are drought-tolerant and need watering less frequently than other container plants, so that if you already look after a few containers the extra work will be minimal. They don't require much food either. A half-strength dose of water-soluble fertilizer once a month during the growing season is quite sufficient.

Keep herbs looking good and producing lots of new growth by trimming regularly with scissors or pruners. If they are allowed to get leggy, trim them right back to encourage a new flush of foliage.

Recycling growing bags

Growing bags that have been used to produce a crop of tomatoes or peppers can be recycled by planting them with herbs, such as parsley, chives or mint, which are used in large quantities. Make sure there are plenty of drainage holes cut along the side of the growing bag about ½ inch from the ground. Water sparingly and feed with a half-strength houseplant feed every two weeks.

Old growing bags also are useful for producing a crop of early strawberries in April or May—up to ten can be planted in one growing bag. Pot up new plants and keep outside until January. Then plant in the growing bag and move to a cool greenhouse. Good varieties to try include 'Honeoye', 'Annapolis', 'Jewel' and 'Sparkle'.

Steps to success with herbs

- Select easy-to-grow herbs and plant them in well-drained soil.

- Choose the herbs that you use most often for kitchen and household purposes.

- Position the container in full sun in a convenient position, so the herbs can be harvested easily.

Planting a windowbox

A windowbox is one of the most convenient ways of growing herbs. During the winter the container can be placed indoors on a south-facing kitchen windowsill to provide fresh herbs all year round.

Herbs, such as chives and basil, that are used in large quantities are best plunged rim-deep into the soil while still in their pots, making replacement a lot easier when the herb has been used up. Sow chives thickly in a pot of soil, like mustard and cress, and use them while young.

1 Cover the bottom of the windowbox with a layer of pot shards to improve drainage. Then fill the container with potting soil.

2 Plant the herbs, starting with the central ones. Choose clump-forming and mat-forming herbs like marjoram and sage and avoid using tall herbs such as fennel. Top with a layer of fine gravel and water the box thoroughly.

Herbs in a strawberry pot

A deep strawberry pot with cupped planting pockets around the sides is a good way of growing a number of herbs in a small space. Soak the strawberry pot thoroughly and cover the drainage holes with pot shards. If you live in a high rainfall area, put a 2-inch deep layer of drainage material, such as gravel, in the bottom of the container to help improve drainage. Fill the container up to the first planting pocket with potting soil. Then position the first plant before adding more soil around the rootball and firming it gently with your fingers.

1 To make watering easier, place a 6-inch-long drilled plastic tube in the center of the pot so the top is level with the rim and fill the tube with some gravel. Then top up the container with more potting soil and plant the rest of the planting pockets.

2 Plant the selection of herbs in the top of the container and then mulch with a 1/2-inch layer of fine gravel as the finishing touch, making sure the soil is covered right up to the plant. Water well.

VIRGIN GARDENER'S BEST BETS

 Containers in full sun
Basil, bay, borage, chives, cilantro, dill, fennel, marjoram, oregano, rosemary, sage, tarragon, thyme.

 Hanging baskets
Basil, marjoram, nasturtium, sage, thyme, winter savory.

 Containers in light shade
Apple mint, bergamot, chervil, chives, lemon balm, parsley, sage, salad burnet, spearmint, sweet Cicely.

 Windowboxes
Basil, chervil, chives, marjoram, nasturtium, oregano, parsley, sage, thyme, winter savory.

FAQs – HERBS IN POTS

 What's the best way of buying herbs?

You can buy herbs in spring as vigorous young plants. Pot them up immediately using well drained potting soil. If you're on a tight budget, many herbs including basil, borage, chervil, chives, coriander, dill, lemon balm and parsley, can be successfully raised from seed. Sow in spring.

 Which herbs should I start with?

Choose the herbs you like and use a lot in cooking. The most popular are sage, basil, chives, parsley and oregano or marjoram, but cilantro, mint and rosemary are also widely grown and used.

What kind of container do I need?

You can grow herbs in almost any container, although small pots will require watering more often. Ideally, choose a container over 8 inches in diameter but windowboxes, tubs, strawberry pots, growing bags and even hanging baskets can be used. Terra cotta is ideal for most herbs, but use non-porous plastic for moisture-loving dill, fennel and coriander.

 How do you get the best flavor?

The flavor of sun-loving herbs such as rosemary, thyme and tarragon can be intensified if you grow them in full sun and water sparingly. Feed them with a half-strength water-soluble fertilizer about once a month during the growing season.

 How long will the herbs last?

Annual herbs such as borage, chervil, coriander and dill will last one season. Hardy perennial herbs such as chives, fennel, lemon balm, lovage, mint and oregano will last several years, while shrubby herbs such as rosemary, bay and thyme can be grown for many years.

Water features

Water features have an atmosphere and charm all their own. Adding one to your back yard will open up a whole new world of gardening opportunities. Nothing else quite captures the soothing ambience of the sight and sound of moving water. You don't need to have a large yard or have years of experience to create a beautiful water garden. With modern starter kits, a simple pond or moving water feature can be put together in just a few hours.

Water features can take many forms. Which one you choose should reflect the style of your garden and the atmosphere you are trying to create. In a formal design, for example, you could use either a traditional square, rectangular or round pool, but if you are trying to create an air of informality, a simple kidney-shaped or irregular pool would be a better choice.

A conventional pool brings light, color and movement to the garden. It should be in proportion with the rest of the garden, so the size and shape of the pool will be determined to some extent by nearby features and your garden's overall layout. Choose a sunny site to get the best reflections. To successfully integrate the pool into your garden's design, aim to echo existing lines and shapes in the garden and create an area of transition using lush planting schemes.

In a modern garden design, creative water features have become a key ingredient. Made from unconventional materials, such as old watering cans, hand pumps and washboards, they can be used to add drama and give a central focus to the garden, or offer a sense of discovery and humor when hidden from view to be chanced upon by the casual visitor. Wildlife ponds have also become popular. If well planned and properly looked after, they will become a magnet for wildlife and home to a wide range of native plants and animals.

small water features

The Virgin Gardener will find small water features ideal because they are easy to construct, require little time to maintain and are safe for children. There are various types available in kit form to suit almost any garden, but if you want to be more creative or tailor a feature to fit in a specific spot in your garden, then you can build your very own water feature easily from widely available materials. Small, reliable submersible pumps enable you to create a water feature in almost any size container.

Bubbling fountain This is the simplest and perhaps the most versatile of small water features. Its simple shape is easy on the eye and its gentle sound creates a relaxing atmosphere. A bubbling fountain consists of a single burbling spout of water that splashes over a pile of rocks, through the center of a millstone or another decorative centerpiece to create a soothing yet enticing sound **(1)**. A small fountain looks effective as a raised feature or when sunken into the ground where it can be used as a focal point—try placing one near a seating area, for example, or subtly hidden from view elsewhere in the garden where it can be heard but not seen.

Bell fountain The domed shape and a sparkling appearance of a bell fountain make it ideal for the modern garden. The spout protrudes from the rocks or water feature and water is forced through a thin nozzle to create a dome-shaped water jet. Like a bubbling fountain, it can be installed in the ground, but is perhaps even more eye-catching when placed in a large pot or raised bed so it becomes the focal point of your garden (see the page opposite).

Wall fountain A traditionally-styled wall mask, such as a lion's head or gargoyle spitting water **(2)**, is an eye-catching way of adding moving water to a formal setting. It can be combined with a pool or simply aimed into a reservoir concealed with pebbles. Novelty wall masks can be used to add humor and drama wherever it is wanted.

Unusual features Don't be constrained by convention, you can use all sorts of household items to create unusual small water features. For example, this child's watering can **(3)** has been fitted to the outlet pipe of the pump to make a wonderfully modern fountain with novelty appeal (see also page 134).

Choosing a pump
Low-voltage submersible pumps are very easy to install. The size of pump you require will depend on the height to which the water is to be raised (known as lift) and the amount of water flowing through (known as flow rate). The lift is the distance between the surface of the water in the reservoir and the nozzle outlet of the cascade. For a small water feature you will need a flow rate of around 120 gallons per hour, but for a fountain or water spout, such as a wall mask, look for a pump which can deliver around 170 gallons per hour. To supply sufficient water for a water cascade and waterfall look for a pump that will produce 265 gallons per hour. Check the packaging for information.

Making a miniature container pond

A miniature pond makes an attractive water feature for any patio or balcony. They are very easy to create in a half-barrel or any other large waterproof container. They are ideal for growing a range of dwarf aquatic plants (see FAQs on page 137). However, a miniature pond is unsuitable for fish because the water temperature fluctuates too much. Even a miniature pond full of plants will need to be covered with an insulating layer in frost-prone areas to prevent it from freezing solid; in cold-winter regions, it will need to be stored in a garage or drained for the winter. Drain the pond in the fall and keep the plants in a bucket of water in a cool but not freezing place over the winter.

- Position the barrel on a firm level base. If it is a genuine hand-crafted half-barrel it will seal itself as the wood becomes saturated. If not, you will need to line it with black plastic or a flexible pond liner.

- Half fill the barrel with water. Then trim the liner **(1)** so it is just below the rim. Fold the top ½-inch over neatly and fix it to the inside of the barrel using a staple gun or tacks.

- Place a ½-inch layer of pea gravel **(2)** over the base to protect the liner and top up with water.

- Leave it for a week to check for leaks and to allow chlorine to disperse. You can now add any planted aquatic baskets **(3)**.

Bell fountain in a pot

You can buy container water features in kit form or you can create your own from scratch. When self-contained in a pot, a water feature can be moved around to change the focal point of your garden—to draw the eye to seasonal features, for example.

- Select a container that has a base at least 12 inches wide and is deep enough to hold the pump covered with at least 4 inches of water. The smaller the container, the less water it will hold so you will have to top it up more often. Bell fountain kits often contain a float to indicate whether the reservoir needs topping up with water.

- If you have chosen a porous container, such as terra cotta, line it with thick black plastic or flexible pool liner, or stand a waterproof plastic pot inside the ornamental porous pot to create the reservoir.

- Position the pump in the bottom of the container, so that the outlet nozzle is roughly level with the rim. Cut a piece of plastic-coated, heavy-duty mesh using a pair of bolt-cutters until it is the correct size to lodge just below the rim on the inside of your container. Then cover the mesh with a layer of pebbles.

- Fill the container with water. then plug the pump in and adjust the flow rate of the pump until a pleasing fountain is achieved and all the water falls back into the container.

Wonderful ways
with water

Imaginative water features lead the way in contemporary garden design. No longer are you restricted to a simple pond or fountain: with a little creative thought you can give life to a modern work of art.

Water features have much to offer the Virgin Gardener who wants to impose individuality and personal style on a garden environment. The interplay and juxtaposition of water, rock and plants has the power to produce evocative atmospheres, particularly if the water feature is accompanied by restful sounds and hypnotic motion. A creative water feature can add subtle humor, provoke spontaneous thought, even spring a surprise on the casual visitor, and in a city can mute the passing traffic.

All the active water features pictured here are based on the same simple construction outlined on page 132. You don't have to buy an original piece of art to be stylish—with a little imagination you can use practically any materials you have on hand, from a pile of log slices to an interesting thrift-shop find. Bear in mind, however, that the different elements need to be connected by a theme.

Natural contrast
Some materials and shapes have a natural affinity, while others seem to be poles apart. This underlying linkage is often used to create effective designs in good contemporary gardens. The bronze heron spouting water from the security of a reed bed (see the page opposite), for example, contrasts completely in color and texture with its surroundings, but both sit comfortably together. In a comic undertone, the bird stands guard over the very fish that its wild counterparts would find a tasty meal.

This idea of contrast can be turned on its head by combining the most unlikely materials that have a distinctly common theme. The metallic water chute, opposite, is an excellent example. It has a formality of shape that is at odds with the natural flow of water, yet the sparkling cascade and watercourse connect well with the vertical galvanized monolith.

The surprise element
Every garden benefits from the surprise element—the unexpected sound or view which makes you sit up and take notice. Still water features are particularly useful for this purpose, because they can be hidden out of sight to be chanced upon seemingly by accident. Bear in mind they do need to be discovered to be effective, so don't camouflage them completely.

Another good design technique is to take advantage of natural human curiosity by providing enticing glimpses of a feature or statue associated with water, or using the sound of moving water to hint at the existence of a pool. The water itself can then be completely hidden from view.

Adding a touch of humor
Light-heartedness is a particularly effective technique in contemporary garden design. The pond at top left, for example, is dominated by a spiral of large white pebbles on a bed of slate. The curving shape draws you in as it threads its way relentlessly to the center of the feature, creating a visual whirlpool effect so adding virtual movement to a static scene.

Humor doesn't have to be surreal to be effective. The bronze swimmer at bottom right, which seems to be emerging from a barrel to spout water at passers-by, is a more literal comic touch which works really well. It is particularly effective, however, when the water spout is intermittent. The rest of the time, the water can gently cascade and circulate from one barrel to the other.

Water enlivens a contemporary garden
A spiral of white pebbles suggests a visual whirlpool **(1)**; light and dark are united in this silver water chute edged by black grassy ophiopogon **(2)**; the bronze heron stalks the margins of its pond **(3)**; and a spouting swimmer adds a comic touch **(4)**.

building a new pond

A conventional garden pool **(1)**, stocked with plants and fish, has much to offer the Virgin Gardener. If well designed and constructed, it makes a wonderful year-round feature. If you build the pond large enough, it will require little maintenance because a natural equilibrium will be reached. With a surface area of over 40 square feet and a maximum depth of about 3 feet the temperature of the pond water will not fluctuate greatly and so is less likely to produce problems such as green water (see page 138).

Raised ponds

A raised pond **(2)** is one that is constructed on top of the ground in a raised bed or free-standing container. Although less popular than a conventional pond, it offers several advantages. You don't have to dig a hole or get rid of the excavated soil. The water and any wildlife the pond contains is raised

Steps to success with water features

- Choose a style and size that reflects the design and layout of the garden.

- Site it in the open where it will be most appreciated, well away from nearby trees and buildings that will cast dense shade or drop leaves in the fall.

- Choose the right combination of easy-care aquatic plants so the pond becomes largely self-sustaining.

up where it can be appreciated more easily. Moreover, the pond is easier to care for because you do not have to bend as much. If you have young children, a raised pond with sides at least 18 inches high is also a safer

1

option than a conventional sunken pond. A variety of raised ponds are now available in kit form.

Using a preformed liner

Most ponds are built using a pond liner. There are two main types: preformed rigid liners and flexible liners that are supplied as a sheet that can fit any shape. The easiest way to build a standard pond is to use a rigid liner made from either plastic or fiberglass. Although quite expensive, rigid liners are simple to install. They last about 15 years and you can be sure of the end result. Mark the outline on the ground then dig a hole sufficiently deep and wide following the liner's contours. Line the hole with sand, then position the liner and check that it is level in all directions. Carefully fill around the sides with sand making sure there are no gaps, before filling the pond with water.

2

Installing a free form pond

To create a pond in the shape of your choice, you will have to use a flexible liner. There are two main types: plastic, which is cheapest but punctures easily and only lasts about five years; and rubberized (PVC, LDPE or butyl) which is stronger and more durable. Even though it is relatively easy to build a pond, you should be aware that it does take a fair amount of strength to install, so if you don't feel up to digging, employ the help of a willing friend or a professional.

• First, choose a suitable site for your pond (see FAQs, below). Then, mark out the desired shape using bamboo canes for straight lines and a hose for curves.

• Once you are happy with the shape, dig the hole so the main part of the pond is at least 18 inches deep and the shelves around the edges that support the marginal plants are around 10 inches deep. Make sure the sides slope slightly inward and check the levels carefully.

• Remove any sharp stones, then cover all surfaces with a 2-inch layer of sand. On a warm day, lay out the flexible liner over the hole and partly fill it with water. Gently pull at the edges of the liner to remove creases, before topping it up with water. Trim the liner to leave a 6-inch overlap on all sides, then cover the overlap with your desired edging such as rocks, pebbles or a mixture of bricks and plants. Finally, stock the pond with plants and fish.

FAQs – SETTING UP A POND

Q What is the best position for a pond?

A Choose an open, sunny site away from overhanging trees and the dense shade cast by buildings. Also check that there are no underground cables or pipes to worry about if you are sinking a pond into the ground. Above all, position it somewhere it will be appreciated, taking into account what will be reflected in the water.

Q What size pond is best for a beginner?

A A mini pond can be the size of a half-barrel, but a conventional pond with plants and fish should have a surface area of at least 30 square feet, preferably 40 square feet—the equivalent of an 8 foot x 5 foot rectangular pond.

Q How deep should it be?

A At least part of a small conventional pond should be about 18 inches deep. Larger ponds should have a deep water area of between 2 and 3 feet. To grow shallow-water plants at the edge of the pool, you will need a 12-inch-wide step about 10 inches below the surface. The walls of the pond should slope slightly inward.

Q What are the best plants for a small pond?

A Choose miniature waterlilies, such as *Nymphaea pygmaea* 'Helvola' (yellow), and shallow-water plants such as the corkscrew rush, zebra rush, water lettuce, variegated iris, pickerel weed, parrot feather, dwarf cattail and water forget-me-not.

Q Which fish should I buy?

A If your pond has a surface area of over 40 square feet, choose brightly colored goldfish. They are cheap and easy to look after, but most important of all, they will swim close to the surface where they can be seen. Fancy, costly koi can become a prized part of the garden pool.

adding plants and fish

Fish add movement and color to a pond and the plants help to integrate the feature into the surrounding garden landscape. Plants are also important for maintaining a natural balance in the water, so the pond becomes largely self-sustaining. Choosing the right combination of plants is important because this will not only affect the ornamental appeal of the feature but dictate how much time you will have to spend looking after it.

Pond plants can be grouped into three types: those that are planted in the shallows around the edge of the pond, known as marginals; those that cover the surface; and submerged plants that can be scattered across the floor of the pond. The submerged plants produce oxygen while using up the nutrients in the water that would otherwise encourage the pond water to turn green with algae. The floating plants also help prevent algae by effectively preventing sunlight penetrating the water.

To work out how many of each type of plant you need, calculate the surface area of the pond then allow one bunch of submerged plants per square foot and introduce sufficient floating plants to cover at least one-third of the surface area. Add a combination of marginal plants to give flowering interest throughout the growing season.

Planting your pond

Use a special aquatic planting baskets which have wide bases for stability and micro-mesh sides to prevent the soil washing out into the water. Older styles of baskets with lattice-work sides should be lined with burlap before filling with soil. Do not use standard potting soil because it will release soluble plant food into the water, encouraging algae. Special aquatic soil is available. Marginal plants can be planted on their own in small baskets or in groups in a larger one, but waterlilies should be planted individually.

Adding fish

Do not add fish until the plants have become established. To give fish sufficient room to grow, do not add more than 2 inches of fish per square foot of surface area. Fish need to adjust gradually to the temperature of pond water, so to prevent distressing the fish you need to leave the fish in their bags and float them on the surface of the pond for about three hours. This will enable the water inside the bag to cool slowly until it reaches the same temperature as the pond water. Do this during the evening, then after the designated period, open the bag and allow the fish to swim away.

Green tip

Preventing green water
If you want to avoid using special chemicals to clear ponds of algae, simply place a pad of barley straw (available from garden retailers) on the pond surface before the algae has a chance to build up. You can also use loose barley or wheat straw—apply 1 ounce in a pond that contains about 2 cubic yards of water. As the barley or straw decomposes, it releases an anti-algae chemical into the water.

VIRGIN GARDENER'S BEST BETS

Marginal shelf
Acorus calamus 'Variegatus', marsh marigold (*Caltha palustris* 'Flore Pleno'), *Iris laevigata* 'Variegata', pickerel weed (*Pontederia cordata*), corkscrew rush (*Juncus effusus* 'Spiralis'), *Typha minima*, umbrella grass, zebra rush (*Schoenoplectus* subsp. *tabernaemontani* 'Zebrinus').

Submerged plants
Hornwort (*Ceratophyllum demersum*), hairgrass (*Eleocharis acicularis*), willow moss (*Fontinalis antipyretica*), goldfish weed (*Lagarosiphon major*), water milfoil, curled pondweed (*Potamogeton crispus*), water buttercup (*Ranunculus aquatilis*).

Surface-floating plants
Fairy moss (*Azolla caroliniana*), cape pondweed (*Aponogeton distachyos*), waterlily, pictured left (such as *Nymphaea odorata* 'Sulphurea', *N.* 'Rose Arey', *N. pygmaea* 'Helvola', *N. pygmaea* 'Rubra'), floating heart (*Nymphoides peltata*), frog-bit (*Hydrocharis morsus-ranae*), water soldier (*Stratiotes aloides*), water chestnut (*Trapa natans*), water hyacinth (*Eichornia crassipes*) and water lettuce (*Pistia statiotes*).

Positioning waterlillies

Thread two cords through the mesh of the basket and use these to lower the waterlily to its correct position. Dwarf forms of waterlily should be placed with about 4 inches of water above the basket and other forms where there will be 12 to 18 inches.

Lowering the basket should be done in stages; by standing the basket on various sized blocks you will give the leaf stalks time to grow. Alternatively, trim off the fully expanded leaves and lower the plant to the correct depth straight away. The emerging leaves will then naturally grow up to the water's surface.

Where to position your water plants

Different types of aquatic plants require particular depths of water to thrive, so need to be placed in the most suitable area of the pond. Marginal plants which have roots submerged, but stems and flowers held above the water's surface, are placed on a special shallow shelf at the edge of the pond (1). Deep-water plants, such as waterlilies, are placed in the deeper areas (2), so that their leaves float on the water's surface, and submerged plants are scattered across the bottom of the pond.

Planting a basket

The best time to plant aquatic plants is while they are actively growing between spring and fall. Keep the roots moist at all times by placing them in a bucket of water until you are ready to plant.

Use a special aquatic planting basket with a wide stable base and open-mesh sides rather than other types of container. Choose one that will fit on the marginal shelf of your pond (see above) and, if necessary, line it with burlap to prevent the soil escaping. Then cover the base with a layer of special aquatic soil.

Next, position the plant in the center of the container and fill in around the roots with soil (1).

Firm down well. Now, cover the surface of the compost with a ½-inch layer of fine gravel and firm again (2). The gravel will help to prevent fish from stirring up the soil and muddying the water.

Before placing the basket in the pond, you need to remove any trapped air. This prevents the soil bubbling up when the container is lowered into the pool. To do this, submerge the planted basket in a bucket of water until the strings of air bubbles stop emerging from the basket. Then place the soaked aquatic basket into the appropriate position in your pond.

wildlife ponds

It is quite possible to turn a new or existing pond into a haven for wildlife by including a few simple design features.

The edging materials of a pond are important for attracting wildlife. They should be natural and provide a safe route to and from the pond. A gently sloping beach made from pebbles or of slate scree is ideal and should be used on at least one side. This would provide easy access for the wildlife and shallows for birds to drink and bathe. Sod laid up to the water's edge can look good, but tend to cause the water to turn muddy. Avoid using paving because this will get too hot for amphibians to cross in summer. Do not site your wildlife pond near to your patio or too close to the house, because it will be a breeding ground for many insects, including mosquitoes.

Use a thick and lush planting along the margins and outside the pond to obscure the edges and provide a seamless transition into the surrounding garden. Choose native plants where possible, but make sure they are not too invasive or grow too big for your size of pond. Allow clumps of grass to grow longer around the pond and heap up at least one pile of logs to provide extra cover. A large log can be partially laid into the pond to provide a convenient perching position for birds and a gangway for amphibians.

If you are building a wildlife pond from scratch, include some deep water areas—at least 24 inches

deep, but preferably 36 inches deep. These areas will remain cool even during the summer months and will be deep enough to protect pond creatures during winter. Do not stock a wildlife pond with fish as they will eat many of its inhabitants.

Plant all the aquatic plants in baskets to keep them within bounds (see page 139); submerged plants are the exception, which can be scattered over the floor of the pond or planted into the sediment layer.

Maintaining a wildlife pond

If you choose the right plants, a wildlife pond should require little maintenance. Be prepared to allow some algae growth and common pond weeds such as blanket weed and duckweed, but do not let them take over. Keep more invasive plants in check by removing them from the pond and cutting them back using pruners in spring or the fall (see page 139).

Take a closer look
Visiting wildlife can be studied at close quarters if you incorporate a viewing platform, using a material such as decking, when designing your pond.

Natural setting
Situated in a natural dip and surrounded by a bog garden filled with moisture-loving plants, this pond is in a perfect spot.

VIRGIN GARDENER'S BEST BETS

 Marginal shelf Bog bean (*Menyanthes trifoliata*), lesser reedmace (*Typha angustifolia*), flowering rush (*Butomus umbellatus*), water mint (*Mentha aquatica*), water plantain (*Alisma plantago-aquatica*).

 Floating plants
Fairy moss (*Azolla filiculoides*), frog-bit (*Hydrocharis morsus-ranae*), water soldier (*Stratiotes aloides*), water hawthorn (*Aponogeton distyachos*), waterlily (*Nymphaea alba*).

 Submerged plants
Curled pondweed (*Potamogeton crispus*), hornwort (*Ceratophyllum demersum*), water violet (*Hottonia palustris*), water crowfoot (*Ranunculus aquatilus*).

 Bog garden
Variegated Japanese rush (*Acorus gramineus* 'Variegatus'), *Astilboides tabularis* (syn. *Rodgersia tabularis*), *Astilbe chinensis* 'Pumila', *A.* 'Gnom', *A.* 'Perkeo', cuckoo flower (*Cardamine pratensis* 'Flore Pleno'), variegated meadowsweet (*Filipendula ulmaria* 'Variegata'), *Gunnera manicata*, *Iris ensata*, variegated yellow flag (*I. pseudoacorus* 'Variegata'), *I. sibirica*, *Lobelia* 'Queen Victoria', *Lythrum virgatum* 'The Rocket', *Lysimachia punctata*, *L. nummularia* 'Aurea', *Ligularia stenocephala* 'The Rocket', golden groundsel (*L. dentata* 'Desdemona'), *Rodgersia aesculifolia*, *R. pinnata* 'Superba', *R. podophylla*, ornamental rhubarb (*Rheum palmatum* 'Atrosanguineum'), *R.* 'Ace of Hearts', kaffir lily, (*Schizostylis coccinea*).

Creating a bog garden

A bog garden goes hand-in-hand with a wildlife pond, but can work equally well with more ornamental water features. Filled with moisture-loving plants it naturally bridges the transition between pond and the rest of the garden. Alongside a wildlife pond a bog garden also provides a rich habitat for the creatures that live around and visit the pond.

If you have naturally moisture-retentive soil, simply add plenty of well-rotted manure before planting. If not, you will have to create an artificial bog garden using a flexible pond liner. If you are building a pond from scratch using a flexible liner, you can make the bog garden at the same time using a piece of the same liner.

- Dig a hole 12 to 18 inches deep and up to 6 feet across. Smooth the surface and remove any protruding stones, then line the hole with about 1 inch of sand.

- Lay the liner on top of the sand, then make ½-inch holes in the liner spaced every 2 feet across the bottom of the bog garden.

- Fill the liner with a rich moisture-retentive soil made from one part well-rotted manure to three parts good garden topsoil.

- Trim the liner to leave a 6-inch-wide flap on all sides, then cover these with large pebbles. Alternatively, bury the edges and cover with gravel, grass sods or paving stones.

- Scatter 2 ounces per square yard of general-purpose fertilizer over the soil, then plant the bog garden starting at the center with the largest plants and finishing at the edge. For best effect, make sure the plants along the pool side overhang to obscure the edge.

- Bog gardens must be kept constantly moist, so it is worth your while installing an automatic watering system (see page 119).

a garden with natural balance

Kevin and Joanna Gibb have recently bought an old brownstone house with a long narrow garden that has been completely neglected. They would like to redesign the space so that it feels less claustrophobic. They want to include a modern formal water feature as well as a secluded area for sitting, with some storage space for outdoor furniture and garden equipment. Joanna wants the garden to exhibit a modern style but to retain many of the original plants; and Kevin would like the design to be innovative with plenty of intrigue and unexpected surprises.

A question of space

When designing a long, narrow garden it is important that you don't emphasize the plot's shortcomings. Dividing a garden into sections or "rooms" with an open water feature in the center can increase the amount of light and feeling of space. Also, a series of parallel lines used across the plot would make a long, narrow garden seem much wider.

Deciding that the necessary construction was beyond their abilities, Kevin and Joanna employed a professional garden designer to ensure their ideas and aspirations were realized in a coordinated and well-thought-out plan. The resulting garden consists of two rectangular courtyards linked by stepping stones that run through a central pool and water feature.

Hot and cool courtyards

Lines of bricks have been used to define the boundaries of each courtyard. The "hot" courtyard, at the far end of the garden, is the only area that catches the sun and has been slightly sunken to improve privacy. The low retaining stone walls are made from brick-shaped granite blocks and have had soil pressed into the cracks allowing flowers to seed themselves naturally and create a more harmonious effect.

Nearest to the house, the "cool" courtyard is made all the more relaxing by the gentle sound of water. This cascades from the copper monolith water feature with novel drip-fed containers filled with small aquatics. A living screen of ivy, jasmine and Virginia creeper adds to the seclusion, making it an ideal place for contemplation or entertaining.

The formal geometric pool is ingeniously integrated into its surroundings by blending the rock and water elements. The granite blocks and recycled slabs used in the access path continue into the pool, appearing to float on the surface of the water. No mortar is used between the blocks, which form a "tadpole maze" of watery corridors. Clam-like carved pods, that were inspired by the seedpods in the film *Alien*, stand alongside the pool and open out to form single seats with back supports (see the picture at right).

Building the water feature

The overgrown plants were removed from the area and the pond design was marked out on the ground using pegs and string. The whole water area was excavated, firmed and covered with a sheet of flexible butyl rubber. Retaining walls that form the formal pool were built up and the main water feature elements positioned (pictured left). The flexible liner was then trimmed and the paving laid, starting with the spaced granite blocks and recycled slab stepping stones.

expert tips   Recycling plants & materials

You don't need to start from scratch to create a stylish and practical garden. Even a dramatic makeover like this can make intelligent use of plants, such as the leaning pear tree and climber-clad fences, that were part of the original garden. Indeed, incorporating existing plants with thought into a new garden plan will help to give the design an established look, providing instant maturity and credibility.

Practical storage

The design cleverly incorporates a storage shed in the middle of the garden without making the garden seem smaller. This is achieved by extending the roof of the shed, which, combined with the existing leaning pear tree, forms a feature gateway linking one garden courtyard to the other. To soften the overall effect, the extended shed roof has been covered in sod of meadow grass dotted with wildflowers such as buttercups, daisies, clover, cranesbill, and dandelions. The grass is kept moist by automatic watering and needs cutting just twice a year using a pair of shears. At ground level, the two courtyards are linked by all-weather, ground-covering materials including gravel, recycled slabs and granite blocks.

Planting themes

A modern theme is achieved by planting eye-catching specimens with bold outlines such as loquat, yucca, alliums, and acanthus with ornamental grasses of contrasting softness. The foliage theme continues into the margins of the pool where dwarf cattails are planted as a visual counterbalance to the saucer-shaped floating leaves and flowers of the dwarf waterlilies.

The greening effect was continued at every level, with lush planting of walls and fences, which helped to obscure the boundary line and add to the sense of space within the garden. In the shady corners, ferns have found their perfect niche, and vines sprawl both upward and along the ground to cover the surfaces and provide extra seasonal color.

Perfect balance
Equal areas of light and shade have been achieved in this practical yet innovative design. The dramatic copper monolith (below) stands out against an evergreen back-drop of ivy. Carved wood planters filled with miniature aquatic plants are drip-fed with water by an underground pump.

a watery retreat in the country

Greg and Sarah Black have busy lives in the city. Wanting to get away from it all on weekends and vacations, they bought a house in the country with plenty of acreage on which to create a natural retreat. They want an informal garden where nature is the dominant element and where they can relax. Neither of them have much free time, so it will have to be able largely to look after itself. Their property boasted a natural pond which was fed by an underground spring, but it was completely overgrown and needed an overhaul.

The natural garden
To achieve the Blacks' dream of creating a functional garden with ornamental appeal that blends perfectly with the countryside, the design had to take into account the garden's immediate natural surroundings. It was decided that the garden design would become progressively more natural and wild the farther away you got from the house. Greg wanted to keep at least a small area of well-manicured lawn outside the picture windows, but the grass further away from the house was allowed to grow longer and, therefore, needed cutting less often. This basic principle was applied to all the different elements of the garden design.

Spring-fed pond
If neglected, a pond becomes a tangled mass of growth as the more vigorous plants swamp their neighbors. Some plants that are essential for maintaining the natural balance in a pond cannot compete with the other plants and soon die out. This is exactly what had happened to Greg and Sarah's pond.

Since the pond was fairly small and could not be seen from the house, Greg decided to take the opportunity to have it enlarged—he wanted it to form the central focus of the garden's wildlife theme. This was a big job, so instead of doing it themselves, they opted to bring in professional contractors with earth-moving equipment. Before the contractors arrived, Greg removed a few of the better-behaved aquatic plants including a large clump of iris that could be reintroduced after the pond was enlarged.

The contractors reshaped the pond so it had sweeping curves and a long 10-inch deep shelf running down both sides. This shallow area was planted with marginal aquatic plants (see page 138), which like their roots in water but prefer their leaves and flowers to be held well above the surface. To maintain the natural appearance, native aquatic plant species were introduced.

Pond weeds, such as blanketweed (1) and duckweed (2), can be a problem in small ornamental ponds but they are tolerated in the Blacks' wildlife pond. If you spot these two species in your pond, and you notice that they are covering large areas of the surface, scoop out as much as possible using a fine-mesh fishing net.

Boggy patch
On the side of the pond farthest from the house, Greg and Sarah planted moisture-loving bog garden plants so that the pond integrated faultlessly into its surroundings. Along the grassy access paths that lead to and from the pond, they sowed a wildflower mixture of grass seed and added clumps of container-grown purple loosestrife (*Lythrum*) and meadowsweet (*Filipendula*) to complete the transition.

Water meadow
The low-lying ground adjacent to the pond remained very wet for most of the year, so the Blacks decided to make it into a water meadow feature filled with wetland species,

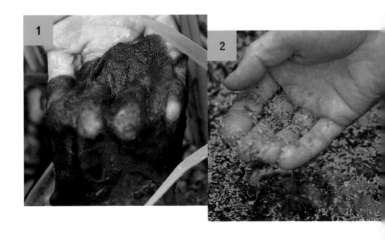

such as Sarah's favorite, snake's-head fritillary. To create this type of water feature in your garden, the ground needs to be thoroughly prepared, then sowed with a special wetland soil mixture of grasses and wildflowers. Sarah chose ragged robin, cowslips and snake's-head fritillaries and then added further drifts of fritillaries as bulbs in the second year. The grass was allowed to grow long, only to be mowed twice a year, with a meandering country path cut through the area so weekend visitors can lose themselves among the hazy grasses and busy bees—the perfect antidote for a hectic city life.

From the house, the water meadow stretches away into the distance to merge with the surrounding fields and hills. Beyond the water meadow, the property was partly bordered by a mixed hedge. This was improved by planting native species around it which bear heavy crops of winter berries to feed the resident wildlife.

Butterfly borders

The other end of the country path in Greg and Sarah's garden starts close to the house. It was decided to border this with a simple combination of massed sedums, asters, butterfly bush and lavender. A rose and honeysuckle-clad fence was added to run behind. This created a heady mixture of scents in spring and summer, and was alive with pollinating insects and butterflies.

If you have a pond, it is important to split up any overgrown aquatic plants to keep them vigorous and flowering well.

The old baskets in Greg and Sarah's pond were damaged by shoots and roots growing through the sides. So the baskets had to be cut from the plants to avoid damaging the plants' roots. The plants and their roots were then divided carefully into clumps using a sharp garden shovel, making sure each clump had plenty of healthy roots and shoots. Several healthy looking sections from the outside of the clump were selected to be replanted in new aquatic baskets (see page 138) and the rest were put on the compost pile.

Ornamental touch

To add a sense of spectacle to the pond, a floating fountainhead was installed, powered by a submersible pump. It is switched on only when Greg and Sarah, or their visitors, take a stroll down the country path or sit by the water.

keeping it
looking good

8

spring

patios & containers

ESSENTIAL TASKS

Water Keep watering winter containers as required. Remember that plants protected by the eaves of your house or situated by a wall or fence will need watering more often.

Plant Hanging baskets and other containers can be planted with tender summer annuals during late spring, after the danger of frost has passed, or whenever the plants are available at garden centers in mild-winter areas.

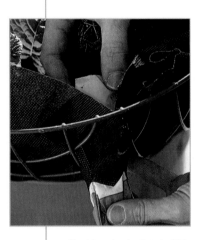

Plant hanging baskets p. 116

Feed plants Push slow-release fertilizer tablets into the soil of permanent plants and when planting seasonal displays to keep them well fed all season.

Uncover pots Containers that were wrapped to protect them from winter cold can be unwrapped during mid- to late spring.

Save water Cover the surface of planted containers with a layer of pebbles or fine gravel to help conserve moisture during the summer months.

TROUBLESHOOTING

Tidy up Remove any dead flowers and leaves from winter containers to keep them looking their best. Clear heavy snow from container plants. Sweep the patio.

lawns

ESSENTIAL TASKS

Mow When the weather is fine and the grass is dry, mow your lawn. The grass will be lush, so collect the clippings and place on the compost pile.

Flowering lawns Leave the foliage of bulbs growing in the lawn for six weeks after flowering has finished. This will give the bulbs time to build up sufficient food reserves to flower well next year. After this period, the leaves can be cut back and the lawn mowed as normal.

Feed Give your lawn a boost during late spring using a spring-formulation lawn fertilizer. If weeds or moss need to be tackled, use a combined lawn treatment.

Plant new lawn Sow seed or lay sod as soon as soil conditions allow (see page 44).

Neaten lawn edges Repair damaged lawn edges (see page 47) or lay a mowing strip (see page 49).

Kill weeds Pull out weeds by hand or use a dab-on weed killer. For a widespread problem, apply a selective weed killer once the lawn starts growing.

Remove moss Control moss by raking vigorously; improve drainage for permanent control.

TROUBLESHOOTING

Improve drainage Spike your lawn with a garden fork. Make rows of holes at least 3 inches deep every few inches across the soggy area. Fill holes with an equal-parts mixture of sieved garden soil and sharp sand. If the whole lawn is affected, rent a mechanical aerator to do the job.

Improve drainage p. 47

 beds &
borders

 pools

ESSENTIAL TASKS

Get pruning Cut back late- and early-flowering shrubs (see page 182), including early-flowering clematis. Quick-prune shrub and bush roses by trimming shoots

Get pruning p. 182

back by about two-thirds (see page 184). Prune dead, diseased and weak growth from climbing roses.
Plant If the weather is mild, plant bare-rooted trees and shrubs while they are dormant. Late spring is the ideal time to plant evergreens, hardy perennial flowers and summer-flowering bulbs.
Provide supports
Prevent top-heavy perennials from collapsing when in full bloom by placing supports around the emerging shoots. Use bamboo canes and string or wire supports that are available from garden centers.
Feed permanent plants Apply a general-purpose fertilizer or aged manure around shrubs and trees. Scatter 1 to 2 ounces of commercial fertilizer per square yard over the shrubbery or about 1 ounce around individual plants.
Divide flowers Large clumps of herbaceous perennials can be divided during mid- to late-spring to keep them vigorous and flowering well (see page 70).
Deadhead bulbs Remove the fading flowers from plants, such as daffodils, but leave flower stalks and leaves to die naturally for six weeks after flowering.

TROUBLESHOOTING

Slugs and snails Protect susceptible border plants such as delphiniums and hostas using copper barriers or commercial slug products before new shoots emerge.

ESSENTIAL TASKS

Feed fish Start feeding when the water temperature begins to rise and the fish become more active. Feed sparingly at first, but more regularly by late spring.
Tender plants During late spring, replace tender floating plants that were removed from the pond the previous fall and overwintered somewhere frost free.
Feed plants Push special aquatic fertilizer tablets into the compost of established aquatic plants. Keep the tablets toward the center of the basket to prevent nutrients from leaching out into the water and encouraging the growth of algae.
Divide large plants Some shallow-water plants and many bog garden plants will need to be divided every few years to keep them flowering well (see page 145).
New plants Add new plants during mid- to late-spring. Plant in flat-bottomed aquatic planting baskets using special aquatic soil (see page 139).

TROUBLESHOOTING

Rotting leaves Remove netting covers and scoop out any wind-blown leaves before they have a chance to sink to the bottom and rot.

early summer

 ## patios & containers

ESSENTIAL TASKS

Water Plants should be watered as required, which may mean watering twice a day in hot, dry weather. Move containers to a shady spot to reduce the amount of water they need. Consider installing an automatic watering system if you have a lot of containers to maintain (see page 119).

Plant Plant hanging baskets and other containers with tender summer annuals during early summer, if not already done. Line porous terra cotta with plastic and use drought-tolerant plants to reduce the need for watering (see page 117).

Automatic watering p. 119

Feed plants If you didn't insert slow-release fertilizer tablets when planting in spring, container plants will need feeding about six weeks after they were planted. To improve flowering displays, apply a high-potash liquid fertilizer, every other watering.

Tidy containers Remove fading flowers to tidy displays and encourage further flower production. Also, remove any dead or yellowing leaves.

TROUBLESHOOTING

Weedy areas Hand-weed gravel, patios and other paved areas, or use a commercial spot weedkiller. Cover nearby ornamental plants with plastic or upturned buckets and leave in place until the spray has completely dried.

 ## lawns

ESSENTIAL TASKS

Keep in trim Mow the lawn regularly. This may mean cutting twice a week while the lawn is growing strongly. Clippings can be left on the lawn to feed the grass if they are less than 1 inch long, otherwise put them on the compost pile.

Neaten edges Trim the lawn edges each time you mow for the cleanest effect, but you can reduce this to every other mowing if you are pushed for time. To get a really neat appearance, pick up the clippings after edging. This will also prevent them from rotting in the border and becoming a weed problem.

Worn areas Over-sow patchy lawns or re-seed (see page 44). Frequently used areas can be reinforced with heavy-duty plastic mesh (see page 48).

Wildflower meadow Areas of spring-flowering meadow can be cut once the plants have finished flowering and shed their seed. Check the seedpods to make sure the seed has been scattered before you mow.

TROUBLESHOOTING

Weeds Remove individual weeds with an old kitchen knife and weaken patches of coarse grasses by mowing regularly. If the whole lawn is weed infested, apply a selective weed killer.

Brown grass Don't worry if your lawn turns brown in summer due to lack of water, it will soon regain its green appearance when the rains come. But if you want to keep it green all summer, apply ½ inch of water twice a week using a sprinkler.

beds & borders

ESSENTIAL TASKS

Harden off seedlings Tender annuals and vegetables need to be acclimatized to the cooler environment outdoors before they are planted. Place in a coldframe or in a sheltered spot for a week or two prior to planting in their flowering position.

Replace annuals Spring annuals that have come to the end of their display should be replaced with tender summer annuals that have been acclimatized.

Trim hedges Trim fast-growing ornamental hedges, such as privet, in early to mid-summer. Prune informal hedges after they have finished flowering.

Mulch beds Apply a 2-inch layer of wood chips, compost, or other organic material around shrubs, perennials, and annuals to smother weeds, conserve moisture, and improve soil.

Pruning Cut back shrubs that flower as soon as the display has finished (see page 182).

Frost damage Severe frost can kill exposed tips of many plants, so you need to cut out dead stems. To check if it is dead, scrape away a little bark with a fingernail; if it's creamy-yellow or green it is alive, if it is brown it's dead.

Check supports Make sure all tall perennial plants that are prone to flopping over while in flower have been securely staked.

Deadhead flowers Remove dead flower heads from rhododendrons and azaleas after flowering has finished. Continue deadheading late varieties of daffodil and tulips, leaving their foliage to die down naturally. Deadhead roses to improve the display.

TROUBLESHOOTING

Spray roses Mildew, blackspot and rust can seriously weaken susceptible varieties. Spray with fungicide every two weeks to keep these diseases at bay.

Pest patrol Watch out for tiny insects on the new growth of many plants including roses. Wash off small colonies with soapy water; spray severe outbreaks with a suitable insecticide.

pools

ESSENTIAL TASKS

Top up reservoirs Regularly top up the water reservoirs of small water features, especially if the weather is hot or windy.

Plant Early summer is the best time to plant tender aquatic plants after the threat of frost has passed. It is also a good time to revamp neglected ponds (see page 144).

Plant aquatic baskets p. 144

Water bog garden Keep the compost in the bog garden moist, but not waterlogged. In hot weather, it may require watering every day, so it may be worth your while installing a seep hose to make watering easier or plumbing it into an automatic watering system.

Improve displays Remove faded blooms and yellowing stems and leaves using a pair of scissors or pruners before the dying growth falls into the water and rots.

TROUBLESHOOTING

Green water Prevent the water from turning green with algae by reducing the amount of water exposed to sunlight; add more floating plants if necessary.

late summer

patios & containers

ESSENTIAL TASKS

Water Continue to water plants as required.

Feed Give all container plants some liquid fertilizer every other watering.

Vacations Arrange to have a neighbor or friend water all container plants each day while you are away. If you are away for a short period of time you could set up a temporary watering system instead (see page 120). If you are away a lot, consider installing an automatic watering system.

Take cuttings Prepare cuttings from tender perennials as insurance against any winter losses of plants to be left outside.

Tidy plants Continue to tidy up displays by removing dead flowers and leaves. Use a pair of pruners to trim back over-vigorous plants from time to time to prevent them from overwhelming their neighbors and spoiling the balance of the display.

Take cuttings p. 180

TROUBLESHOOTING

Pest alert Watch out for aphids in the buds and shoot tips of container plants. Wash off small colonies with soapy water; use a ready-to-use insecticide to deal with more severe outbreaks.

Disease check Plants in containers are usually more susceptible to diseases, such as powdery mildew, if they run short of water. Remove any badly affected leaves and spray the rest of the plant with a suitable fungicide. Pay particular attention to keeping all containers well watered.

lawns

ESSENTIAL TASKS

Mow and edge Keep mowing your lawn regularly. Clippings can be left on the lawn to feed the grass if they are less than 1 inch long, otherwise put them on the compost pile. Continue to trim the edges of the lawn every time you mow.

Vacations Ask a neighbor to mow the lawn for you if you are away for more than a week during the summer months; the edge trimming can wait until you return.

Edge the lawn p. 47

Heavy wear Lawns can suffer from excessive wear and tear during the summer vacation, especially under children's play equipment and areas used for ball games. Either move the play equipment around to spread the wear more evenly or reinforce the worn patches using heavy-duty plastic mesh before the damage is done (see page 48).

TROUBLESHOOTING

Weeds During prolonged dry spells, the grass may stop growing, but weeds don't. They will flower, set seed and then spread if you let them. Stop this from happening by running the mower over the lawn once a week to remove the flowers.

beds & borders

ESSENTIAL TASKS

Pruning Cut out one stem in three from summer-flowering shrubs after they have finished flowering. Prune the sideshoots from wall-grown pyracantha to a few leaves to enhance the display of berries over the winter months (see page 185).

Plant bulbs Autumn-flowering bulbs such as colchicums, hardy cyclamen, nerines and autumn crocus should be planted during mid-summer.

Trim hedges Give hedges their final trim. This will allow any new growth time to mature before the onset of winter.

Water There is no need to water established plants, but it is essential that any plants added this spring or early summer are kept watered through their first growing season. It is also worth watering annuals, such as fuchsias and impatiens, as well as leafy and pod-producing vegetables during long, dry spells.

Tidy borders Remove dead heads and yellowing leaves. Also cut back straggly pansies and untidy leaves of perennials, such as hardy geraniums, which will produce a fresh mound of attractive foliage and may produce another flush of flowers.

Take cuttings Remove semi-ripe cuttings of shrubs (see page 180) to increase stocks. Also take cuttings from not-so-hardy shrubs, such as hibiscus, myrtle and olearia, so that you have ready replacements for any losses caused by winter cold and wet.

TROUBLESHOOTING

Save water Prevent moisture loss from the soil by adding a layer of organic material (known as a *mulch*) around trees, shrubs and climbers.

Disease check Inspect perennial flowers for powdery mildew disease. Spray affected plants that have not flowered with a suitable fungicide (check instructions on the packet). Those that have finished flowering can be cut back and the diseased leaves disposed of. New disease-free foliage will then be produced.

pools

ESSENTIAL TASKS

Top up ponds Continue to top-up ponds and water features as necessary. Do this often so that the temperature of the pond remains more or less constant and the fish are not distressed.

Feed fish Continue to feed fish regularly throughout the summer.

Tidy plants Continue to remove fading flowers and yellowing stems and leaves from plants before they fall into the pond to rot. Thin out floating plants if they are covering more than two-thirds of the pond's surface area and scoop out dense growths of submerged plants using an old colander.

TROUBLESHOOTING

Gasping fish During hot weather, the oxygen levels in still water are depleted and fish can often be seen gasping at the surface. If you have a fountain or cascade, switch it on to oxygenate the surface water. If not use water from a hose to do the same job.

Duckweed Like tiny seedlings floating on the surface of the water, duckweed can soon multiply to cover the entire pond. Use an old colander to scoop out as much as you can.

Blanketweed Use a rake to scoop this rapidly growing weed or twist the thread-like growths around the end of a bamboo cane. Leave the weed on the side of the pool

Duckweed p. 144

to give any pond creatures the chance to get back into the water. Then add the dry weed to the compost pile.

fall

 patios &
containers

ESSENTIAL TASKS

Plant winter displays Patio containers, hanging baskets and windowboxes can be planted with hardy plants, including colorful foliage, berries or flowers. Use winter annuals, such as pansies for intermittent blooms over several months and dwarf bulbs to give displays a color boost in spring.

Tender plants Move containers filled with permanent tender plants into a frost-free place. If your garden only gets light frosts, almost-hardy container plants can be overwintered successfully outside. Move them to a sheltered spot and wrap the pot with a double layer of bubble wrap and the plants with a double layer of spun row cover. Leave an opening so the plants can be watered if necessary.

Plant winter displays p. 115

Clear out containers Pots and tubs containing summer displays should be emptied and the pots cleaned. Salvage as many plants as possible, re-using hardy plants, such as ivy, in winter displays and over-wintering tender perennials, such as geraniums, in a frost-free place. Cut back plants and store them in boxes or take cuttings (see page 180) if space is limited.

TROUBLESHOOTING

Frost-proofing Some garden containers, notably those made from terra cotta, are not reliably frost-proof. Empty and move to the safety of a shed or garage any that are susceptible to frost damage in your garden.

lawns

ESSENTIAL TASKS

Mow Continue to mow your lawn until it goes dormant.

Edge Continue edging your lawn to keep it looking neat. Consider adding a mowing strip, if not already done in spring (see page 49).

Clear leaves Fallen leaves should be cleared from the lawn regularly. If they are allowed to remain for more than a week, the grass underneath will suffer. Use a bow rake to collect leaves for the compost pile. For larger lawns, consider renting or buying a leaf blower which will clean up leaves quickly.

Feed Apply a fall lawn fertilizer to give your lawn a boost, particularly if it suffered heavy wear during the summer.

Plant bulbs Daffodils and crocuses can be planted in small areas near the edge of the lawn to create an attractive display next spring.

Rake If necessary, remove the dead and decaying stems that build up within the grass (known as *thatch*) using vigorous strokes with a rake.

Create a mowing strip p. 49

TROUBLESHOOTING

Moss To prevent moss in shaded areas, you will have to reduce the amount of shade or replace the grass with more shade-tolerant groundcover plants.

Bare patches Sow grass seed to thicken up patchy grass or re-sow bare patches (see page 44).

beds & borders

ESSENTIAL TASKS

Lift tender bulbs Tender plants such as gladioli need to be lifted and stored somewhere dry and frost-free in frost-prone areas.

Get planting Plant spring bulbs, woody plants and winter flowers. Trees, shrubs and vines should be watered thoroughly and planted at the same depth as they were in the container (see page 102). Plant bare-root specimens immediately.

Tender plants To ensure tender perennials produce displays year after year, keep them frost-free over winter. Box up a selection of your favorite plants in soil that is moist and place in a frost-free garage (see page 121). Alternatively, take cuttings (see page 180).

Clean borders Remove the dying top-growth from herbaceous plants and protect the central root (known as the crown) of not-so-hardy types with a blanket of leaves or straw held in place with netting. Leave dead stems of grasses to provide architectural interest to borders, especially on frosty mornings.

Tie climbers Check climbers and wall shrubs to see if they are well secured. Tie any stems that need it.

Dig vacant ground Areas that you intend to plant next spring should be cultivated during the fall so that the frosts can break down any large clods over the winter. If your soil is light and sandy, leave digging until the spring.

Hardwood cuttings Now is the time to take hardwood cuttings from many shrubs (see page 181).

TROUBLESHOOTING

Protect climbers Give borderline-tender climbers a protective double layer of spun row cover or a layer of insulation made from straw held in position by fine-mesh netting. This will prevent them from dying during the cold weather.

pools

ESSENTIAL TASKS

Clear ponds Remove any dead or dying foliage from plants growing in the shallow areas by cutting stems back to about 1 inch above the surface of the water.

Feed fish Give your fish a high-protein feed to allow them to build up sufficient reserves before winter.

Divide large plants Remove baskets of large plants from the pond and divide them up using a sharp shovel, before replanting and replacing in the pond (see page 139).

Divide large plants p. 139

TROUBLESHOOTING

Net ponds Prevent fallen leaves from blowing into the pond by covering it with a fine-mesh net. If your pond is too large or if wind-blown leaves are the main problem, it is worth putting up a 2-foot high netting barrier around the pond to catch the leaves. Clear accumulations of leaves as necessary.

winter

 patios & containers

ESSENTIAL TASKS

Water Keep watering all containers filled with plants if soil is not frozen. Containers under the eaves of your house or shed and those next to walls tend to receive less rain and so require watering more often. Don't forget to check plants that were wrapped up in the fall, because they will need occasional watering too.

Protect winter displays Small pots and hanging baskets may require protection in moderately cold winters because they contain a relatively small amount of potting soil that is more prone to freezing. Wrap pots in bubble wrap to protect the plant roots. In cold-winter areas, move susceptible plants to an unheated porch or garage or to the shelter of a thick hedge.

Tidy displays Remove dead flowers and foliage from winter containers to improve the displays and prevent them from rotting.

Protect winter displays p. 121

TROUBLESHOOTING

Protect from snow Some evergreen shrubs, especially conifers, are susceptible to damage by large accumulations of snow. If heavy falls are forecast, either wrap the conifer with soft string to prevent it from being pulled out of shape, or be prepared to knock snow off before damage is caused.

lawns

ESSENTIAL TASKS

Mow Avoid walking on your lawn while it is wet or frosty. Mowing may be necessary throughout winter in very mild areas, but elsewhere the grass will practically stop growing.

Clearing leaves Keep clearing leaves that blow onto the lawn during early winter. Do this at least once a week if you have a lot of deciduous trees in your area.

New lawns In mild-winter areas, where the soil is not too wet, you could lay grass sod in early winter. Otherwise, it is better to wait until spring.

Mower maintenance Clean and maintain your mower (see mower instructions for details). Check that blades are in good condition, clean and wipe with an oily rag to stop them from rusting while in storage. If you are getting it serviced, make an appointment now because service centers will be very busy come the spring.

Clearing leaves see p. 168

Tool care Clean and sharpen all tools. Wipe metal surfaces with an oily rag before storage.

Overhanging plants Shrubs and trees that are starting to overhang the lawn or cast deep shade can be pruned back or thinned. The plants will not suffer so much stress at this time of year and you will be able to see where to make the cuts more clearly.

TROUBLESHOOTING

Lawn protection Keep pets from using the lawn as a bathroom to prevent dead spots in spring.

 beds &
borders

ESSENTIAL TASKS

Check supports Take the opportunity to check the condition of supports while climbers are dormant and leafless. Make repairs as necessary and loosen any constricting ties.

Check roses Check woody plants such as roses after a hard frost or severe winds and refirm the soil around their roots if they have become loosened.

Early sowings If you have the facilities to grow plants somewhere frost-free until the end of the spring, sow sweet peas during late winter. For nearly all other flower crops wait until early or mid-spring before sowing (see page 178).

Boundary repairs Check walls and fences to see if they are in need of repair, especially if they are used to support a climber. Carefully take down climbing plants and protect them with plastic before applying wood preservative or repointing crumbling mortar.

Feed birds Place bird food out in a cat- and squirrel-proof feeder. Feed birds nuts, seeds, suet and fruit, and give them fresh water every day. Once you start feeding, keep it up all winter because the local bird population will come to depend on you.

TROUBLESHOOTING

Clear leaves from roses Wear thick gloves to gather all fallen leaves carefully from bush and climbing roses or use a leaf blower to make the job easier. This will help prevent disease from infected fallen leaves from carrying over to next year's new foliage.

 pools

ESSENTIAL TASKS

Remove the pump In cold-winter areas, remove submersible pond pumps and clean thoroughly before storage. If your pool contains fish, replace the pump with a low-voltage pond heater (available from specialist suppliers), which will keep at least part of the surface ice free all winter.

Clear leaves Continue to clear up wind-blown leaves from around the pond and netting so that they cannot find their way into the pond, rot and foul the water.

Feeding Continue to feed fish with a high-protein fish food until the weather turns really cold and the water temperature reaches 50°F (10°C)—once this occurs, the fish become less active.

Winter protection Cover small water features with bubble wrap. Protect small pools by covering with planks and laying insulation materials over the top.

Ice-free hole Fish ponds need to have at least part of their surface kept free of ice to allow toxic gases produced by decaying plant materials at the bottom of the pond to escape from the water. If your pond freezes over, melt a hole using a saucepan full of hot water. Never smash a hole in the ice because the shock-waves may kill the fish.

TROUBLESHOOTING

Big freeze When sub-zero temperatures last for a period of time, use a hose to siphon off a couple of inches of water from below the ice-sheet on the pond to prevent it getting any thicker. The trapped air under the ice-sheet will help prevent the pond surface from freezing totally shut again.

virgin
basics

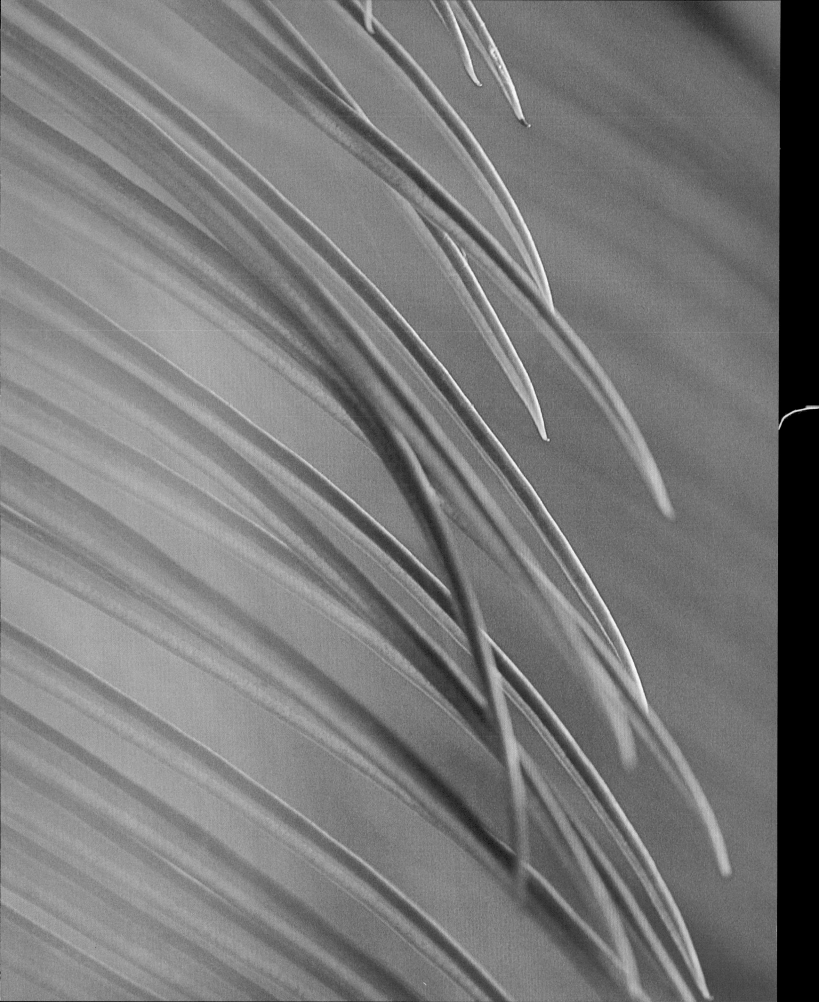

know your garden climate

The climate in your garden is determined by several factors. The most important is the geographical location of your garden: how far north it is, its altitude and distance from the coast.

Coastal gardens tend to have more rain and experience less extremes in temperature than those inland. For these reasons, within the USA, there is a huge variation in temperature and rainfall between regions. Local geographical factors such as mountain ranges and large plains or lakes also can have a significant influence on the climate in a particular area.

What plants can you grow?

Temperature, sunlight, rain and wind are the main factors that affect the plants you can and cannot grow.

Temperature Plants vary greatly in their ability to tolerate high and low temperatures, so it is essential that you choose varieties that are able to cope with your garden's conditions.

Apart from your garden's geographical position (see chart opposite), air temperatures are affected by the lay of the land. A garden with a slightly north-facing slope, for example, will be slower to warm up and quicker to cool down than a garden with a slight south-facing slope, which captures more of the sun's energy.

The temperature of the soil is affected by the type of soil you have: sandy soil warms up quickly while heavy clay soil takes its time. Dark-colored soils also warm up more quickly than light-colored soils.

Tender plants, such as summer annuals, are very susceptible to damage and easily killed. Even a plant considered hardy can be damaged if the cold period is prolonged, very severe or occurs just after the plant has put on new growth in spring. It is essential that all tender plants are protected from frost. The easiest way to do that is not to plant them out until the last likely frost date in your area (see chart for rough guidelines). If a frost is forecast after planting out tender plants, cover them with a double layer of spun row cover to protect them. If you are caught by an unexpectedly late frost, cover affected plants early in the morning with sheets of newspaper to slow down the rate of thawing, because this is when most of the damage to plant tissue occurs.

Choose plants according to the USDA hardiness zone in which you live. Plants available at local nurseries and garden centers are usually well suited for your regional climate.

Sunlight This obviously increases temperatures, so the more sunshine a garden gets, the warmer it will be. Any south-facing areas in your garden will provide a warm growing environment. Many plants like sunny conditions and do best in a site that gets direct sunlight for most the day. Others, such as rhododendrons **(1)**, are adapted to growing under trees and so prefer a partially shaded site.

It is important to assess how much sunlight each part of your garden receives, and then choose suitable plants for each area.

Rain Water is essential for plants to survive and most is supplied by rainfall. Levels of rainfall vary considerably from area to area. There

1

2 3

are also variations in how much rain falls from month to month throughout the year.

In dry areas, rainfall may only occur just once or twice each year. Even where rainfall is more even, droughts can occur, which put plants under stress and if prolonged, can kill them. If you live in a drought-prone area, choose plants that have evolved to reduce water loss. Plants which have gray, hairy, glossy, needle-like or thick succulent leaves, such as *Echeveria* (2), will do well in these conditions.

Wind The dramatic damage caused by strong winds is all too obvious, but even a light breeze has an effect on plant growth.

Air movement is beneficial as it reduces the incidence of disease and helps plants to keep cool. Wind is not a problem in most gardens, except in exposed, windy sites. A steady breeze, however, reduces humidity and increases evaporation of water from the plants' leaves, which means the plants need more water to compensate. This can put the plants under stress, especially

during prolonged drought—reducing growth and potential yields from fruit and vegetable crops. Fortunately, it is very easy to protect plants from the effects of wind by putting up windbreaks that help to slow down the air movement.

In some gardens, currents of air are accelerated by the funnelling effect of buildings or natural weather patterns. Wind damage is particularly severe on the coast, as the air is laden with salt. Use salt-tolerant shrubs such as *Pittosporum* (3) to help shelter coastal gardens.

AT-A-GLANCE GUIDE TO HARDINESS ZONES

ZONE	STATES COVERED	LAST LIKELY FROST	FIRST LIKELY FROST	FROST-FREE SEASON
1	Eastern Alaska, northern Canada.	mid-June	mid-July	30 days
2	Central Alaska; northern Manitoba, Ontario, Saskatchewan, Quebec.	mid-May	mid-August	90 days
3	Western Alaska; southern Alberta, Manitoba, Ontario, Saskatchewan, Quebec; northern Maine, Minnesota, Montana, North Dakota, Wisconsin.	mid-May	mid-September	120 days
4	South Dakota, Wyoming; coastal Alaska; central British Columbia, Colorado, Idaho, Maine, New Brunswick, New York, Vermont; southern Minnesota, Montana, North Dakota, Wisconsin; northern Idaho, Iowa, Michigan, Nebraska, New Hampshire, Utah.	early May	mid-September	125 days
5	Central British Columbia, Oregon, Utah, West Virginia; northern Idaho, Illinois, Indiana, Kansas, Massachusetts, Missouri, Nevada, New Mexico, Nova Scotia, Ohio, Pennsylvania, Washington; southern Maine, Iowa, Michigan, Nebraska, New Brunswick, New Hampshire, New York, Vermont; eastern Colorado.	end of April	mid-October	165 days
6	Rhode Island; central British Columbia, Oregon, Nevada, New Mexico, Utah, Washington; southern Connecticut, Idaho, Illinois, Indiana, Kansas, Missouri, Massachusetts, New Jersey, Ohio, Pennsylvania; northern Arizona, Arkansas, California, Oklahoma, Maryland, Tennessee, Texas, Virginia, West Virginia.	mid-April	mid-October	180 days
7	Narrow strip of central Arizona, British Columbia, California, Nevada, Oregon, Washington; southern New Mexico, Oklahoma, Tennessee, Utah, Virginia; central Arkansas, North Carolina, Texas; northern Alabama, Georgia, Mississippi, South Carolina.	mid-April	mid-October	180 days
8	Coastal British Columbia, Oregon, North Carolina, Washington; central Arizona, California, Texas; southern Alabama, Georgia, Mississippi, New Mexico, Nevada, South Carolina; northern Louisiana, Florida.	early March	mid-November	245 days
9	Coastal California, Louisiana, Texas; southern Arizona; central Florida.	mid-February	mid-December	265 days
10	Coastal California; southern Arizona, Florida.	late January	late December	335 days

planning a garden redesign

You may want to redesign your garden for a number of reasons: if you have moved into a new house, for example, and inherited a design from the previous owners that doesn't suit your particular needs; or if your circumstances have changed and you require different features in your garden, such as a safe play area for children. Whatever your situation, the first step is to draw up a scale plan of your existing garden. This will give you an accurate vision of what your garden can accommodate.

Making plans

First make a rough sketch of your garden, then use a measuring tape to measure accurately the position of major features such as the house and garage as well as any boundaries. A 10-foot retractable tape is suitable for measuring a small garden, but for larger areas use a 100-foot surveyors' tape (available from do-it-yourself stores or rental shops). Measure and jot down any changes in level, both from front to

back and from one side of the garden to the other. Now sketch the location of permanent plants such as trees and large shrubs and other large features that may be present, such as a garden shed, pool or arbor. To get accurate measurements of the position of each feature within the garden, measure its distance from two fixed points of reference, such as two corners of the house.

Using the measurements that you recorded on the sketch, draw up an accurate plan on graph paper. Make it reasonably large—a scale of 1-inch to 1-yard is ideal for most gardens. Include on the graph paper all the features you intend to keep in the final garden plan, then add all the other features on an overlay of tracing paper or a sheet of clear acetate placed on top.

On a sunny day, return to your garden with a pad and crayons in hand and note which way is north (use a compass if you are unsure) and how the shadows fall across the garden. Use different colors to indicate different levels of shade. For example, use red for areas that are shaded in the morning, orange for areas that are shaded in the evening, and yellow for any areas that stay shady for most of the day. Transfer these shaded areas onto a second overlay.

Also note any obvious problem spots where plants struggle to grow, such as deep shade next to the house or under the canopy of a maple tree, for example, or boggy soil that stays wet for long periods or soil that dries out too quickly in summer. Finally, take a soil sample

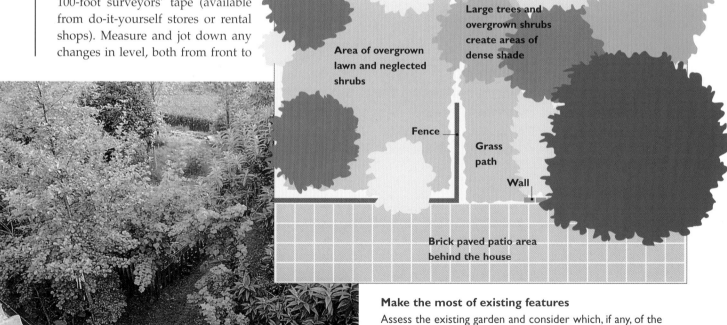

Area of overgrown lawn and neglected shrubs

Large trees and overgrown shrubs create areas of dense shade

Fence

Grass path

Wall

Brick paved patio area behind the house

Make the most of existing features

Assess the existing garden and consider which, if any, of the features you want to retain. In this garden, most of the large shrubs were overgrown and had to be removed to allow more light into the house. Two compact evergreens, however, were retained to give the new design a sense of maturity.

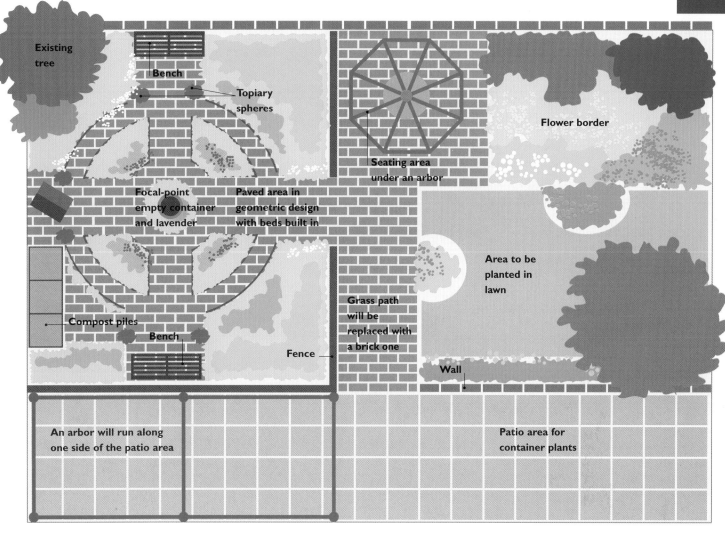

Existing
tree

Bench

Topiary
spheres

Focal-point
empty container
and lavender

Paved area in
geometric design
with beds built in

Seating area
under an arbor

Flower border

Area to be
planted in
lawn

Grass path
will be
replaced with
a brick one

Compost piles

Bench

Fence

Wall

An arbor will run along
one side of the patio area

Patio area for
container plants

Plan out the key elements on paper

Sketch out your ideas to see how the different elements fit together in the new garden design. Start with the boundaries, paving and other ground covering materials, then add other features such as seats and garden structures.

and check the soil acidity levels in different areas using a simple pH kit (see page 166).

The plan should now contain enough information for you to finalize the position of features, decide on planting schemes and develop your garden design with confidence. The graph paper layout can be used as many times as you want to try out a variety of ideas. Cut out shapes in colored paper to represent different features, such as a shed, patio area or pool and try them out in different positions

around the garden. You could also try changing the size or shape of different features, to see how this affects the overall design. Don't be afraid to change your mind: a well-designed garden usually goes through several revisions during the planning and building stages as unexpected problems or new ideas emerge. Building features such as patios and pools, however, are difficult and costly to alter once work has begun, so make sure you have considered everything before committing yourself.

trying out your ideas

Before you make any changes to your garden, it is worth marking it out to help you visualize the overall effect. Straight lines such as the edges of a patio or formal pond are easy to mark out with pegs and string, but to create the sweeping curves of a new border or lawns a rope or garden hose would be more suitable. If you want further reassurance, you can try mocking-up other key features. For instance, you could use bamboo canes and string in the place of arches and other garden structures to see what impact they have on their surroundings.

Creating the new garden

Your garden will be viewed and accessed from your house, so to ensure that you have a good view plan the design from the house.

Changing boundaries It is always a good idea to start with the garden boundaries because they can have a great influence on the style and feel of the design. Boundary fences and walls are difficult and often expensive to change, although if totally inappropriate for the garden design you are hoping to create, they can be disguised with paint or camouflaged with relatively inexpensive trellis and climbers.

In this garden, a new wall was built to provide privacy. It was made from salvaged bricks to match the materials used in the house. If you want to change a boundary wall or fence, be sure to have your property surveyed, and notify local zoning officials to get a permit and find out any restrictions on height or materials before you begin.

Decorative paving Patios designed for sitting in the sun or enjoying outdoor meals need to be carefully positioned if they are to be successful. So it is a good idea to establish where you are going to have your patio before you add any other features to your plan.

In the garden featured, the overgrown lawn area was paved over to create a low-maintenance patio in a modern geometric design. Small beds for planting form a circular shape around the large terra cotta pot, which provides a focal point. To minimize the impact of so much paving in a relatively small garden, the design combines different paving materials and uses plants to soften the harsh outlines.

Covering the ground The influence of a grassy lawn or other ground covering on the appearance of a garden is often overlooked by the beginner. Here, a well-proportioned lawn has been shaped to complement the overall design of the garden. It provides a natural open space that is restful on the eye and offers the opportunity for creating attractive vistas, even in a small garden like this.

Special features Desired garden features such as arches and arbors should be included on your design plan, along with practical features, such as a shed or compost pile. Bear in mind that some features, such as a pool or areas for growing herbs and vegetables, need an open, sunny location. The arbor in this garden is a decorative feature with a practical function—a table and chairs have been placed there and a small candelabra provides soft lighting for evening entertaining.

Using garden dividers Dividing a garden up into "rooms" is a useful design technique for disguising the size of a garden. It also allows you to

Planting plans
A detailed planting plan was drawn up for each border taking into consideration how much sun each area receives. The ground was thoroughly dug and cleared of weeds before the plants were due to arrive, so they could be planted immediately.

combine different styles. Here, a picket fence has been retained to separate the area for growing herbs and vegetables from the arbor and mini-orchard. Anything that breaks the direct line of sight can be used as a garden divider—hedges and fences work well in large gardens, while trellis and rustic fence panels are suitable in a small one.

Borders and plants Like other features, beds and borders should be in proportion to the rest of the garden design. Do not make them too wide unless you provide access, such as stepping stones, through the middle to carry out routine maintenance. In this garden, a balance of deciduous and evergreen plants that offer more than one season of interest was chosen to give the garden year-round appeal.

Focal points
The two main points of focus in the garden were both combined with fragrant plants to help soften their appearance. The arbor was planted with climbing roses and colorful clematis, while the large terra cotta urn was surrounded with lavender.

understanding your soil

Soils vary in quality and fertility. The easiest way to grow a satisfying garden is to accept your type of soil, and select only those plants that will thrive in these conditions. Garden centers and catalogs are packed with adaptable plants, and also offer many for conditions like dry shade, very dry soil, heavy clay soil, or wet areas. (See below for advice on assessing your soil.)

If your soil has been damaged— the topsoil removed during building works, perhaps, or the soil compacted by heavy equipment—you will need to make major changes to loosen it or increase fertility. Otherwise, it is unlikely to support the healthy growth of plants. If you have less than ideal soil, consider building raised beds. You can make the walls of lumber, stone, or other materials, or simply mound topsoil into informal raised beds.

Most gardeners prefer to improve their soil as much as they can. Digging in aged manure, compost, and applying organic matter as mulch, supplies nourishment to the microorganisms that thrive at and below the surface. These tiny creatures create the food for the roots of plants, and improve soil drainage.

Assessing your soil

If you have a new garden that is completely bare or an area of a garden you intend to replant, it is worth checking that the soil is in good shape before you start.

Dig several 24-inch deep holes over the area and check the soil profile—that is, the two layers of soil. The top layer (called topsoil) contains most of the nutrients and supports most of the plant growth. It is usually about 6 inches deep and is often a darker color than the second layer of soil (called subsoil).

How to test your soil

Different plants require a certain type of soil to grow healthily: some love acid soils, others thrive in more alkaline conditions, while most prefer a neutral or slightly acid soil. You can test the pH (the level of acidity) of your soil very easily using a soil test kit (available from garden retailers), which tell you whether your soil is alkaline, neutral or acid. To get an accurate reading, you need to gather a sample of soil that is representative of your garden as a whole.

1 Lay out 6-foot long bamboo canes in a W-shaped pattern over the area. Then dig small holes where the canes cross and collect soil samples from about 4 inches into the hole. Avoid contaminated areas or those that are not typical of the plot as a whole, such as around a swimming pool. Mix the samples together in a clean bucket and use a garden sieve to remove stones and other debris.

2 Place a small amount of the soil into a folded piece of paper or card and gently pour the soil into the testing bottle.

3 Add water as directed on the testing kit and then shake vigorously. Allow to settle before checking the sample against the color chart supplied.

For a more accurate analysis or an indication of the nutrient levels in the soil, send a sample to a soil laboratory. Check the package for a lab address, or call your USDA extension service agent.

To test the drainage of your soil, fill each hole with a couple of gallons of water. If it drains away completely within 24 hours, all is well. If not, you will have to dig the soil (see below). If the water drains very poorly, you may have to install extra drainage (ask your garden center about your options) or grow plants in raised beds or pots instead.

Simple digging

The traditional way of overcoming poor drainage is to dig vacant areas of soil once a year. This helps to bury weeds and break up any surface compaction, allowing water to drain freely. It also allows you to incorporate organic matter, such as manure, deep into the soil where a plant's roots develop.

Different soils require digging at different times of the year. But only dig when soil conditions allow, or you will do more harm than good. You can use a shovel on most soils, but if your soil is very stony, a garden fork may be easier.

Steps to success when digging

- Dig heavy soils in late fall before the soil becomes too wet. If it sticks to your tools and boots it is too wet. Leave lighter, sandy soils until spring.

- Choose a spade with a handle that is comfortable and sufficiently long to prevent you from stooping while digging. Wear sturdy boots.

- Push the blade vertically into the ground and turn over small amounts of soil at a time, keeping your back as straight as possible. Take regular breaks.

Heavy soils If your soil has a high clay content, dig in the late fall so that any large lumps of earth are exposed to frost action, which breaks the clods down.

Loamy soils (not clay or sandy) These can be dug any time during the winter months provided the soil is not too wet or frozen.

Sandy soils Light, sandy soils are best dug during the spring, a couple of weeks before planting.

Deep digging

Some soils can develop hard compacted layers about 12 inches below the surface, which are impenetrable to roots. This causes shallow rooting, so that plants grow poorly and are more susceptible to periods of drought. Ordinary digging does not break up the soil at this depth, so a special technique called deep or double digging has to be employed. Even though very simple, it is hard work.

- Dig a 24-inch-wide trench with a shovel to a depth of about 8 inches and move the soil to the other end of the plot being dug.

No digging method

If you don't like the idea of digging every year, you don't have to. Take a leaf out of the organic gardeners' book—if you don't walk on the soil, you won't cause the damage which makes digging necessary. The secret is to prepare the soil thoroughly to begin with by deep digging (see box below) and then to add a thick layer of organic matter to the soil surface once a year. Thereafter, you can simply leave the worms and beetles to do the work for you.

- Break up the bottom of the trench using a garden fork and incorporate some organic matter, such as well-rotted manure as you go along.

- Move back 24 inches and dig out a second 24-inch wide trench, moving the soil forward to fill the first trench. Fork over the bottom of the second trench as before, adding the organic matter.

- Repeat this process until the whole plot has been dug, then use the soil from the first trench to fill the last trench.

improving your soil

Knowing how to feed your soil properly is one of the basic principles of good gardening and should be the starting point for every Virgin Gardener.

Using organic matter

Nearly all garden soils can be improved by adding some sort of bulky organic matter, such as well-rotted manure, bark or wood chips, or home-made garden compost or leafmold (see below).

How does it work? Organic matter is broken down by microorganisms (free-living bacteria and fungi), releasing nutrients to plants and improving growth. The way bulky organic matter benefits your soil, however, will depend on the type of soil you have. On light and sandy soils, which are very well drained,

organic matter acts like a sponge helping the soil to hold onto water. Organic matter also provides food for soil-borne creatures, such as earthworms, which burrow through the soil opening up the structure, improving drainage and aeration, which is of particular benefit to heavy, clay soils. This, in turn, encourages deeper roots and better plant growth.

How much should you use? The amount of organic matter you add depends on your soil type. Loam garden soils will need about a bucketful for every square yard each year, but if your soil is either especially heavy and clay-based or very light and sandy, you will need to add about ten-times this amount to see any improvement. If you don't have enough organic matter to

treat your whole garden, concentrate on areas which will benefit most, such as prominent flower borders or where you intend to grow fruit and vegetables.

When is it applied? If you are cultivating your soil, incorporate the organic matter as you dig (see page 166 for advice).

If your garden is already filled with established plants, however, simply place the organic matter on the soil's surface during the spring where it will also help to prevent moisture loss and suppress the growth of weeds. In the first year, place a 3-inch layer over the soil around each plant, taking care not to spread it directly against the plant's stem. Renew the mulch to this depth once a year or as needed, as it decomposes.

Making leafmold

Piles of leaves can be used to make a particularly useful and pleasant garden compost known as leafmold. The process is remarkably simple.

1 During the fall, rake up any fallen leaves (provided they aren't diseased), and fill large, heavy-duty plastic leaf bags with them.

2 Add a few handfuls of grass clippings to the bag, water well if the leaves are dry and place the bags in an out of the way place for a year.

The resulting leafmold can then be used as a mulch or a soil improver before planting. To make potting soil, leave the leafmold for two years, then sieve before use.

For large amounts of leaves, make a "leafmold bin" out of heavy-duty plastic mesh held up by 4 sturdy posts. To prevent the leaves from blowing around, cover the bin with a piece of old carpet once it is full and the leaves are wet.

expert tips   **Reliable compost**

A good way of making sure a new pile has all the necessary creatures to carry out the composting is to inoculate it with a shovelful of well-rotted compost from a previous pile. If this is your first compost pile, add a shovelful of soil or a commercial compost activator (available from garden retailers) to each 6-inch layer of organic waste instead.

Using garden compost
Spread well-rotted garden compost as a surface mulch or incorporate it into the soil at planting time to improve the soil's structure.

A compost pile

If you have the space, it is a good idea to have a compost pile in your garden where you can recycle organic garden waste such as grass clippings, prunings and weeds. This makes getting rid of garden and kitchen waste very easy and provides you with lots of free garden compost that can be used to improve your soil at planting time or as a surface layer (known as *mulch*) around established plants to conserve moisture and suppress weeds. What's more, a compost pile also benefits the environment because it recycles waste materials that would otherwise end up in a land-fill site.

Making garden compost

This couldn't be easier. All you need to do is to use the right ingredients in roughly the right quantities (see below) and mix well, adding water as necessary. Then simply allow the pile to "cook" for a year. During this period, unseen microorganisms and garden creatures do all the hard work, turning your waste into a useful material, generating a lot of heat in the process.

Use the best ingredients if you want good results—any organic kitchen or garden waste can be used, including potato peelings and grass clippings. Don't add thorny or evergreen prunings because they take far too long to decay, and avoid adding flowering weeds because they may release their seeds in the compost pile and be spread when you use the compost. Any meats, fats and bones should also be avoided as they decompose slowly and may be smelly or attract pests. Avoid disproportionate amounts of any one ingredient or results will be disappointing. Instead, mix two parts of green materials such as non-flowering weeds or grass clippings with one part of something dry, such as straw, shredded newspaper or dead leaves to get rich, sweet-smelling compost. You can either mix the materials together before adding them to the pile or add them in alternate layers, up to 6 inches thick, until the bin is full.

Within a week, or so, the compost should heat up as the micro-organisms get to work, reaching a temperature of about 120°F (50°C) in the center. After "cooking" for about a year, your garden compost is ready to use.

During winter, insulate the pile with a piece of old carpet to prevent it from cooling down. You should also add a lid to prevent it from getting too wet, especially if you live in a high rainfall area. You can improve the consistency of your compost and speed up the composting process by turning the pile when it starts to cool. To do this, move the material that was around the outside of the pile toward the center and spread the core of the pile on top. This is much easier to do if you have more than one compost bin side by side, because you can simply move the compost from one bin to another when you turn. If the compost becomes too dry, add some water.

Compost made easy
If you have the space, construct three compost bins side by side. One should be in the process of being filled, the second filled with decomposing material and the third being emptied of ready-to-use compost. This makes turning the compost very easy, as you can simply transfer it into the third bin when it's empty.

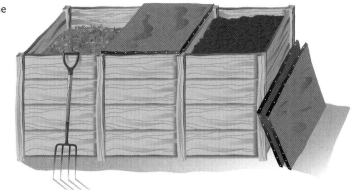

feeding your garden

Plants need a range of nutrients to grow well. All the essential nutrients are available in good border soil, so most plants will not need feeding every year unless your soil is poor. Plants which grow very quickly, however, such as vegetable and fruit crops, and those that put on dramatic flowering displays, such as roses, are worth feeding more regularly. Plants grown in a confined amount of soil, such as in a container, require feeding about six weeks after planting.

The most convenient way to feed all plants is by applying fertilizer. Deciding which fertilizer to buy, however, can be very daunting, because so many types are available. To be able to make the right choice, you need to know what nutrients plants need and the type of growth you are trying to promote.

Essential nutrients

Plants need a balanced diet of nutrients if they are to grow well. The three main plant nutrients are nitrogen (N), phosphorus (P) and potassium (K). They are often called the macro-nutrients or primary nutrients and expressed as a ratio of N:P:K on fertilizer containers. These three nutrients promote different types of growth in plants. Nitrogen generally encourages plants to grow quickly, producing lots of leaf and shoot growth; phosphorus is essential for the healthy growth of roots; and potassium promotes flower and fruit production.

Calcium, magnesium and sulfur are also required by plants, but in smaller amounts. These are known as secondary nutrients. Boron, iron, chlorine, copper, manganese, zinc and molybdenum are needed in very small quantities and are known as micronutrients or trace elements.

Applying organic matter

Using lots of organic matter in your garden, such as well-rotted farmyard manure or garden compost, is not a substitute for adding fertilizer. Bulky organic matter can, however, help to improve the structure of your soil, improving drainage and allowing more air in. If applied regularly enough and in sufficient quantities, it will also make the soil more fertile, but this takes a long time (see "Improving your soil," page 168).

Organic or inorganic?

Fertilizers are classified as organic or chemical according to their origin. Organic fertilizers come from natural sources such as dead plants and animals; chemical (or synthetic) fertilizers are mostly manufactured, although a few, such as rock potash, are naturally occurring minerals which are mined.

The nutrients in fast-acting chemical fertilizers are immediately available to plants and useful for feeding fast-growing crops, such as vegetables, that are showing signs of starvation. However, the nutrients are easily washed out of the soil, particularly in winter, during periods of high rainfall and on free-draining soil.

On the other hand, organic fertilizers, such as aged manure or commercial products, are much slower acting and continue to benefit the soil—and thus your plants—for a longer period. They release their nutrients more slowly because they need to be broken down by microorganisms before the nutrients become available to plants. The rate of breakdown varies with soil conditions: when soil is warm and moist, the action is faster than when soil is cold or very dry. Although the results of using an organic fertilizer are not apparent as rapidly as with many chemical products, the plants benefit just as well as the nutrient

levels slowly increase. Slow-release chemical fertilizers are available for similar effects.

Types of fertilizer

Fertilizers can be divided into three main groups: specific, simple and complete fertilizers.

Specific fertilizers are a good choice for the Virgin Gardener, because they have been produced for a particular type of plant: for house plants, lawns, roses and

vegetables such as tomatoes. They are convenient and easy to apply, but are generally more expensive than other types of fertilizer.

Simple fertilizers supply one or predominantly one nutrient. Products that supply only a nitrogen (N) boost are most common, but you can also find phosphorus-only and potassium-only fertilizers. Manufacturers use various sources of these nutrients, but no matter what the source, all provide the percentage of nitrogen, phosphorus or potassium specified on the label. Commercial products include a comprehensive label that shows you the formula of major nutrients and their organic or chemical sources.

Fertilizers that contain all three of the main nutrients (NPK) are often called complete fertilizers. This does not, however, mean they contain all the nutrients necessary for healthy growth. Complete fertilizers that supply the three main nutrients (NPK) in roughly equal amounts are also called balanced or general fertilizers—they are ideal for using all around the garden to boost general plant growth.

You can also buy combination fertilizers that include a fungicide, insecticide, or herbicide. The latter is often used in lawn fertilizers, to control crabgrass or other weeds. If you buy these products, read the label carefully to make sure the contents are safe for all of the plants in the area in which you will be using it.

Applying fertilizers

Manufacturers have devised a variety of ways to make delivering essential nutrients to your plants as easy as possible.

Granular fertilizers can be scattered onto the soil surface over the rooting area of border plants. Water areas thoroughly after applying, so that the nutrients are made available to the plants. In dry areas or periods of prolonged drought, consider applying a liquid fertilizer instead (see below).

Apply granules to the lawn using a shaker pack **(1)** for smaller lawns or a special fertilizer spreader for larger areas. For lawns covered with weeds or moss, there are special formulations that deal with these problems at the same time.

Liquid fertilizers are fast-acting fertilizers designed to promote quick growth. The balanced formulation is good for applying generally and the high-potash version is useful for flowering and fruiting crops and plants. They can be applied with a watering can, sprayer or via a special feeder that can be attached to the end of a hose.

Slow-release or controlled-release fertilizers **(2)** are coated in a special resin which releases the nutrients slowly over a set period of weeks or even months.

Making liquid fertilizer

Nettles can also be used to give annuals and vegetables a boost of nutrition during the summer. You can easily make a good liquid fertilizer from stinging nettles (*Urtica dioica*), which grow wild in many areas.

1 Wearing gloves, gather some nettles and tear them up by hand. Alternatively, lay the nettles on the lawn and run over them with your mower.

2 Place 1 pound of the chopped nettles into a two-gallon bucket of water, cover with a piece of burlap and allow to stand for two weeks. The liquid fertilizer can then be used as required, diluting it with an equal amount of water before use.

weed control

Weeds are uninvited plants growing in the wrong place. They are harmful because they compete with other plants for soil moisture, nutrients and space. If unchecked, they will smother your plants and eventually take over the whole area. In an informal garden, however, you may be prepared to allow some weeds, such as stinging nettles, to thrive to provide habitats and food for wildlife.

Annual weeds, such as shepherd's purse and chickweed, grow, flower, spread their seed and die all in one season. To prevent them from reappearing year after year, you need to remove them before they release their seeds. This is fairly easy to do if you weed regularly. Perennial weeds, such as couch grass and Bermuda grass, which live for more than one year, are more troublesome as they will spread via underground or low-growing stems that root and produce new shoots as they spread. When weeding, you must remove all the roots because many perennial weeds can regenerate from even a tiny piece left in the soil.

Green tip

Preventing weeds
Most weed problems can be prevented without using chemicals. Apply a layer of well-rotted organic matter to the soil surface around permanent plants, or plant through a special weed-proof sheet called sheet mulch or landscape fabric (available from garden retailers). Any weeds that do appear should be controlled early by pulling them out by hand.

Mulch

The easiest way to control weeds is to use mulch. A layer of wood chips, bark chips, chopped fall leaves or other organic material will smother young existing weeds. Pebbles, lava rock and gravel can also work as mulches, but apply landscape fabric first to prevent weeds from sneaking into the spaces between stones. Mulch also keeps soil moist, cutting down on watering, and keeps the roots of plants cool. Organic materials benefit the soil by increasing the activity of earthworms and other soil organisms. As the creatures travel through the soil to feed on the mulch, they add air spaces that improve growing conditions and drainage, and work nutrients from the mulch deeper into the soil.

Weeding tools

A garden hoe and hand tools, such as a dandelion digger or Cape Cod-style weeder, are excellent aids for removing weeds. Hand weeders are available in many styles, so experiment to find the one that suits you best. Use a long-handled hoe to weed rows of vegetables quickly.

Slice off young weeds by pulling the hoe toward you, or lift and remove clumps of bigger weeds. Shake off soil and toss uprooted weeds onto the compost pile to decompose. If the weeds have already formed seeds, avoid adding them to the compost pile, where their seeds may be spread when you apply finished compost.

Hand weeding

The most precise, but most laborious, way to weed is to do it by hand **(1)**, which is useful for dealing with isolated weeds or for removing weeds that are close to ornamental plants. Grab the weed at its base and pull. For stubborn weeds such as dock, dandelion and stray tree seedlings, give the weed a twist as you pull, to free the root.

When an ornamental border is heavily infested by perennial weeds, dig up everything in the border, so that the roots of the plants and weeds can be untangled, and then the ornamental ones replanted.

Weed killers

Chemicals are an effective way of tackling weeds, but it is essential to apply them accurately, to stop them from coming into contact with any ornamental plants.

Individual weeds You can spot treat individual weeds using a dab-on applicator which allows you simply to wipe the chemical directly onto the weed. Alternatively, you can try ready-to-use weed killer sprays **(2)** which are available in hand-held spray bottles. These are especially useful for small groups of patio weeds. Spray only on still days when there is no chance of the spray drifting on the wind. If applying weed killers among ornamental plants, protect the plants with a plastic sheet **(3)** or upturned buckets before spraying. Don't remove the protection until the spray has dried.

Treating large areas It is easier to treat large areas using a pressurized sprayer or watering can for soluble weed killers, or a special applicator or granular types. Concentrated weed killers are available as liquids, soluble powders or crystals, and need to be mixed with water before applying. Granular weed killers are supplied ready to be sprinkled.

Weeding around the garden

Weeds can appear in all areas of your garden, so it is important that you know how best to remove them.

Unused ground You can try pulling weeds, hoeing or digging out all the weeds, but this is very hard work. You may be better off covering the area with a heavy-duty black plastic sheet that will smother the weeds and kill them. Unfortunately, it can take up to two or three years to kill persistent perennial weeds.

For faster results, you can use a total weed killer that is deactivated on contact with the soil, so the area can be planted just a few weeks after treatment. Several applications may be needed to kill persistent weeds.

Lawns Individual lawn weeds can be removed using an old kitchen knife, a dandelion digger or other hand tool or a chemical dab-on weed killer. If the problem is more widespread, most weeds are easy to control using a selective lawn weed killer—this kills the weeds but does not affect the grass. Coarse weed grasses, however, are immune to the effects of selective lawn weed killers; to weaken and kill these, dig up the weeds and re-sow the area with grass seed (see page 44).

Paths and patios Use a special weeding tool to hook out weeds from between paving slabs and rake gravel periodically to uproot any seedlings. Tackle severe problems with a path weed killer, which not only kills existing weeds but prevents new ones from germinating for a year. A spray bottle or watering can fitted with a dribble bar **(4)** will direct weed killer to crevices.

Mixed borders Control weeds in borders and around shrubs with mulch, which smothers existing weeds and reduces further outbreaks. You can also hoe or pull weeds by hand. Spot treatments of weed killer will work, but be sure to protect neighboring plants.

3   4

pest and disease prevention

Plants that grow vigorously will shrug off most pest or diseases. Remain vigilant, though, so you can spot problems early and take the appropriate action to ensure the affected plants are not weakened and the problem doesn't spread.

Preventing problems

Clear away dead and dying leaves promptly. Place diseased leaves in the trash (if you put them on the compost pile, the disease will spread when you use the compost). Keep weeds under control, because these can act as hosts to many problems.

Buy disease-resistant plants Many disease-resistant plants are now available. Read the label of the plant or check mail-order catalogs to find disease-resistant varieties. If mildew on phlox is a problem in your garden, for example, you may want to replace your disease-prone plants with a cultivar such as pristine white 'David'. Vigorous old shrub roses and climbers, such as 'New Dawn', are often more disease resistant than modern tea roses.

Encourage beneficial insects Many species of tiny wasps and other beneficial insects attack garden pests, by laying the eggs of their larvae on the pest insects or their eggs. The larvae eat the pests, but the adults dine on nectar and pollen. Encourage these natural enemies of pests to patrol your garden by including flowering plants with clusters of tiny blossoms, such as oregano, dill, fennel and yarrow, among your beds and borders. Praying mantises, spiders, ladybugs, and green lacewings also eat many garden pests. Try to avoid insecticides, which destroy beneficial insects.

Barriers Putting up suitable fencing and/or underground barriers can help to keep out deer, groundhogs, rabbits and other large pests. Fine-mesh netting also can be used to protect vulnerable plants and crops from birds. Flying insect pests can be kept away from vegetable crops by covering the plants with insect-proof mesh as soon as they have been planted. Low-flying carrotfly can be foiled by erecting an 18-inch high netting barrier around your crop or vegetable patch.

Traps Slugs can be trapped in dishes sunk rim-deep into the border soil, then filled with beer. Pheromone traps (available in garden centers) can be used to lure fruit tree pests, such as male codling and plum fruit moths, before they can mate. Use some corrugated cardboard to trap earwigs and pupating caterpillars, which hide in the grooves. Sticky spheres that attract flying insects, and sticky bands that wrap around tree trunks to trap caterpillars, may also help eliminate pests.

Dealing with problems

If a more severe outbreak occurs, hand-pick the insects or use mechanical means to remove them. If the pest is still not controlled, or if the problem is disease, snip off the affected plant parts and dispose of them. Should all else fail, you can turn to chemical aids such as pesticides and fungicides. The first step is to identify the problem, so inspect your plants regularly to make sure

The natural predator
You can prevent pests in your garden by encouraging wildlife that feeds on them. To encourage lots of slug-eating frogs to take up residence in your garden, add a pool or water feature.

you catch problems early. The chart on pages 176–177 details the most common plant diseases, telling you how to spot problems, how they are caused and how to treat them. If a plant starts to look sickly or foliage is being damaged, check the plant for the culprit causing the damage.

Biological controls Your garden already includes many biological controls—in the form of creatures that devour pests. Birds are tops at eating insects, so attract them with feeders and birdhouses. Spiders are already at work in your garden. You may also have predatory insects at work. You can boost your population of some predatory insects by buying them at garden centers or by mail-order. If a caterpillar infestation is severe, you may want to use a product containing Bt (available at discount stores and garden centers), a bacterium that kills caterpillars but not other insects. When you notice pests, give your helpers time to control the outbreak before you reach for insecticides.

Physical controls Pick off or rub off small colonies of insects between your finger and thumb or use a blast of water from a hose to dislodge them. Some flying pests can be encouraged to leave by giving the plant a vigorous shake.

Chemical controls Aim to reserve these as a last defense. Chemicals can be either organically derived or

synthetic. Organic controls, such as rotenone and pyrethrins, are both effective insecticides. Many synthetic chemicals are available either for specific problems or for more general use.

A general systemic insecticide is absorbed by the plant and will kill all the insects feeding upon it; a selective insecticide will kill only those insects targeted by its particular ingredients. If you are having severe aphid problems, for example, you can choose an insecticide for those particular pests.

Disease-control products fall into three categories, depending on the way they work. Some are preventive in nature, helping to keep disease from getting a start. Others are eradicants, which control disease once it has begun. Systemic products combine both attributes.

Besides choosing a product that is formulated for your particular pest or disease problem, make sure it is safe to use on the plants you intend to apply it to. Products for ornamental plants may not be safe for use on vegetables and other food crops.

problem solving

SYMPTOMS	PROBLEM	TREATMENT
LEAVES		
Leaves have holes		
irregular holes in lily leaves, bright red beetles	lily beetle	pick off by hand
irregular notches in leaves, ½-inch-long beetles	vine weevil (adults)	collect at night
irregular holes with slime trails	slugs and snails	scatter slug pellets, collect at night, biological control
ragged holes or leaves stripped to veins	caterpillars	pick off by hand, biological control
ragged holes in deciduous trees	leaf weevil	collect at night
yellow spots turn brown and drop out leaving holes	shothole canker	spray with a copper fungicide
young leaves tattered and misshapen	capsid bugs	spray with a systemic insecticide
young leaves with small holes, shiny black beetles	flea beetle	encourage vigorous growth
Leaves marked		
black or green scabby patches (apples and pears)	scab	prune out affected shoots, spray with systemic fungicide
brown leaves often curled, dieback may occur	salt damage	avoid contaminating soil with salt or salt spray
circular or angular brown, yellow or gray spots	leaf spots	clear up fallen leaves
orange (spring) or dark brown (winter) raised spots	rust	remove affected leaves, spray with systemic fungicide
purple-black spots with yellow edges (roses)	blackspot	spray with systemic fungicide, clear up fallen leaves
scorched leaves on one side of the plant	wind damage	protect with windbreak or move to a sheltered spot
shiny, raised white spots on undersides of leaves	white blister	remove affected leaves
transparent white or brown patches	slugworms	pick off by hand
yellow or brown patches	leaf blights	cut back into unaffected growth, clear up fallen leaves
Leaves misshapen		
pale green and waxy growths	azalea gall	pick off galls, spray with a copper fungicide
raised often brightly colored areas	galls	pick off affected leaves
rolled, sometimes with silk webbing	caterpillars	pick off by hand, biological control
shoot tips distorted, turn brown, often bark split	frost	prune out affected shoots, insulate plant next winter
small leaves, poor growth often discolored	nutrient deficiencies	apply fertilizer
stunted leaves, distorted edges, swollen stems/bulbs	stem/bulb nematodes	destroy affected plants, clear up fallen leaves
thickened yellow margins, some curled (sweet bay)	bay sucker	pick off affected leaves, spray with systemic insecticide
tightly rolled leaves, grub inside	sawfly	remove affected leaves, spray with systemic insecticide
Leaves discolored		
black soot-like coating to upper surfaces of leaves	sooty mold	control insects that excrete honeydew, wash leaves
discolored foliage and stems wilt and die	wilts	destroy affected plants
discolored areas on upper surface, gray furry threads	downy mildew	pick off affected leaves, spray with systemic fungicide
discolored or pale leaves which often fall early	waterlogging	improve drainage
pale bands or spots	weed-killer damage	destroy badly affected plants
pale green or cream mottling, tiny insects jump away	leafhoppers	spray with a systemic insecticide
pale streaks, often mosaic, stunted growth	viruses	destroy affected plants
silver sheen, affects whole branches, leaves fall early	silver leaf	cut back into unaffected growth after flowering
tiny pale flecks, dull foliage, sometimes webbing	spider mites	cut out affected parts, spray with a systemic insecticide
white powdery coating to leaf surface	powdery mildew	spray with a systemic fungicide
yellow spots, often distorted	smut	cut out affected parts, avoid splashing water

SYMPTOMS	PROBLEM	TREATMENT

SHOOTS

Shoots wilt

greenfly, blackfly and other color insects on shoots	aphids	rub off, spray colonies with systemic insecticide
poor growth, plants wilt, cream C-shaped grubs	vine weevil (grubs)	biological control
shoots die back usually from tip, leaves often wilt	dieback	prune out affected shoots into unaffected growth
shoots wilt and die, discolored leaves	wilts	destroy affected plants
shoot tips slowly die back and remain brown	fire blight	cut back into unaffected growth after flowering
stems die back to near ground level (clematis)	clematis wilt	prune wilted stems, spray growth with systemic fungicide
tips on young trees wilt and die, tunnels in branches	leopard moth	skewer caterpillars in holes, or prune affected shoots

Shoots damaged

flattened stems	fasciation	prune out affected stems with secateurs
bark raised and rough, often brown sunken patches	canker	prune out affected shoots into unaffected growth
shoot tips of shrubs eaten overnight, ragged cuts	deer	protect susceptible plants with suitable fencing
soft shoots grazed, gnawed bark	rabbits	protect plants with suitable fencing, use tree guards

Shoots discolored

bracket fungi or toadstools	wood rots	destroy affected plants, practice good garden hygiene
hard, roughened lumps present	galls	prune off affected stems
orange or red raised spots on stems	coral spot	prune affected shoots, practice good garden hygiene
spotted stems with small hard brown scales	scale insects	prune out affected shoots
stunted shoots and twisted stems	nematodes	destroy affected plants

FLOWERS

Flowers have holes

irregular holes with slime trails	slugs and snails	scatter slug pellets, biological control
ragged holes in buds and flowers	caterpillars	pick off buds and caterpillars, biological control
tattered holes in petals	earwigs	trap in pots filled with straw or newspaper

Flowers fail to open

buds brown and eventually dry	balling	pick off affected flowers
buds dry up and harden (rhododendron)	leafhopper	destroy affected buds
flowers die followed by nearby leaves and shoots	fire blight	cut back into unaffected growth after flowering
greenfly, blackfly and other colored insects on flowers	aphids	rub off, spray colonies with systemic insecticide
ragged blooms, leaves tattered	capsid bugs	pick off affected buds, spray with insecticide
swollen buds, distorted leaves	gall midges	prune off affected buds

Other flower problems

buds and flowers turn brown early in season	frost	pick off affected flowers, protect from frost
buds fall off while apparently healthy	bud drop	water plants in late summer
flecked petals, buds may not open	western flower thrips	spray with systemic insecticide before buds open
flowers infested with shiny beetles	pollen beetle	not necessary, shake blooms before cutting
flowers stripped	birds	net affected plants or use bird scarers
no flowers, normal foliage (bulbs)	blindness	dig up and divide affected plants

growing plants from seed

Raising plants from seeds can be very rewarding, inexpensive and a lot of fun. For gratifying results, grow only fast-maturing annuals such as annual poppies, zinnias and marigolds from seed. Seed packets and catalogs will tell you how many days or weeks to maturity. Those that take a very long time to bloom are best bought as plants. Most vegetables are also easy to grow from seed.

You can sow seed directly in the garden, or in pots or flats. If your winters are cold, starting seeds indoors will give you a jump on the season and provide the pleasure of gardening during late winter.

How to plant seeds

If you are planting outside, simply sow directly into well-prepared soil. Indoors, you will need seed-starting mix or potting soil and clean containers. Special seed trays, known as flats, are the best containers because they provide the correct depth of soil and have drainage holes. Use small trays or multipart plastic containers divided into separate cells (known as cell packs), which mean you don't need to separate seedlings into individual containers later.

Some seeds have to be kept in the dark for reliable germination (check the packets for details). Cover the planted trays with cardboard or other light-blocking material. Check for signs of germination every day and move the seedlings promptly to a warm, well-lit position once it occurs. Other types of plants need light to germinate. In this case, cover the seed tray with plastic wrap or dust with a layer of vermiculite, which allows light through but keeps the seeds moist.

Sowing large seed

Some seeds are large enough to sow individually in cell trays or in pots. Fill the container with soil and make a hole to the correct depth using the end of a pencil. Drop one seed into the hole and cover with soil.

Sowing seed step-by-step

Growing your own seedlings is simple, cheap and satisfying. Here's how to do it.

1 Fill the seed tray with seed-starting mix or potting soil, spreading it out evenly and removing any lumps. Gently firm the surface with the bottom of an empty seed tray or a tamper so that the soil is about ¼ inch below the rim of the tray. Place the tray in a bowl containing ½ inch of water until the surface of the soil darkens and becomes moist. Place to one side to drain.

2 Empty a small amount of seed into the palm of your hand and then sprinkle it evenly over the surface of the soil. Aim to space the seed about ½ inch apart.

3 Cover the seed with a layer of fine soil mix. Label clearly, then place in a well-lit position out of direct sunlight at the correct germination temperature (see seed packet for details on depth and germination).

Sowing fine seed

Some plants have such tiny seeds that they are impossible to pick up and sow individually. The technique described below will ensure an even distribution of seeds.

1　Mix very small seed with dry sand before sowing. This effectively dilutes the seed and the light color of the sand enables you to see how much you have sown.

2　Moisten the surface with a spray bottle and cover the container with plastic wrap to prevent the surface from drying out.

Aftercare

Seedlings need warmth to germinate. The top of your refrigerator is usually suitable. You can also buy electric heating cables to lay under trays for even warmer conditions. Once seeds sprout, remove the plastic wrap or light-blocking covering and transfer the trays to a sunny, south-facing windowsill.

Before seedlings start to touch in the seed tray they need to be spaced out in another container using fresh soil. This is known as *pricking out*. Do this by lifting the seedlings out, holding them by a leaf and supporting the roots with the pencil or a dibber (available from garden centers). Place the seedling at the same depth into a cellular seed tray or pot filled with soil. Firm gently to hold the seedling upright. Add a light sprinkling of water.

Keep the seedlings in well-lit conditions so they remain stocky, but out of direct sunlight, which can cause scorching. Turn the containers every day to prevent lopsided growth or place aluminum foil reflectors behind the seedlings.

Trouble-shooting

Uneven germination This is caused by seed being sown at slightly different depths. Level the soil before sowing and cover seed with a thin, even dusting of sieved soil.

Shriveled seedlings This is due to lack of moisture. If the soil dries out, stand the tray in a bowl containing ½ inch of water until the soil is moist.

Disease problems Seedlings can flop over after germination because of a disease called "damping off." Always use clean containers and commercial soil mix, which is free from disease organisms, and use fresh water from the faucet, not from a rain barrel. Also, water seed trays by placing them in water rather than pouring water on them.

Good air circulation decreases susceptibility to damping off. Keep some space between individual pots, and avoid crowding trays altogether. Fungicides are also available for control.

VIRGIN GARDENER'S BEST BETS

 Annuals to start indoors in cold-winter areas
Ageratum, alyssum, calendula, celosia, dahlia, dianthus, ice daisy (*Mesembryanthemum*), lavender 'Lady', rose moss (*Portulaca*).

Annuals to start outdoors
Annual poppies, annual sunflower, bachelor's-buttons, catchfly (*Silene armeria*), cleome, cosmos, garden balsam, larkspur, love-in-a-mist, marigold, morning glory, nasturtium, zinnia.

Easy perennials to grow from seed
All species of *Centaurea*, columbine (*Aquilegia*), Cupid's dart (*Catananche caerulea*), *Delphinium*, dianthus, feverfew (*Matricaria parthenium*), four-o'clock (*Mirabilis japonica*), foxglove (*Digitalis*), *Gaillardia*, lavatera, perennial sunflowers (*Helianthus*), purple coneflower (*Echinacea*), *Rudbeckia*, shasta daisy (*Leucanthemum* x *superbum*).

new plants from cuttings

Taking cuttings is a quick and easy way to start new plants from an existing specimen (this is known as vegetative propagating). Try making cuttings to multiply your stock of any favorite plant. The Best Bets at right are among the easiest, but you can have success with many other plants, too.

There are three main types of cuttings, each of which is taken at a specific time of year using growth that is at a different stage of maturity. Softwood cuttings are taken from soft, rapidly growing plants during the spring and early summer; semi-ripe cuttings are taken in summer and early fall using stems that have started to produce woody tissue at its base

of new growth; and hardwood cuttings are taken in fall and early winter from dormant plants that have reached their fully ripe stage.

To root cuttings successfully you will need clean pots, and potting soil. Semi-ripe cuttings often root better if the cut ends are dipped in a special hormone rooting powder (this is available from garden centers). A brand that also contains a fungicide will help to prevent the roots from rotting.

Softwood cuttings

These are very simple to root, but wilt easily, so they need to be kept as described below, or they will quickly deteriorate. Collect suitable material in early morning while it is

Steps to success with cuttings

- Before you take a cutting, ensure that the plants are healthy and prepare them using clean tools.

- Always take more cuttings than you need as some will not root.

- To stop your cuttings drying out, protect them from direct sunlight and place a plastic bag over the pot to create a humid atmosphere.

Preparing softwood cuttings

1 Use a sharp knife to trim the stem below a leaf joint so the cuttings are 3–4 inches long. Remove flower buds and pull off the lowest pair of leaves.

2 Insert the cuttings around the edge of a 3-inch pot containing moist potting soil.

3 Label and date the pot, then cover with a plastic bag held in place by a rubber band. This will help to stop the cuttings from wilting.

Place in a warm spot out of direct sunlight and check the cuttings regularly to see if they need watering. When new growth

appears, acclimatize the cuttings to conditions outside by first puncturing the plastic to improve ventilation and later by removing the bag completely. Then individually plant the rooted cuttings into 3-inch pots filled with fresh potting soil.

cool. Choose healthy, vigorous non-flowering shoots with three to five pairs of leaves. Trim material just above a leaf joint. To prevent it from wilting, place it immediately into a plastic bag and label clearly. Then, prepare the cuttings as directed below left.

Hardwood cuttings

Some trees and shrubs are best propagated from fully ripened wood produced during the past growing season. For best results, take hardwood cuttings as soon as the leaves have fallen from deciduous plants. Although you can take hardwood cuttings in winter, they don't root as easily at this time. You need to make sure that you choose healthy stems which are about pencil thick.

Using a pair of pruners, make each cutting about 6 to 12 inches long (the faster the growth rate of the plant, the longer the cutting will be) trimming just below a bud at the base and just above a bud at the top. Make the top cut at an angle so it sheds water and makes it easier to tell which end is which. Remove all but the top three or four leaves from evergreen cuttings.

Choose a sheltered but sunny border with well-drained soil. Using a spade, make a narrow V-shaped trench about 9 inches deep. Fill the bottom of the trench with sand, then insert the cuttings into the sand 3 inches apart, leaving about one-third of each cutting above the ground. Refill the trench and firm each cutting in well. Water during dry spells and remove all weeds.

VIRGIN GARDENER'S BEST BETS

Softwood cuttings
Abelia, abutilon, blue marguerites (*Felicia*), clematis, diascia, fuchsia, geranium, helichrysum, hydrangea, impatiens, marguerite daisies, osteospermum, potentilla, privet, *Prunus*, smoketree (*Cotinus*), verbena, wisteria.

Hardwood cuttings
Flowering currants, forsythia, honeysuckle, jasmine, mock orange, poplar, roses, spirea, willow.

Semi-ripe cuttings
Barberry (h), broom (h) butterfly bush, camellia, ceanothus (h), daphne, deutzia, false cypress (h), juniper (h), lavender, mahonia, olearia (h), pyracantha, red cedar (h), rhododendron (h), rock rose, skimmia (h), viburnum, weigela.

Semi-ripe cuttings

Many shrubs and conifers are easy to root from semi-ripe cuttings taken in mid-to-late summer. You need to wait until early fall for evergreens, which often root better at this time.

1 Choose healthy shoots that have started to go brown and woody at the base. For those plants in the Virgin Gardener's Best Bets above marked with an "h," you need to create what is known as a heel, as follows. Gently tear the stems from the parent plant so that a small thin strip of woody bark, the heel, is formed. For those not marked with an "h," you can simply make a straight cut. Use a sharp, clean knife to trim the stem just below a leaf joint so the cuttings are about 3 to 6 inches long. Cuttings with a heel should be trimmed to remove any rough snags. To reduce the water loss from large-leafed shrubs, cut the

leaves in half. To encourage rapid rooting, wound the cuttings by removing a 1-inch-long sliver of bark from one side at the base of the cutting.

2 Dip the prepared cuttings in hormone rooting powder, shake off the excess and insert around

the edge of a 3-inch pot filled with fresh seed and cuttings soil. Then follow the instruction from steps 2 onward as described for softwood cuttings, left.

pruning made easy

Woody plants such as shrubs, trees and climbers may need pruning to look their best and to keep growth under control. There is a certain mystique about pruning that puts off even some experienced gardeners, but don't worry, pruning is a very simple technique as long as you follow a few basic rules.

The best equipment

Always use sharp, clean pruning tools. You should use pruners for stems up to ½ inch in width and loppers for stems between ½ and 1½ inches thick. If you wish to prune larger stems than this, use a special pruning saw.

Check that the blades of your pruning tools are in good condition before you begin. If cutting out diseased stems, remember to wipe the blades with a garden disinfectant between cuts to prevent spreading the disease to healthy tissue or other plants.

Simple pruning

The aim of pruning is to keep an established plant healthy. This amounts to cutting out any dead, diseased or damaged wood, known as the three Ds. Most plants do not require any more attention than this.

Simple pruning can be carried out at any time of the year. Spotting diseased or damaged wood is often easiest when the plant is in leaf. If the plant is dormant, scrape off a bit of bark with your fingernail to make sure it is dead. Living branches will be greenish under the outer bark.

Pruning shrubs

Even though most shrubs don't require regular pruning, it can be used to encourage more attractive displays of colorful leaves and flowers.

To prune successfully, you must know when the shrub flowers, or else you risk losing the flowering display the following year.

Steps to success when pruning

- Use sharp, good quality tools to guarantee a clean cut and reduce bruising to the plant.

- Choose a sunny, dry day to prune as wet weather makes the foliage soggy and the job unpleasant.

- Make sure you cut in the right place (see opposite).

Early flowering shrubs Shrubs that bloom in spring and early summer, such as forsythia, produce flowers on the previous year's growth. You need to prune these plants as soon as the flowers fade. Simply cut back about a quarter to one-third of older flowering shoots, cutting back to the highest new shoot or bud.

Pruners and loppers

There are two types of pruners: "by-pass" **(1)** which have a scissor-like cutting action where a curved blade passes against a solid edge; and "anvil" **(2)** which have a single straight blade that cuts against a block of soft metal or plastic. The by-pass type allows you to make cuts at any angle. Position the pruners so that the blunt edge is higher than the sharp blade and pressing against the section to be cut off. Cuts made with the anvil type should be made square with the stem so that the pressure from the block is even. Loppers **(3)** work in the same way but are suitable for thick stems and their long handles make them ideal for high branches.

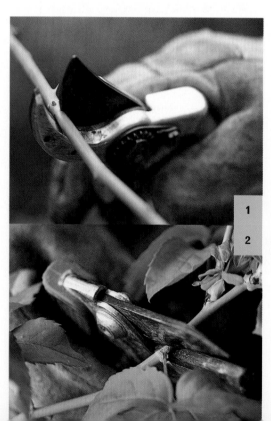

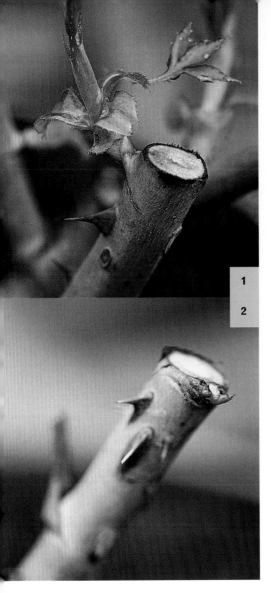

Prune in the right place

It is important to cut back a stem in the right place **(1)** in order to prevent diseases gaining access to the plant. This means making your cut where it will heal the quickest.

If you are removing whole stems from a plant, cut them off where they meet the main stem. If you only want to remove part of a stem, make the cut just above a bud (about ¼ inch away) at an angle so that the cut surface sheds water. (For plants which produce buds in pairs, you need to make a straight cut so you don't damage either bud.) If you cut too far from the bud, the stub that is left behind can become infected and rot back into the rest of the stem. But if you cut too close to the bud, you risk damaging it **(2)**. Bear in mind that the position of the bud down to which you prune will determine the direction of the new growth. Therefore you should always prune to an outward-facing bud to stop the center of a plant becoming congested with growth.

Late flowering shrubs Shrubs like buddleia that tend to bloom from mid-summer to early fall produce flowers on the current year's growth. These plants need to be pruned in early spring just before new growth starts. Cut back last year's flowering stems or weak growth to within an inch or two of the old wood. Flowers will then develop from this new growth.

Shrubs with colored stems A few shrubs, such as red-twig dogwood, are grown for their colored stems. To encourage vigorous new growth with greater stem color, prune these during early spring. Simply cut back the previous season's growth to near ground level to form a stubby framework of stems.

Shrubs with decorative foliage Some shrubs, elderberry for example, produce attractive young foliage displays when young, which become less decorative as the plant matures. To maintain larger and more colorful leaves, you need to prune such plants in early spring to encourage new vigorous growth each year. Do this by cutting back all of last year's growth until you produce a stubby framework of old wood.

Gray-leafed shrubs Shrubs and shrubby perennials that produce gray leaves, such as blue spiraea (*Caryopteris* spp.), may become less compact with age. Prune in early spring to maintain a compact habit of growth. Cut back old growth to the base of the plant, being careful to avoid new shoots that may have begun to grow near the base.

Neglected shrubs

You can rejuvenate an old shrub, even if you don't know what it is, using the fail-safe one-in-three method. All you need to do is cut out one-third of the stems, starting with the oldest (usually the largest) during early spring. This will encourage new growth from the base of the plant. The following two years cut out another one-third of the stems, starting with the oldest. After three years, all the old stems will have been removed and the shrub rejuvenated. See page 106 for more information about dealing with overgrown shrubs.

pruning popular plants

To make sure that all your favorite plants look their best and grow healthily, it is important that you prune them correctly and at the most beneficial time of the year.

Standard, bush and shrub roses

Recent research has shown that healthy, vigorous roses can cope with quite a lot of abuse and still flower well. Simply prune out any dead, diseased or dying growth (the three Ds), then roughly trim all the shoots back by about half. Don't worry about making an angled cut or pruning just above a bud. If you have a bed of roses, you can even prune them with a pair of shears or a hedge trimmer.

Climbing and rambler roses

These are often confused because they both cover large areas, need support and are both early-flowering roses—they bear their blooms on growth produced last year—so should be pruned as soon after flowering as possible. They do, however, differ in height and flowering periods.

How to prune a climbing rose (above)
Cut out one old shoot for every new vigorous shoot that has been produced. Cut the old shoot back to a new shoot near the base, or to ground level if there is not one. Old stems left on the climber should have their side shoots, which flowered last year, trimmed back to three leaves.

How to prune a rambler rose (below)
If the rose produces vigorous new growth from ground level, cut about half of the stems right back to the ground. If only a few stems are produced, cut back about one-third of the stems, starting with the oldest.

Climbing roses These have strong stems, produce large flowers and reach a height of between 8 and 15 feet. If the variety in your garden flowers just once a year, prune it between mid- and late summer. If, however, it flowers throughout the summer, leave pruning until winter. If your climber produces attractive hips (fruits formed by the plant after flowering to carry the seeds), it is worth delaying pruning until the winter anyway.

Rambler roses These tend to be old roses that flower vigorously and grow to a height of 15 to 30 feet. They are often grown along fences. They produce small flowers in large clusters once a year during mid-to-late summer and are best pruned during the fall or early spring.

Pruning clematis

Clematis are another popular plant with a reputation for being difficult to prune, but if you know how and when they flower, you shouldn't have any problems. To work this

Better flowering
It is essential that clematis are pruned correctly to get a good crop of flowers every year.

out, simply note when your clematis is in bloom and whether the flowers are produced on soft new growth only or also on woody stems produced the previous year.

Flowers on new stems The late-summer flowering clematis bear their flowers on new growth produced during the current season. To maintain a good crop of flowers you need to encourage a lot of new growth each year. Prune these in early spring, cutting back to just above the lowest pair of plump buds. If you don't prune regularly, all the flowers will be produced out of sight at the top of the plant where the new growth is produced.

Flowers on old stems Clematis that bear their blooms on old wood need very little pruning. Simply remove any dead, diseased or dying growth (the three Ds) after flowering. If the plants become too large or have been neglected, they can be cut back hard to just above a healthy pair of plump buds about 12 inches above the ground.

Flowers on old and new stems Some popular varieties of clematis flower on both new and old wood. Regular pruning is not necessary except to remove the three Ds. If there are plenty of new stems coming from the base, however, cut back the oldest stems in early spring to just above the lowest pair of plump buds. This will help the plant to produce flowers over a longer period of time because the un-pruned stems will produce large blooms early in the season, while the pruned stems will grow to bear smaller flowers later on.

Honeysuckles
Most popular honeysuckles are early flowering—they bear their blooms on growth produced during the previous year. If you need to prune this type of honeysuckle, cut back the shoots after flowering to a new shoot lower down on the plant. This will then grow and produce flowers next year.

Honeysuckles that are late-flowering and bear flowers on the current season's growth, such as the Japanese honeysuckle, don't need pruning unless the climber has outgrown its alloted space. If this happens, cut back overgrown stems during early spring to just above a healthy bud about 12 inches from the base. New shoots will then be produced from the base and should be trained into the support.

Wall shrubs
Plants such as pyracantha that produce a fine crop of berries in the winter are worth pruning in a special way to make the most of the seasonal display. The trick is to prune in stages.

To keep the plant narrow, cut back one-third of the horizontal stems in early spring. These can be left to flower and carry a crop of berries in the autumn. Prune all other sideshoots after flowering. To help reveal the crop of berries, snip back any new growth that is hiding them to about 1 inch in late summer.

Improving displays of berries
To show off the berry displays of wall shrubs, such as pyracantha, prune back new shoots that cover up the colorful fruit to about 1 inch during late summer.

what's in a name?

The naming of plants can seem very confusing to the Virgin Gardener. There are common names and totally unpronounceable Latin names. To be sure you are buying a specific plant, however, you need to know its full Latin name. To make finding the plant you want easier, many garden centers include the Latin name on labels. Catalogs may list plants either alphabetically by their common name or by their Latin botanical name.

Common names

Many wild plants have acquired a common or folk name from the local citizens who needed to refer to it regularly. This name is usually descriptive but not universally known, so that the same plant may have many common names, each known in different parts of the country. Common names often refer to a group of closely related plants rather than one particular type, making it rather ambiguous. In some cases the same common name is used in different parts of the country for very different plants.

Latin names

Although user-friendly, common names are very confusing and not universally recognized, so a system of naming plants had to be developed to enable experts and scientists to refer to a plant with the confidence that all their peers would understand exactly which plant they were talking about.

A famous Swedish naturalist called Linnaeus (1707–1778) put forward the idea of giving all plants two names that would uniquely identify them: the first word is the genus (a bit like a surname) and the second name is the species (like a first name). This two-name system was then used to name all known plants as well as new discoveries.

What Latin names mean

Although referred to as the "Latin" name, genus names are often based on ancient Greek or have their origins in classical mythology. For example, the genus name *Chionodoxa* for the bulb glory-of-the-snow comes from two Greek words: *chion*, meaning snow, and *doxa*,

meaning glory. *Iris* is named for the goddess of the rainbow. Other genus names may honor a person—*Forsythia*, *Buddleia* and *Fuchsia*, for example, which memorialize Forsyth, Buddle and Fuchs—and still others are descriptive.

Species names are usually used as adjectives to describe the color of foliage or flower, the size of leaves, or other attributes of a particular plant in a genus: *purpureus*, for example, means 'purple', while *macrophylla* means 'large-leaved.'

Example of plant label information

Type of plant	*Evergreen flowering shrub*
Common name	*Rock rose*
Latin name	*Cistus x purpureus*
Use	*Flowering shrub for a sunny border*
Features	*A rounded frost-hardy shrub with small gray-green evergreen leaves up to 2 inches long. It bears masses of large pink showy flowers with slightly crimped edges. Each bloom is about 3 inches across with a darker spot at its center.*
Height after 5 years	*3 feet*
Spread after 5 years	*3 feet*
Position	*Plant in full sun*
Soil type	*Any moderate or poor well-drained soil*
Hardiness	*Survives temperatures down to −5°C (23°F)*
Pruning	*Deadhead regularly. Prune out any dead or damaged stems each spring. Do not prune back hard.*

When two species of the same genus have been interbred to create a plant which shows characteristics from both parents, it is called a cross and the species name is prefixed by a multiplication sign (for example, *Camellia* x *williamsii* is a cross between *Camellia japonica* and *Camellia saluensis*). Where two species from different genera are crossed, a hybrid genus is produced and the genus name is prefixed by a multiplication sign (for example, x *Cupressocyparis* is a cross between the two genera *Chamaecyparis* and *Cupressus*).

If a plant's name includes more than a genus and species name, it is a subspecies, a variety or a cultivar.

Genus (the plural is genera) This is a group of one or more plants that share a range of characteristics, but can be separated from other genera by some major characteristic.

Species This is a group of one or more plants that share a range of characteristics and can be bred with one another to produce offspring that are similar to themselves. They differ from other species within their genus by one or more distinctive characteristics. Subspecies, which are indicated by the abbreviation "ssp." within the name, are a naturally occurring variant that is distinct from the species.

Variety and cultivar A plant which differs from others in the species by a relatively minor but distinct variation, such as the color of the flower or whether or not it is has hairy leaves, may be named a variety or a cultivar. If the variation occurred naturally in the wild it is called a *variety* and given a Latinized third name, preceded by the abbreviation "var." (for example, var. *glauca*). If it is the result of

A typical family line

Common name	Variegated English holly
Family	Aquifoliaceae
Genus	Ilex
Species	*Ilex aquifolium*
Cultivar	*Ilex aquifolium* 'Handsworth New Silver'

selective breeding, it is called a cultivar and given a name in a modern language that is set off in single quotation marks (for example, 'Snow Carpet'). In casual usage, cultivars are often referred to as varieties. Several plants of a species that share minor variations may be called a strain.

Botanical Latin names are occasionally changed as botanists reassess plants and reassign them to other genera or species. The genus *Chrysanthemum,* for example, has been reclassified in recent years, with some former species of *Chrysanthemum* being moved to *Dendranthema, Leucanthemum* and other genera.

You may occasionally see the abbreviation "syn." in plant names, which indicates that the name is a synonym for the chief botanical name by which the plant is referred.

Family The entire plant kingdom has been structured into a family tree according to each plant's main botanical characteristics. Genera are grouped together to form broad families. For example the family Rosaceae contains a wide range of seemingly unrelated genera including herbaceous perennials like *Alchemilla* and *Geum*, hardy shrubs like *Pyracantha* and *Spiraea*, and trees such as *Malus* and *Sorbus*.

Using Latin names
Long Latin names may seem a bit daunting but don't be afraid of them: simply take them one syllable at a time. After all, you already use a number of Latin names without a hint of hesitation—chrysanthemum and rhododendron, for instance.

The Latin name, along with a lot of other useful information, can be found on the plant label. A complete label should give cultural information, such as soil, light and water requirements; cold-hardiness information (for example, "Zones 5–9," or '"Hardy to –10°F"); special advice, such as whether a plant is invasive or poisonous; and, ideally, a photograph showing the entire plant as a mature specimen.

index

acknowledgments

Carroll & Brown Limited would like to thank Van Hague's and Country Gardens for allowing location photography at their garden centers.

US horticultural consultant
Sally Roth
Picture researcher
Sandra Schneider
Indexer
Michele Clarke
Illustrator
John Woodcock

Photography credits
t=top *c*=center *b*=bottom *l*=left *r*=right
DSR=Derek St Romaine; GEPL=Garden Exposures Photo Library; GPL=Garden Picture Library; RHS=Royal Horticultural Society
Des.=Designer

2bl David Murray **8** Photo courtesy of Joanna and Richard Robinson **8/9** Photo courtesy of The Reader's Digest Association. Des. Philip Enticknap **14bl** DSR/RHS Chelsea 1997. Des. Fiona Laurenson **14br** Andrea Jones/GEPL. Channel 4 "Garden Doctors" **14/15** Jerry Harpur. Des. Isabelle C. Greene, California **16** DSR **17tr** Jerry Harpur. Des. Keeyla Meadows, California **17b** Jerry Harpur. Des. Isabelle C. Greene, California **18** Friedrich Strauss/GPL **18/19** DSR/RHS Rosemoor Vegetable Garden **19** John Glover. Tommy and Missy Simpson, USA **19** Friedrich Strauss/GPL **28** John Glover/GPL **28/29** Andrew Montgomery/New Eden/Country Life Picture Library **29t** DSR **29b** Steven Wooster. Des. Anthony Noel **30l** DSR. Des. Johnny Woodford and Cleve West **30r** DSR/RHS Chelsea 1999. Des. James Alexander-Sinclair **32** Steven Wooster. Des. Annie Wilkes

33t Andrew Lawson. Des. David Magson **33b** Steven Wooster. Des. Anthony Noel **34/35** Andrea Jones/GEPL Channel 4 "Garden Doctors." Des. Paul Thompson and Ann-Marie Powell **35** Andrew Lawson. Des. Andy Rees **36l** Photo by Stephen Jerrom. Courtesy Glass Garden, Inc. **36r** DSR/Hampton Court 1998. Des. Johnny Woodford and Cleve West **37t** Andrea Jones/GEPL. Des. Matthew Vincent **37b** DSR/RHS Chelsea 1999. Des. Claire Whitehouse **42/3** DSR/RHS Chelsea 1995. Des. Julie Toll **46** DSR. Des. Mark Rumary **50, 51** Andrea Jones/GEPL. Channel 4 "Garden Doctors." Courtesy of Mari Mower. Des. Dan Pearson **52t, 53** Andrea Jones/GEPL Channel 4 "Garden Doctors." Des. Paul Thompson and Ann-Marie Powell **55tl** Steven Wooster/The Chapple's Garden, New Zealand **55tr** Steven Wooster/Pippa Bishop's Garden, New Zealand **55bl** Steven Wooster/Growable Art Landscape Designs. Ellerslie Flower Show 1998, New Zealand. Des. Jan Latham **55br** DSR/RHS Chelsea 1997. Des. Simon Shire **58tl** DSR/RHS Chelsea 1999. Selsdon and District Horticultural Society **58r** Jerry Pavia/GPL **60/61** Jerry Pavia/GPL **64** Gilda Pacitti **65** David Murray **66/67** DSR/RHS Chelsea 1999. Selsdon and District Horticultural Society **68, 69** Andrea Jones/GEPL Channel 4 "Garden Doctors." Des. Paul Thompson and Ann-Marie Powell **70, 71** Lynne Brotchie/GPL **72t** DSR **72cl** DSR. Chris and Stan Abbott, Kelberdale, North Yorkshire **72cr** DSR. Dr. Robinson, Howth, Dublin, Eire **72b** Andrea Jones/GEPL Channel 4 "Garden Doctors."

Des./owner Nayla Green **74tr** David Murray **77** Mel Watson/GPL **80, 81t** David Murray **81b** Linda Burgess/GPL **82** DSR **83b** David Murray **84** JS Sira/GPL **85** DSR **86, 87** Andrea Jones/GEPL Channel 4 "Garden Doctors." Des. Paul Thompson and Ann-Marie Powell **88t, 89** Mark Bolton **91tl** DSR/RHS Chelsea 1997. Des. Julian Dowle and Jacquie Gordon **91tr** DSR. Mrs Maureen Thompson, Sun House, Long Metford, Suffolk **91bl** DSR. Mr and Mrs Foulsham, Vale End, Albury, Guildford **91br** DSR **92, 93** Nicola Stocken Tomkins **94bl** Gilda Pacitti **96t, c** David Murray **96b** Brigette Thomas/GPL **99** DSR/RHS Chelsea 1997. Des. Roger Platts **100t** Marcus Harpur **100b** DSR **101** Gilda Pacitti **104, 105** Marcus Harpur/Park Farm, Great Waltham, Essex **106, 107** Mark Bolton/New Eden/Country Life Picture Library **108/9** DSR/RHS Hampton Court 1999. Des. Ruth Chivers **109t** Steven Wooster. Des. Anthony Paul **109bl** DSR/RHS Chelsea 1999. Des. George Carter **109br** DSR/RHS Chelsea 1997. Des. Lady Xa Tollenmache **110tl** DSR **110bl** Linda Burgess/GPL **112t** John Glover **112b** Nicola Stocken Tomkins. Des. Susan Sharkey **118** Steven Wooster. Des. Sue Firth **122, 123** Andrea Jones/GEPL Channel 4 "Garden Doctors." Des. Paul Thompson and Ann-Marie Powell **124** Nicola Stocken Tomkins. Des. Andrea Parsons **125l** Nicola Stocken Tomkins. Des. Sheila Bampfield **125r** Nicola Stocken Tomkins. Des. Katia Demetriadi **126tl** David Murray **126tr** DSR/RHS Chelsea 1999. Des. Terence Conran **126bl** Juliet Greene/GPL **126br** Linda Burgess/

GPL **130tl** Nicola Stocken Tomkins/Hampton Court Flower Show 1999. Des. Karen Maskell **130br** Gilda Pacitti **132t** Iris Water and Design/Pleiadian Enviromental Design Association **132c** David Murray **135tl** Nicola Stocken Tomkins/Hampton Court Flower Show. 1999 Des. Karen Maskell **135tr** Andrea Jones/GEPL Channel 4 "Garden Doctors" **135bl** Steven Wooster/Hampton Court Flower Show 1999. Federation of British Aquatic Societies. Des. Graham Robb **135br** DSR Sculpture by Dennis Fairweather **136bl** DSR/RHS Chelsea 1998 Lambeth Horticultural Society **136/137** Steven Wooster/Himeji Japanese Garden, Adelaide, Australia **138** Gilda Pacitti **140, 141** Andrew Lawson **142** DSR. Des. Cleve West **143** DSR. Des. Johnny Woodford and Cleve West **144t/145** Andrea Jones/Garden Exposures Photo Library Channel 4 "Garden Doctors." Garden owners Oliver Ashbee and Sarah Morgan **160l** David Murray **160c** DSR **162, 164, 165** Andrea Jones/Garden Exposures Photo Library Channel 4 "Garden Doctors." Des. Paul Thompson and Ann-Marie Powell **184/185, 186b** David Murray **187** Jonathan Edwards

Jacket Photography
Front l Mel Watson/GPL
Front r Derek St. Romaine/RHS. Chelsea 1999. Selsdon and District Horticultural Society **Front b** Andrea Jones/GEPL. Channel 4 "Garden Doctors." Des. Paul Thompson and Ann-Marie Powell
Back t, center above Mark Bolton **Back center below** John Glover **Back below** David Murray